COMMONSENSE
ETIQUETTE

COMMONSENSE ETIQUETTE

A Guide to Gracious, Simple Manners for the Twenty-First Century

Marjabelle Young Stewart

with

Elizabeth Lawrence

St. Martin's Griffin ✖ New York

Design by Maureen Troy

Library of Congress Cataloging-in-Publication Data

Stewart, Marjabelle Young.
    Commonsense etiquette / Marjabelle Young Stewart with Elizabeth Lawrence. — 1st St. Martin's Griffin ed.
        p.   cm.
    Includes index.
    ISBN 0-312-24294-8
    1. Etiquette.   I. Lawrence, Elizabeth (Elizabeth K.)   II. Title.
BJ1853.S8735   1999
395—dc21   99-36596
                                                               CIP

First Edition: December 1999

10 9 8 7 6 5 4 3 2 1

To Bill Sr., Jackie, John, Bill Jr., Sherri,

Erin, Shannon, Cole, Chase, and Drew,

sisters Maxine and Eleanor, and cousin Eva,

with all my love,

and to ʌ   Buchwald

CONTENTS

ILLUSTRATIONS

ACKNOWLEDGMENTS

Many thanks to my dear editor, Marian Lizzi, who's provided me with excellent suggestions and devoted assistance all along, and to my agent, Dominick Abel, who has been with me for all of my seventeen books, guiding me along the path.
—M.Y.S.

I am grateful to my late parents, Martha and Pope Lawrence, for teaching me easy manners from an early age; to my husband, Hugh Howard, for his guidance and support; and to my daughters, Sarah and Elizabeth, for their patience while I work.

—E.L.

Trust (along with generosity) is at the heart of civility. Cynicism is the enemy of civility.

—Stephen L. Carter,
Professor of Law, Yale University

THE ART OF CIVILITY

Everything I have ever done in my professional life has been predicated on the simple principle of the Golden Rule, which advises us we should treat others as we wish to be treated ourselves. The biblical phrase "Love thy neighbor as thyself" conveys the same meaning.

For me, treating people with respect and courtesy is what manners are all about. Good manners are characterized by consideration, cooperation, and generosity. That mix of thoughtfulness produces courtesy. Good manners also require the exercise of tact and regard for the wishes of others.

Etiquette, in a very real way, is at the heart of how we like to think of ourselves individually and as a society. Good manners and commonsense etiquette, born of the simple instinct to treat others kindly, produce civility, and civility makes our world a better place in which to live.

By treating people with respect, I don't just mean the outward manifestations of respect but a genuine caring that comes from within. If you can approach the world and all those in it with an attitude of hopeful expectation and trust, you will most likely find that the world is a place to be savored, filled with other wonderful human beings.

This is not to say that everyone is fine, trustworthy, and upstanding. Far from it. But you do not need to evaluate the values of every person you encounter in daily life in order to get along. It is not your job to change them, but the more you treat others as you wish to be treated, the better you will be treated in return. Your courtesy and civility will help you move beyond any slights and missteps by others.

A civilized person will look beyond the moment. Occasionally we are all faced with someone who doesn't return good behavior but is instead rude and insulting. Resist the temptation to reciprocate insults or boorish behavior, or you will fall into the trap of acting badly in return. Trading insults never changes the behavior of the rude person. Try answering politely, absorb any truth in the tirade, then move on. You are not likely to modify someone else's bad behavior by chastising or criticizing. Don't waste your valuable time and energy trying to make people behave well. Your good behavior will serve as an example and might even effect a change, over time if not immediately. Even if you're not a direct beneficiary, you will be better off for having acted with consideration, cooperation, and generosity.

Learning Compassion. The ability to put oneself in someone else's skin is essential to acting with civility. This means that you are aware of and can sympathize with other people's concerns, thereby keeping yourself from becoming judgmental. This ability enables you to experience other behavior, especially that which may be harmful to others; understand where it comes from; and yet still act in the ways you know are right. If you can teach young children the elements of compassion—on the order of "How would you feel if someone hit *you*?"—they are more likely to be caring and therefore well-mannered adults.

Learning Respect. It's such a simple word and so easily bandied about, from Rodney Dangerfield's catchphrase "I don't get no respect" to Aretha Franklin's anthem *"R-E-S-P-E-C-T."* Yet it really is one of the key elements of treating people well—both others and oneself.

With a degree of compassion, you can act with thoughtful and sympathetic regard for others—that is, you act with respect. Once compassion and respect are ingrained, everything else comes naturally. If your manner is to approach people with thoughtful and sympathetic concern, you will almost always treat them well. What it all translates to is an attitude that every person, no matter who it is, is essentially like you, deserving of consideration.

Even when possessed by anger, the wise person struggles to push his or her ire aside at least while in the company of bystanders. Otherwise, you show yourself to the world as a person who cannot cope, who lets anger, bitterness, or disappointment rule you. This does not mean you have to act like a doormat for someone who treats you ill. Nor should you be subservient toward others. Rather, healthy, wise, and civil people have a sense of themselves that enables them to think just as highly of—and do unto—themselves as they do of others.

THE GOLDEN RULE AT HOME

To learn how to greet the world, you need to start with those at home. If we treat our family members with trust and hopeful expectation, courtesy and compassion, we are more likely to be happy among our nearest and dearest and thereby understand how to treat those outside our small world.

It starts with each person. If we value ourselves, we can treat our partners and children with love and respect. I don't think you need to go through heavy analysis to find worthiness within yourself. All you really have to say is, "I am alive and I can contribute to the world in my small way." That alone is a point of origin, a statement of self-worth.

Once you've taken a look at yourself, move on to your spouse or partner. How do you feel about the other person? Is your partner's happiness as important as your own? How do you show your feelings? I find that showing my love in big and small ways helps enhance the life in my house. A loving touch, a little joke, a thoughtful deed, silly little presents—these and thousands of other acts of your own choosing can make life at home just a little sweeter.

If we value ourselves, we can then treat our partners and children with love and respect. By treating our children, from the moment they are born, as sentient beings worthy of love, trust, and admiration, we begin teaching them how to value themselves and others. When you value other people you naturally treat them with consideration, cooperation, and generosity, which is courtesy.

We teach our children, talk to them, hug them, encourage them, feed them, bathe them—we love them. In almost everything we do, we teach them something. The better we model for them how to do things, the better they will be taught.

Treating a spouse with courtesy and love is one of the best teaching devices for children, too. It's natural that if we treat each other well we are more likely to do it for our children. Children who hear parents speaking harshly to one another learn to speak harshly, too. Children who see affection and courtesy between their parents are more likely to develop those positive qualities.

BASIC COURTESIES OWED TO CHILDREN (AND ADULTS)

Children, just like adults, are owed good behavior. In fact, it is just as important, perhaps more so, because they are constantly listening and learning the ways of the world.

Never talk down. No one likes being condescended to, and children are quick to pick up on such behavior. Explain things in simple terms, but not in such a way that they sound simple-minded.

Do not discuss your child in his or her presence. Do you like being spoken of in the third person? Even if you want to relate something complimentary, ask the child's permission.

Do not use baby talk. Baby talk confuses a child who is learning to speak because it seems acceptable. Also, adults sound foolish using gibberish.

Never ridicule a child. Children, even more than adults, are very sensitive to the feeling that their dignity is being compromised.

Try not to discipline your child in public. Again, children are easily embarrassed and can become resentful of what seems to them unfair treatment. You may reprimand a child if needed, but try to save any serious actions and discussions for a more private time. If you need to, remove the child to a private space and conduct your discipline there before returning to a group or public place.

Avoid vulgar language. If you use it, you are tacitly telling your child that it is acceptable.

Solving Conflicts. Adults who can learn to solve conflicts between themselves at home are better able to do the same thing in the world, and to teach their young how to do it, too. The key to solving problems is willingness: If you and your partner *want* to make things better, you can. The more one of you has invested in keeping power or the status quo, the harder it will be. If you can approach issues with trust, compassion, and generosity, most problems can be solved. And if everyone could do this, the problems of the world would be solved, wouldn't they?

Of course, it's not that simple, but if we can take steps in our own lives, among the people we most care about, we will accomplish something important. Start small. Is the conflict worth getting upset about or can you give way? If you feel you must hold fast, be open to discussion. And try to start the conversation with an open mind and a willingness to find areas of compromise. Remember, the position your opposite number is maintaining is probably just as important to him or her.

When discussing a problem, try not to lose your temper. I find it sometimes helps to say to myself, "Will I even remember this issue in a few months?"

Try to listen to the other person before forming your own thoughts. Perhaps you hadn't considered the other person's concerns. The more we practice listening before speaking, the more natural it becomes, and the less important it is to get the first word in. I can't stress enough how important good listening skills are to successful communication of any kind.

Suggest common ground. Once the two of you can agree on something, you may find it easier to move forward toward more common areas of understanding.

When it comes to resolving problems with children, you can use many of the same techniques. Always remember that even though something may seem silly or insignificant to you, it doesn't to a child. And the opposite holds true, too. What is of monumental importance to you may have no meaning at all for a child.

Approach issues with compassion and open-mindedness. A child who feels that he or she is being listened to and taken seriously is generally more likely to comply with a decision than one who has been told flat out there's no room for discussion, just do it!

Some issues, including those of safety, may have to be decided by adults. It helps if both you and your partner can present a united front. Divided opinions are confusing for children.

Don't be afraid to set rules and guidelines and to say no. Children like and need to know the limits you set, even when they chafe at them.

As with everything in a family, if expectations are made out of love, understanding, and fairness, the family ties will be stronger and children and adults will behave better.

Creating Family Rituals. Humans seem to be programmed to ritualistic behavior. We develop methods and schedules to suit our needs for many daily acts, large and small. The more we practice them, the more comfortable we become with them.

We all have certain rituals, from the way we get up and get going each morning to our nighttime routines. Many seem to develop spontaneously over the course of our lives and we hardly even notice, but many we consciously create. These can be useful in developing models for good behavior.

Rituals involving loving ways of treating family members can enhance our lives to a remarkable degree. I often think of the bedtime rituals we create with children. They usually involve undressing and dressing, cleaning teeth and bodies, reading books, telling stories, or saying prayers. Every family does it a little differently, but put together and performed each evening, the actions serve to end the activities of the day, settle children for the night, and make them feel safe, secure, and loved.

We can provide a sense of comfort and security for each other—grown-ups as well as children—from the morning through the day with only a little thought. Probably you already do it without even thinking about it. We can greet each other with kindness every morning. Even if you're not a morning person, you can give grumpiness a softer edge. If you are bright and chipper in the morning, respect a slow-rising loved one's more somber mood by tempering your enthusiasm.

I like to make a practice of telling the people in my life how much I appreciate who they are and what they do on a regular basis. It makes me feel good, it makes them feel good, and it makes us all more willing to treat each other with kindness.

Some people set aside specific periods of time each day or every few days for specific purposes, such as reading to their children and themselves, exercising, checking in with relatives and friends, and on and on. These are all rituals, and they can be used to enhance your own life as well as someone else's.

Perhaps one of the most important things a person can do is set aside time on a regular basis for the company of a spouse or partner. This is often difficult, given the pressures of modern life, but it goes a long way toward building strong family ties and keeping communication open.

Time spent with a loved one doesn't have to be an elaborate night out, although those are nice. It can be a walk after dinner, time spent chatting in the kitchen after the children are asleep and the chores are done (or left until another time). The important thing is to spend time on a regular basis—a ritual time.

Try to make it a time when you discuss the events of the day, not necessarily the petty details. Make the time fun, thinking of the amusing aspects of the hours just passed. It should not be a time for resolving thorny problems but a time to enjoy one another's company.

For many people, family meals are important rituals. Including young children in a daily family meal, even if it's not a full meal, starts them off early with a sense of their place as part of the family. Also, when we treat each other well at the table and serve as good role models for table behavior, we are teaching by example. The busier families become, the harder it is for some to schedule a regular meal together. But do try to maintain the ritual: I think there is no better way to keep lines of communication open than with such daily events. I believe it is more important than many extra activities.

I also believe in the positive value of responsibility within each family. For some, this translates to everyone having chores they are expected to perform. I think this is important, especially as a teaching tool for children, because it helps to show that a family works together as a unit. Such chores can be simple, especially for young children. Even a child of two can be taught to bring a cup to the sink. Later you might move it up to taking the dinner plate into the kitchen, helping to set the table, or making one's bed. And of course the list can go on and on.

Once established, comforting rituals—including meals, fun times, and chores—become second nature and translate into sociable behavior in dealing with the outside world.

THE WORLD AT LARGE

Cary Grant, the quintessential elegant and well-mannered gentleman, wasn't always so.

Grant was born poor in the rough-and-tumble world of East London. As a child, he was not taught the finer points of civilized behavior that later made him known on screen and off as someone who treated everyone he met—whether it was a cabbie or a president— with courtesy and respect.

He once told me, "I acted like a gentleman so long I finally became one."

In many ways those words cut to the heart of civilized behavior. The more you practice being good to people, the more it becomes second nature. Soon you don't have to think about it; you just do it. Once that happens, everything else is easy.

If you practice saying "please" and "thank you" to everyone who does you a service, from waiters to storekeepers, you've begun treating them well. If you answer politely when strangers on the street ask you for directions, you've done them a service. If you hold the door for the person coming in behind you at the store, you send the message "I'm happy to make things just a little easier for you." If you realize that everyone's time is valuable, not just yours, you can reduce the tension in the checkout line.

There are hundreds of small things you can do to make your life and those of others just a little more pleasant. Try to remain patient when a line moves slowly. Say "excuse me" as you brush past or bump someone accidentally.

Try not to take out your own frustrations on the people you encounter (save them for a brisk workout, a long walk, a cleansing meditation). Try to be pleasant to the people you encounter. Just a friendly word or two will do.

Again, it's a matter of attitude. If you approach the world with a chip on your shoulder, you will be sure to find offense. If you don't, you and everyone else will be happier.

Dealing with Difficult People. At one time or another everyone has to deal with someone who is obnoxious, contentious, or perennially angry. Knowing best how to handle the situations that develop with such people isn't always easy, for they can be maddening. Begin by understanding that you probably won't be able to get such people to change and that you need to figure out ways to work around them.

It helps if you can keep emotional distance by telling yourself over and over, "The behavior is not my fault." Don't take another's bad behavior personally. If you've acted with fairness, compassion, and respect, you have no reason to fault yourself.

Don't ignore the person's behavior. If someone desperately needs to be noticed, give him or her some attention. Just don't let it rule the event. If someone seems afraid or intimidated, do your best to be reassuring. If someone is unreasonably angry, listen and respond calmly if you can, and end the conversation if the anger escalates. If someone seems truly disturbed and you are close enough to make suggestions, offer to help find professional help.

Try not to lose your temper with difficult people and attack them. People who are emotionally hypersensitive can take a simple observation and see it as vicious criticism. You're not likely to win in any sort of an argument with a difficult person anyway, so save your emotional energy.

Dealing with Those Who Appear Different. For many people, others who appear different from them are a source of embarrassment or fear. They think they don't know how to treat them, what to say, what to tell their children. Remember, to someone else *you* appear different. All you need to know is that you treat someone who is not identical to you the same as someone who is.

A person in a wheelchair is just a person, the same as you in all the important aspects. A person who is blind is merely a person whose eyes don't see. He or she may be a rocket scientist and an athlete. A person who is deaf doesn't hear. He or she may be an artist or a writer. A person who has cognitive difficulties still has the same feelings and many of the same perceptions as you. A person whose body is somehow distorted in shape doesn't necessarily have a distorted mind or spirit. And even if a person can't do all of the marvelous things that many others can, every person has emotions, feelings, and the right to be treated with respect.

Even a beggar does not deserve a look of disgust or a rude word. You as a person walking by do not know the story of that person's life. Maybe it was upstanding, maybe it wasn't but it is not up to strangers to pass judgment.

If you notice that someone looks as though he or she needs help doing something, you may ask if you can help. Don't automatically assume that the person needs help. If the person accepts your help, ask how you can best be of service and then do it without a fuss.

Some embarrassing moments can happen when we are with children and come upon a person who appears different in any way. Small children tend to stare, point, and ask guileless questions in a loud voice. I find that gently quieting the child and then promising to explain the situation works well. Afterward it's best to explain forthrightly the "differentness" you saw. You needn't dwell on it, but explain enough for the child to understand.

Attending Cultural Events. Any sort of a cultural event at which we find ourselves in a space with other people, all of whom are trying to concentrate on the performance or performer before them, demands courteous behavior. No matter how large the hall, every person has a very limited amount of space with neighbors seated close by. People pay attention at a musical concert, show, or lecture, and thus it is important that we not intrude ourselves and disrupt their enjoyment just as we expect them to leave our enjoyment unobstructed. To that end there are a few rules of behavior that are especially important.

• Be on time. It's true that most cultural events don't start at the stroke of the hour or half hour. One of the reasons they tend to start a few minutes late is that there are always some stragglers. Even given the extra minutes allotted, there are still latecomers who disrupt everyone trying to get to their seats during the show. I was recently at a show that had a compelling opening scene. We had waited the obligatory five minutes plus after the scheduled starting time, the curtain rose, and the shocking scene commenced. Then, wouldn't you know it, a latecomer pushed through the row at a crucial moment, leaving me and ten other people swerving in our seats trying to see the action and hear what was being said over the shuffling and rustling.

• Settle in before the show. We all have to get ourselves settled before a show starts. Our coats need to be put away, our bags arranged, and so forth. It is considerate to your neighbors to get all that done ahead of time. If you feel you must have candy or might need a cough drop or a tissue during a performance, take them out of their wrappers ahead of time and have them in your lap before the show starts. There are few things more irritating to others than the crinkle of paper and plastic while things are unwrapped, invariably in the quiet moments of a piece of music or play. Years ago, when women occasionally still wore gloves at social events, I was at a play seated near a very proper-looking lady who kept her gloves in a cellophane bag. Every ten minutes or so, she felt the need to take them out of the bag. I was miserable and wish to this day that I had spoken up and asked her, nicely of course, to please make up her mind.

Remember, a live performance is not like a movie. This is reflected in a number of ways. Ushers usually show people to their seats. Once the show has started, latecomers are asked to wait until the appropriate moment—when there is a logical break in the action—and then they are shown to their seats.

• Turn off all electronics. Few things are more irritating when you're concentrating on a show of any kind than to be distracted by the electronic beeps of watches and pagers. If you feel it is so important to talk on the phone during a show, step outside. Rest assured, cell phones have become so routine that no one will be impressed with your importance at receiving a phone call.

• Be quiet during a performance. As tempting as it sometimes is to comment, keep your thoughts to yourself while the show is in progress. You are not watching television at home where no one else can hear you. Save your important thoughts for the intermission. Similarly, sing along only when asked to by the performers. If you have a fit of coughing, which sometimes is unpreventable, try to stifle it and leave as quickly and quietly as possible. Finally, try to stay awake, or if you must sleep, do so quietly. Snoring is definitely bad form.

• Be aware of your space. At any performance we are each of us assigned a small amount of space. To go beyond that space into that of a neighbor is thoughtless. Try not to crowd your neighbors by hogging the armrests or letting your legs stray into their leg space.

All of this applies to going to the movies, too. Be on time, settle in as unobtrusively as possible, be quiet during the show, don't make too much noise with your food, try not to extend into other people's space, and turn off your electronics.

• Wear appropriate attire. Rules of dress have relaxed remarkably in the last two or three decades. In fact, society may have gone a little far in the quest to break down barriers, for there is a fine line between being casual and accepting and being disrespectful. For example, I was recently at the Wednesday matinee of a family Broadway musical in New York. It was a popular and terrific show, which, by the way, commanded a high ticket price. Everything was beautifully staged, except for the dozens of children I saw dressed as if they were on their way to the sandbox—T-shirts, shorts, flip-flops. For them this could have been a trip for an ice-cream cone rather than a major cultural event. I tried to imagine what event the children's parents would consider important, and I came up blank.

I'm not saying children must wear their best clothes—although the children who did looked ready to enjoy three hours of magic—or be uncomfortable, but to wear the most pedestrian of everyday clothes sent the message that this event had no importance. It said the work of the actors wasn't worth creating a presentable appearance, that it was the same as going to a movie. It said buying an expensive ticket to a show was no more than buying an ice pop. Finally, it said to the child, I don't expect you to enjoy or understand anything that is not completely in the terms you already understand and completely in your own small universe. Now that's a condescending message to convey that will in no way empower a child learning to meet the world.

PERSONAL GROOMING HABITS

The way we present ourselves to the world is a reflection of how we perceive ourselves and want others to view us. It's easy to say, "Take me as I am," but more often than not we mean, "Treat me as I want you to treat me." For others to do this we must project an attractive image.

Fashion aside, cleanliness matters. No matter how comfortable you may find it not to bathe or change clothes, it offends others. A rebellious part of you may say, "Fine, why should I care?" Yet, I suspect, your whole being does want to be accepted. To do so, we need to follow a few basic rules. We need to look clean. We need to smell clean. Our clothes need to be clean.

Stand Tall. Poor posture, such as slouching, hanging your head, shuffling when walking, sends a signal to the world: "Don't look at me, I'm not worthy." But you are worthy, so hold your head up—you'll see much better—look people in the eye, and walk with confidence (not to be confused with a swagger).

Sit Up Straight. Unless you are at home curled up in front of the fire or your favorite TV show, there is no need to lounge when seated in public. Slide into a seat, don't flop. Keep your feet on the floor, knees facing forward or to the side. You may cross your legs. You may cross them at the ankle. If you are a woman wearing a skirt, you may cross one knee over the other. People wearing trousers and engaged in casual conversation may place an ankle over one knee. Most people look sloppy if they let their legs splay.

Piercing. There is a current fashion among young people in particular to pierce just about every part of the body. Most of these jewelry sites don't really offend, and some can even be attractive, but there is nothing quite so stomach-churning when eating out as seeing someone's lip ring dangling with lettuce or other food. Think not only about what you want to see when you occasionally take a glimpse in the mirror but what others must see whenever they look at you.

Smoking in Public. Attitudes toward smoking have changed in recent years. It used to be accepted practice to smoke almost anywhere and to ask permission only perfunctorily. Today, as fewer people smoke, assume that you may not smoke unless you are outside or in a specifically designated smoking area. This goes for pipes and cigars, too, no matter how popular they are.

Chewing Gum. Until recently chewing gum was considered a private activity or something reserved for children. Today, perhaps because of the increasing lack of tolerance for smoking, public gum chewing seems to be on the increase. Chewing gum may relieve tension, it may keep people from craving a cigarette or a chocolate bar, but to those nearby it is an intrusion. To have to listen to someone popping gum in a public place is an invasion of public space. The person chewing attracts all available attention, as if saying, "Look at me, I look like a cow, and I'm going to make sure you pay attention to me and nothing else!"

I suspect that most of the time people are just thoughtless in their chewing habit, totally unaware of the world around them and how others are affected by their behavior. Nevertheless, the behavior does attract attention. If you need to chew gum in public, do so discreetly.

The essence of etiquette is civility. So much of civility is thinking about the other person's feelings and perspective, and acting with compassion, consideration, and sensitivity. That forms the basis of civilized behavior. Now that we know the basics of how to treat one another and ourselves both in our own world and the one at large, we'll move on to more guidelines for gracious living.

HOW TO USE THIS BOOK

We have attempted in writing and organizing *Commonsense Etiquette* to make it pleasurable to read one chapter at a time, at your leisure, or to browse, here and there, to satisfy your curiosity on a given subject. Using the table of contents, you may find your way quickly to areas of specific interest; an even more immediate approach would be to refer to the index that appears at the end of the book.

Chapter 1, Communicating, offers guidance on making introductions and other form of oral address, as well as the proper styles for writing letters and thank-you notes and employing proper phone etiquette. Chapter 2, Modern Table Manners, together with Chapter 3, The Tools of the Table, provide the rudiments for setting your table correctly as well as using proper manners when at the table. Chapter 4, Entertaining at Home, and its counterpart, Chapter 5, Dining Out, offer wide-ranging guidance on welcoming guests and employing appropriate protocol for business dinners and other events. Chapter 6, Weddings, discusses that most ritualized of events, the wedding, and its attendant parties, while Chapter 7, Milestones and Transitions, describes other ceremonies, events, and rites of passage. What are appropriate gifts for what events? See Chapter 8, Giving and Receiving Gifts, for some sound answers. And in a world where the vast majority of us work, Chapter 9, Office Etiquette, offers some philosophy and basics for enhancing the life of your office by employing some sensible and basic courtesies. Finally Chapter 10, Commonsense Advice, lists fifteen simple ways to make the world a more civilized, enjoyable place.

Good manners needn't be hard, forbidding, or complicated; indeed, once you have the right mindset, all they really require is common sense. And they will make your life just a bit more pleasant.

1

COMMUNICATING

Effective communication—the ability to express and exchange ideas with other people—is a precious tool. Some would say that if people communicated better, we could solve the world's problems. While this lofty goal may be unachievable, no doubt we can learn to exchange ideas clearly. Clear and considered communication can make our lives more productive and happier than if we permit ourselves to stumble around in the dark of misdirection, obtuseness, and plain old slovenly habits. If we can't bring peace to the world by speaking and writing effectively, perhaps we can bring some of the light of understanding and pleasure to our everyday lives.

OUR MANNER OF SPEECH

What we say and how we say it are among the hallmarks of our personalities; our manner of speech has an important impact on how we are perceived by others. People who speak clearly and thoughtfully communicate more effectively. Those who mumble or speak too fast risk being misunderstood. People who shout or speak too loudly can intimidate others. There are times when whispering is soothing, when raising one's voice makes you heard, and when doing something out of character gets a desired reaction. When we are attentive to how we are heard by others, we are more likely to get our messages across.

You make a better impression on everyone around you if you speak thoughtfully. That means taking a moment to think about what you want to say before the words emerge from your mouth. Most of us, in fact, would benefit in many ways from thinking a bit more carefully before speaking.

Strangely, fashion in our culture has reduced speech in some circles to the most basic and guttural, full of profanities that accomplish nothing except to punctuate the air. The sloppy words and phrases once used to shock and convey urgency, anger, or despair at the deepest level are so overused they have little meaning today. All they really convey is that the speaker has so little regard for the listener that he or she can't be bothered to think of a more precise way to say something.

No one remembers stock vulgar phrases for their meaning, but one does remember the person who uses them as being vulgar. Do you want to be classified with the pack, or do you want what you say to be remembered?

If you've ever wondered why children seem to use more vulgar language than in generations past, then just look at the people whose behavior they're modeling: the adults around them. If you or your partner use and tolerate bad language, you must expect your children to do the same. On the other hand, if you set a good example by using words for their meaning and forming expressive sentences rather than stock phrases and clichés, you and your children will have an easier time communicating when a subject being discussed requires more subtle language and shades of meaning.

GOOD CONVERSATION

Few things are as energizing, thought-provoking, and just plain fun as a good talk. To have good conversation, however, you must pay attention, consider what is being said to you, and be sensitive to the mood of those with whom you are speaking.

A considerate conversationalist has the patience to *listen* to what others say. If you appear to listen but are actually thinking of what you plan to say next, more than likely you won't hear everything that is being said and you will end up with parallel or even diverging conversations. If you constantly engage in conversational one-upmanship or rattle on like some out-of-control monologuist, you will soon become known as a bore and people will avoid your company. If you finish other people's sentences, you risk frustrating them and distracting them from their own lines of thinking. If you actually stop to listen before responding, you might learn something and the conversation may advance to your mutual benefit and pleasure.

• Include others in the conversation. If you find yourself in a group of people, those on the periphery will be more likely to remain interested if you try to include them in the discussion. When one or two people monopolize a group exchange, others will drift away.

• Try not to preach but rather to engage the opinions of others. Once opinions have been solicited, disagree if you wish but don't simply dismiss other people's views. Try to find common ground or accept their opinions as different from yours.

• Try not to interrupt. I know this seems a simple lesson that we were all taught as children, but adults need to remember it, too. Often in an effort not to lose our own thoughts, we forget to let others finish expressing theirs. The joy of conversing is in listening and not just hogging the airspace.

• Try to keep up on world and cultural events. I don't mean you have to read every issue of the *New York Times, Wired, Fortune,* and *The Utne Reader.* But having a basic knowledge of, say, cultural and business trends and world affairs does help when mingling with other people. A common pool of information is usually the best source for conversation.

• Keep a sense of humor. Good conversation often relies on the give-and-take of humor and seriousness. You may find that being able to keep a light touch, especially with people you don't know well, eases a conversation. You don't have to tell your favorite off-color jokes; just try not to take everything too seriously, unless it is patently obvious you should.

Gossip. Let's be honest: Just about everyone likes to gossip. It's human nature to want to know what other people are doing and to judge or order their actions according to some sort of hierarchy. The downside of gossip, however, is that it can be hurtful to discuss and judge our friends and neighbors out of their presence. There's an inherent unfairness about allowing only one side of a situation to be dissected. Few of us have all the answers, and rarely do we know what it's like to be someone else. Hearsay about other people's marriages, finances, child rearing, and careers can be particularly damaging.

Don't be a rumormonger. Not only can it hurt others, but the talk can also reflect back on you. Other people notice if you indulge in talking and speculating about friends and neighbors too much. You can become known as a gossip and soon people will begin to mistrust you, thinking, "If nosy Nancy says that to me about her, what is she saying about me to others?" When people begin to distrust you, they begin not to talk to you and soon you will find yourself left out.

MEETING AND GREETING

Introductions enable two strangers to meet one another. It's a natural part of social discourse. There's no reason why being introduced to someone (or making introductions) should cause anxiety. Perhaps people feel apprehensive because they fear doing it wrong, but that's really unnecessary—introducing people isn't difficult, and it only makes things go more smoothly. Proper introductions give people a sense of place in a group, thus allowing conversation to begin. An introduction is also the first verbal impression you make on someone, and for that reason every person should know how to handle introductions graciously.

There was a time when convention held that even in social situations people could not introduce themselves directly to others, that the host or hostess was obliged to do the honors. Now introductions can be made by a third person who knows each of the parties or, in these less formal days, by anyone willing to help. In fact, most people feel grateful when someone takes the responsibility for making sure people sharing the same social space have met one another.

When introducing yourself, use both your first and last name. If you can, include a word or two of relevant information. For instance, you could say at a cocktail party at Bob and Diane's home, "Hello, I'm Hattie Carmichael. I work with Bob at All-Tech." The same holds true for introducing someone else. If a couple is married and uses the same name, you can introduce them as a pair; in all other situations, however, use the full name of each person.

Now comes the question of who to introduce to whom. There are a few general rules that make it easy. Younger people are introduced to older people as a sign of respect. Men are traditionally introduced to women, again as a sign of respect. Guests are presented to the hosts of a party. If you are in a room with dignitaries or clergy, they are deemed most important, and guests are introduced to them. If you are in a group of people of the same age and sex, no dignitaries or clergy present, introduce people as you come upon them.

When speaking with dignitaries or clergy, you should address them by title. For dignitaries, for instance, you would use the appropriate title, addressing them as Ms. Mayor, Father Cleland, Senator Thompson, or Judge Alvarez.

When introducing someone in a formal situation, the most common form of address is to say, "Ambassador Roth, may I present . . ." If you find this too old-fashioned, you might say, "Mayor Smith, I would like you to meet . . ." Doctors, dentists, and people with doctorates do not use these titles in social situations.

When someone is introduced to you, it's best to say "How do you do" or "I am pleased to meet you." You can elaborate a little if you have the information, saying something like, "Oh, I've heard so many nice things about you" or "Did I hear that you've just returned from a long trip?"

The Informality of First Names. Informality is commonplace today; many people have been brought up to address people they've just met by their first names. There are, however, some situations when we rush to use first names too hastily. Knowing how best to address people when introducing them, or when talking together, is most helpful.

Never assume that someone whom you have just met wishes to be called by his or her first name, especially a person older than yourself. It's not appropriate to use nicknames or pet names for people unless they have asked you to do so. Many people regard it as irritating and condescending to be called by their first names by people they don't even know. The privilege of calling you by your first name is something you offer to people, not a privilege they should presume. This is less true in social settings, but in professional settings, and the world at large, it is important to treat people with respect—and this extends to their names.

Perhaps one of the reasons people become nervous about making introductions is they are afraid they will make a mistake and everyone will be embarrassed. Maybe they are afraid they will forget a name or a face, or mispronounce a name. It happens to everyone and, when it does, you should just apologize, saying something simple like, "I'm so sorry. I've forgotten your name." If you're not sure of how to pronounce someone's name, simply ask. If someone introduces you incorrectly, pleasantly correct the error. The momentary embarrassment will be nothing compared to a person persistently calling you by the wrong name.

In most families, aunts and uncles are usually called "Aunt" or "Uncle" by the younger generation, followed by the first name, unless there isn't much difference in age between the generations. When introducing your aunts and uncles to others, use the same form as introducing any younger person to an older one: "Uncle Dick, I'd like you to meet my friend Dorothy Davies. Dorothy, this is Richard Gearing."

What to call your in-laws can be tricky. Many people, shy of asking, try not to call them anything at all, which is both awkward and inadequate: By rendering them anonymous, you're relegating your spouse's parents to the land of no-name. A better approach is to ask them early on what they would like to be called. If you didn't do it before the wedding, do it shortly after. If you called them by their surnames before the wedding, ask now that your status has changed.

Whatever you call them, don't assume. I know of one woman who automatically used "Mother" to address her fiancé's mother, to the older woman's continuing irritation. Her other daughters-in-law and all her friends called her by her name and treated her as a respected friend. To assume a family intimacy without even asking what the older woman preferred seemed diminishing.

Family Identifications. When introducing a relative, as with anyone else, be sure to identify the connection. For instance, when introducing your brother's wife you would say something like, "Aunt Jane, I'd like you to meet Stephanie, my brother Paul's wife." Technically, the spouse of your sibling is the only one related to you, not the spouse of your spouse's brother or sister. In practice and general conversation, this fine distinction is rarely made.

If you are divorced or widowed, your in-laws become your ex-in-laws, but whether you choose to make this distinction is up to you and them. Often the best policy when introducing ex-in-laws to others is keep it simple, saying something like, "Bob, I'd like you to meet Shana. Shana was married to my brother Steve." When introducing a widowed ex-relative, you can say, "Gretchen, I'd like you meet Sylvia. Sylvia is my brother Pete's widow. She is now married to Harry Brown."

Children and Introductions. Children should be taught how to introduce and greet people at an early age. This is part of a parent's job of giving them tools to make life easier.

At times, all children become shy and will need to have the talking done for them, but there is no reason why they, as natural mimics, can't know how to use introductions and greetings. After all, if you use them routinely, they already know them.

If you've ever listened in on a game of pretend you've probably heard the child's version of decorous greeting and introducing. It's rather stylized, but kids get the idea quickly, so you can call upon them to use this knowledge in life as in playtime. You, too, can practice with them in play so that when the time comes for an actual introduction the exchange won't seem hard.

Children no longer need to curtsy and bow to adults when being introduced. A simple handshake and a pleasant "How do you do?" will do nicely. In less formal settings, just getting a child to say "Good morning" may be an accomplishment. But with a little role playing and instruction, even a five-year-old child can manage the basics.

The Handshake. In our culture, men greet one another by shaking hands, and they greet women they do not know well or at all by shaking hands. Women greet one another by shaking hands, too, especially when they first meet, or in formal social situations. In business, men and women meet and greet one another using a business-like handshake.

In times past, a man had to wait for a woman to extend her hand to shake it. Today, a man or a woman can offer a friendly hand. The most straightforward approach is to simply offer your right hand to be grasped. A handshake should be firm but not too hard. (A bone-shattering handshake communicates little and can inflict pain on older people and those with delicate hands.) It used to be considered polite for a man to take only a woman's fingers. This is acceptable in social settings (especially with elderly women), but for business a full, firm handshake is best for both parties.

The Social Kiss. This has nothing to do with a romantic kiss. When it comes to greeting friends or acquaintances at a social rather than a business function, men and women tend to greet one another with a light peck on the right cheek. In Europe the greeting involves a quick bob on each side. If you wear a lot of lipstick you might consider a quick bob near the cheek, too. American men generally stick with the handshake or a bear hug when greeting one another.

WHO COMES FIRST?

For many people the hardest part of introducing one person to another is knowing which person should come first. These guidelines should make it easier.

Women take precedence over men. This means that men are introduced to women roughly like this: "Sarah, I'd like you to meet Jake Coan. Jake, this is my sister Ms. Howard."

Elderly people take precedence over younger people. This means that younger people are introduced to older people, something like this: "Granny, may I present Wayne Walker, a school friend of mine. Wayne, this is my grandmother, Mrs. Lawrence."

Guests are always presented to the hosts. Guests should also be presented to the guest of honor, if there is one, unless they are elderly or are dignitaries.

Dignitaries take precedence. In the hierarchy of etiquette,

(Who Comes First?, cont'd.)
people who hold high-ranking office, such as governors, mayors, judges, ambassadors, senators, members of Congress, and church officers, outrank women, the elderly, and other guests. People are introduced to them as a mark of respect for the offices they hold.

THE WRITTEN WORD

Much of our formal communication is done through writing. Some say the art of writing is being lost in our ever-more electronic world, but I think the ability to put words together in a thoughtful way will always bring pleasure and grace to those who practice it.

WRITTEN FORMS OF ADDRESS

In general, the opening of a letter is more formal than if you were to communicate in person or on the phone. When writing to someone you don't know, you will probably want to use the person's title. Thus, a woman you know to be married would be addressed on the envelope using the respectful "Mrs." She may use her own first name, so "Mrs. Annabelle Abercrombie" would be appropriate. If the woman is older, she may customarily use her husband's name and thus would prefer "Mrs. Charles Abercrombie." If you know a woman is married but does not use her husband's name, she would be addressed using her own name as "Ms. Annabelle Ames."

The greeting of the letter might be "Dear Mrs. Abercrombie," though, if it's someone you know slightly or well, you may elect to use the first name or even her chosen diminutive ("Dear Annabelle" or "Dear Belle"). As with spoken forms of address, dignitaries and clergy are referred to by their titles: "Senator," "Congressman," "Pastor."

Thus, a letter might open like this:

Mrs. John Adams
The Springs
East Templeton, WI 68926
October 25, 1999

Dear Mrs. Adams,

I was so pleased to meet you last Saturday at the Wrights'
home.

If unsure of how to address a woman, you are generally safe using
the title "Ms." for young women. Rarely is the title "Miss" used
except for older women whom you know to be unmarried, and for
young girls. The greeting for such a letter might be "Dear Ms.
O'Neil" or, if you choose, you might use the person's full name, as
in "Dear Maureen O'Neil."
    Traditionally, writing a woman's name as "Mrs. Maureen O'Neil"
conveyed her status as a divorced woman. These days, however, that
is not implied. Many women simply elect to use their own name
despite their married status; some divorced women take back their
maiden names. Others use a combination of their maiden and married
names. In any case, a divorced woman does not use her ex-husband's
first name as part of her own.
    Men are generally addressed by the title "Mr." If a man or woman
uses the title "Dr." before the name, that takes precedence over Mr.,
Mrs., or Ms.
    When addressing a married couple, one of whom is a doctor, you
always use the title. When the doctor is the woman, the names would
read "Mr. and Dr. Jensen." When the doctor is the man, "Dr. and
Mrs. Lincoln" is appropriate.
    We would never write "Mr. and Ms. Anderson" unless addressing
a man and his sister. If you are addressing a man and his sister and
they share a last name, she is probably a "Miss" (although she might
not want to be called "Miss"). Getting the title right can be tricky.
    Should you find yourself writing a letter to a member of the clergy,
an elected official, or another dignitary, use the title both on the
envelope and the greeting. For instance, if you were to write to your

state senator (or congressman) you would address the envelope in this fashion:

> The Honorable John James
> The State House
> Salem, OR 97401

and the greeting would appear like this:

> Dear Senator James:

If you were to write to the president of the United States, you would not need to put his or her name on the envelope. You would simply write:

> The President
> The White House
> Washington, D.C. 20500

For clergy, use the appropriate title ("Father," "Reverend," or "Rabbi") along with his or her name. Some have doctorate degrees that they also use, after the clerical title, as in "The Reverend Dr. Anna Smith." For government officials, the standard closing is "Respectfully." For members of the clergy it is "Sincerely."

FORMAL INVITATIONS

For casual parties and events, a telephone invitation may be enough. However, for formal or large events, a written invitation is called for. For any party, casual or not, a proper response is necessary.

We'll start with the formal invitation, which can seem intimidating. The most common formal invitation is for a wedding, which is covered elsewhere in this book (see Chapter 6, Weddings, page 154). A wedding invitation is by no means the only kind of formal invitation; others include anniversary parties, dances, balls, coming-of-age parties, and other such major events.

Formal invitations are conservative in wording and appearance. The wording is usually centered on the page. The invitation is engraved or printed in black ink on heavy plain white or off-white paper. The paper may be paneled or plain.

Often the invitation is enclosed with a piece of tissue in a second envelope on which the name of the person receiving the invitation is written. Both of these customs harken to an earlier era. The tissue was used as a blotter when printing inks were not as sophisticated as they are today and ink could smudge. The extra envelope dates to the time before postal services, when all mail was delivered by messenger.

A formal invitation for a party would look much like this:

Mr. and Mrs. John Jones
request the pleasure of your company
on Saturday, the twelfth of June
at eight o'clock
192 Winthrop Lane
Cambridge, New York

R.S.V.P.   Black tie

A formal invitation should be mailed at least three weeks in advance of the event.

The invitation might also include the reason for the party—if, for example, the party is being held in honor of someone or to commemorate an event or holiday. If you are giving a party for yourselves, however, you would not mention that fact.

The manner of dress is only mentioned when the hosts expect everyone to really dress up. Mentioning "black tie," which these days implies formal dress, or "white tie" (truly formal dress) would only appear on an invitation for an evening. It would not be appropriate for a daytime event.

R.S.V.P. stands for *Repondez s'il vous plaît* and means "please let us know if you are coming." You should respond as soon as you can.

A formal invitation requires a formal response. If a response card is included along with the invitation, as has become common with wedding invitations, you may use it. If not, then you should send a handwritten reply, written on heavy plain stationery, that reads like this:

Ms. Samantha Egerton
accepts with pleasure
your kind invitation
for Saturday the twelfth of June

A formal regret might resemble this:

Ms. Samantha Egerton
regrets that she is unable to accept
your very kind invitation
for Saturday the twelfth of June

Alternatively, you may put everything in the third person, saying:

Ms. Samantha Egerton
regrets that she is unable to accept
the kind invitation of Mr. and Mrs. John Jones
for Saturday the twelfth of June

Notice that the date is spelled out in a formal invitation and acceptance or regret.

INFORMAL INVITATIONS

Preprinted invitations or handwritten notes can be used for less formal occasions and casual parties. Stationery stores usually carry a wide variety of decorated invitations. Among the most useful are those that are plain, with blanks to be filled in with the particulars of time, place, and so on. You may also use your own stationery to write invitations.

You might take a somewhat formal approach such as this:

Open House
Susan and Peter Jackson
New Year's Day
Noon to 4 P.M.

Or you might write a short note, create your own invitations, or invite people using the telephone. In issuing written invitations, be sure to include a telephone number, which your guests will want to use when responding.

It's also sometimes helpful to give an indication of the nature of the party and how formal you expect it to be. This can be conveyed casually along with the other pertinent information, as in this example: "We would love to see you for dinner around 7:30 on Friday, September 1. We're cooking out, so dress casually."

Again, an invitation of any kind should be accepted or declined as soon as possible after you receive it. If you can't accept right away when invited by telephone, make sure you call back just as soon as you can. If a telephone number is included in a written invitation, use that. If not, write a note.

How you respond to an invitation is important, too. It's best to sound genuinely pleased when accepting. If you must decline, show your disappointment. You don't need to give details about why you cannot come, but a brief explanation is often welcome.

PERSONAL CORRESPONDENCE

The personal note has definitely fallen out of favor in recent decades, a victim of the convenience of the telephone and E-mail. This is a genuine loss of civility, since nothing is as gracious as the written word, and telephone conversations and electronic communications seem so temporary and disposable.

Writing long informational letters filled with anecdotes is an art form, one that these days is only practiced for the most part by those who enjoy writing. Even if you take little pleasure from your pen, that doesn't mean you should give up on note and letter writing altogether. Notes don't have to take all your time, and letters often mean a great deal to the people who receive them. There are even a few instances in which it is rude, even today, not to write a note. These instances include:

- Thank you for a wedding present
- Thank you for spending the night in someone's home
- Thank you for presents not opened in the giver's presence
- Letter of acceptance or regret to a formal invitation
- Letter of condolence to a friend on the death of an immediate family member

There are a few other instances in which notes are particularly appreciated. These include:

• Thank you to someone who has done a special favor

• Note of congratulations in response to an important event, accomplishment, or honor in a friend's life

• Thank you to the hosts after a special dinner or party

Personal notes and letters follow a simple format. You begin with the date in the upper right corner, beneath the letterhead if using personalized stationery. If using a folded note card, you start inside, to the right of the fold. The letter begins with a salutation ("Dear Anna"). The body of the letter is next, followed by a closing. Closings for personal correspondence are a matter of choice, and they depend on your relationship with the person addressed. "Love" is the usual choice for family members and close friends, but "Fondly" and "Yours" work well for people whom you may not know well but feel warmly toward. "Sincerely" is used for strangers and in business letters.

You may either type or handwrite almost all personal notes and letters, with two exceptions: Thank-you notes for wedding presents and notes of condolence should always be handwritten.

Envelopes are addressed in a straightforward manner. Address the envelope using the names of the recipients. (If a married couple goes by different names, use them with the titles Mr. and Ms., as in "Mr. James Forester and Ms. Jane Winston.") For most correspondence, you can abbreviate names of streets and states, though for formal correspondence, everything except the titles Dr., Mr., Mrs., Ms., Jr., and Sr. is to be spelled out. Formal correspondence also includes the return address. In the past, it was *de rigueur* to put this information on the middle at the top of the back flap of the envelope, although that convention has largely been superceded, given the needs of the postal service, and return addresses are now often recorded on the upper left-hand corner of the envelope face.

Thank-You Notes. This is an area I feel strongly about. A quick note sent to thank someone for a favor, a party, or a present is a simple way to let that person know that you appreciate the efforts expended. You don't have to write an epistle; you only need a few specific lines remarking on the cause of your note and another sentence or two pertinent to the person you are addressing. The generic "Dear Cynthia, Thank you for the lovely evening. Fondly, Mary" is not quite enough for a grown-up to write, but something along these lines is:

> Dear Cynthia,
>
> Thank you so much for the lovely time spent at your house on Saturday. The evening couldn't have been better orchestrated, from the lively conversation of the guests (I never knew Bill had so many jokes in him!), to the delicious food you prepared. We're still talking about the luscious coconut cake.
>
> Fondly,
> Mary

Children and Thank-You Notes. Thinking of what is appropriate for grown-ups to write brings to mind children and thank-you notes. Children should be taught to thank people, too, not only because it is the polite thing to do, but as part of teaching them to value people and things. In fact, the earlier you start, the easier the habit is to ingrain. Even before children can write they can draw and dictate thank-yous to be written on their pictures. As soon as they can form letters they can, with your help, write notes. Children take great pleasure in such simple tasks, especially if you can make it fun by having them talk about what they like about the present, or draw what they like best. Needless to say, the thank-you notes of small children need be only a sentence long.

Letters of Condolence. Nobody likes to think about death, but death is as much a part of life as birth and thus needs to be acknowledged to grieving relatives. I can tell you from personal experience that a handwritten note, telling the person that you are thinking of them, really does help. If you knew the deceased, it helps if you can recall a memory associated with the person. A phone call in addition is fine, too, but it is not a substitute for words put on paper. A printed sympathy card conveys little. The personal touch at these times *is* important.

A condolence note to a close friend might look something like this:

> Dear Max,
>
> I was so sorry to hear of your mother's death. I'll always have a fond memory of that weekend we spent at the beach listening to your mother's great stories and enjoying her lively sense of humor. Remember when we all danced the limbo, your mother included?
>
> I know the next weeks and months will be difficult for you and the rest of your family, but please know that we are all thinking of you. I would like to be of use if possible, so if there is anything that I can do, please just let me know.
>
> > Love,
> > Hilary

A slightly more formal note, to an acquaintance or less close friend, might look something like this:

> Dear Sue,
>
> I just learned of the death of your father. I've often heard you speak of him warmly and I know how very much he meant to you. I just wanted you to know that you have my deepest sympathy and that I'm thinking of you. If there is anything I can do for you in the weeks and months ahead, don't hesitate to call on me.
>
> > Fondly,
> > Sam

If you know that your friend and the person who died had a complicated or tumultuous relationship, you need not pretend that all was sweetness and light. People's feelings often remain complicated. You may tactfully allude to the problems that were common knowledge between you. Such a note might read:

Dear Clarice,

I just learned of the death of your sister Amy and am so sorry. I know you two had your ups and downs over the years, but I also know that you always did your best to try to see things from her perspective as well as your own.

Please know that I am here for you, should you need me. Please don't hesitate to call.

Love,
Bernadette

A condolence note should be written as soon as you learn of the death, but no one should hold it against you if it is not within the first few days. Up to several months after the event is acceptable, but *don't* wait six months or a year.

A note of condolence should be answered with a handwritten thank-you note, although I do feel that people shouldn't be held as accountable for the follow-up note as at other times.

PERSONAL STATIONERY

Ironically, in an era when letter writing is in decline, beautiful paper and stationery designs seem to be on the increase, as is interest in fine pens and inks. So, what should you use?

Everyday Writing Paper. The most essential supply in your stationery "wardrobe" is probably everyday writing paper for personal correspondence. This paper is used for writing letters to friends, thank-you notes, letters of congratulation and condolence, and so on. A woman's paper may be colored pastel or vivid; it may be white, pale blue, or gray (the latter is specially suitable for condolence notes). It can measure about 5 by 7½ inches or up to 8½ by 11 (standard business size). If white, beige, or gray, these sheets may double as business paper, making it the most versatile of papers. It may be personalized with a monogram or a name and address.

Men's paper is usually larger, often business size, and may be printed with his name and address. If full size, it can double for personal business as well. Men's paper does not usually have a monogram.

An option for a couple to share stationery is to have what is called house paper. This stationery, 7 by 10 or 8½ by 11 inches, is printed with the address but no names.

Paper for children can be whimsical and fun, and a good way to interest a child in letter writing.

Formal Writing Paper. This paper is used to respond to formal invitations and to write condolence notes. It should be plain white or cream of fine heavy (usually thirty-two-pound) stock. Formal paper has a fold on the left side, giving it a face that measures about 5¾ by 7¾ inches. It may be plain or engraved with your name at the top. The letter is folded once again to fit into its matching envelope.

Correspondence Cards. Measuring about 3½ by 5¾ inches, these are used for quick short notes. They may be decorated with a monogram, colored, or plain. You never write on the back. If you have that much to say, use a sheet of paper.

Personal Cards. These used to be called calling cards, but formal calls have gone the way of gaslights. Today, these small cards (about 2 by 3½ inches) are engraved or printed with your name and sometimes address and often are used for gift enclosures. They also can be used for business cards.

Blank Decorated Cards. Beautifully decorated cards in which you write your own greetings and notes can be great for informal notes and responses. Don't rely on ones with preprinted messages.

HOLIDAY GREETING CARDS

For so many of us, December is a time of year for catching up with friends and acquaintances through letters and greeting cards. It has become one of the shared rituals of the season. I know I always look forward to receiving news from friends I rarely see. However, sometimes I feel overwhelmed by the amount there is to do at such a busy time of year.

No one is socially obliged to send cards. They should be sent out of free will. If you don't send greetings, however, don't be disappointed if others do not send them to you.

If you would like to send a yearly greeting but find the Christmas holiday season just too busy, you could create your own ritual. Some people send New Year's greetings after the December rush has slowed. Sending them at the close of December may enable you to remain on other people's active card lists.

For people who enjoy participating in the pleasant custom of sending holiday greetings, there are a few guidelines to follow. For friends and acquaintances:

• Always include a personal line or note, even on preprinted cards. After all, your personal touch is what makes a holiday wish special.

• If you send a copied letter detailing your year, keep it brief. A few special news notes will do.

• If you use cards preprinted with your name for both business and personal acquaintances, be sure to write in your first names when sending to family and friends.

• Avoid religious cards for those who don't share your faith.
For business acquaintances:

• Avoid sending a personal letter. Stick to a handwritten sentence or two.

• Cards preprinted with your name should still be signed, although not necessarily by the whole family.

• Avoid comic cards unless they specifically relate to business.

• Send only secular cards.

Newspaper Announcements

There's an old saying that a well-bred woman had her name in the newspaper three times in her life: when she was born, when she married, and when she died. I don't know what the rule was for men back then, but today most women and men are more likely to have their names in the papers for many reasons, including business success, public service, and social prominence. Yet, for all the community and business announcements that we see in our local papers, the most common remain those for birth, marriage, and death.

Birth Announcements. In small towns and cities local newspapers often announce local births. Usually the parents need do nothing, as the reporter in charge regularly checks in with the local hospitals. In some large cities parents must pay for the announcement. If you wish to announce the birth of your child, call the newspaper and ask their requirements.

Wedding or Engagement Announcements. The most common announcement is that of an upcoming wedding, either well in advance of the event (this is an engagement announcement) or on the day of or immediately after the wedding. Such announcements usually appear in weekend editions, since most weddings take place on Saturday or Sunday. Weekly newspapers run announcements on the day they publish. The wording of most announcements is fairly standard, although some newspapers have their own requirements. (See Chapter 6, Weddings, page 131, for more information and examples of wedding and engagement announcements.)

Death Announcements. The announcement of a death in the newspaper is not the same as an obituary; rather it is a paid announcement. These announcements are placed in the newspaper by the funeral director and are based on information provided by the family. (See also Chapter 7, Milestones, page 192, for information on obituaries.)

Other Announcements. Should you find yourself in the position of wishing to announce an important event, such as a fiftieth wedding anniversary, confirmation, bar or bat mitzvah, the debut of a daughter into society, the formation of a new business, or a community-service event, call the local newspaper and ask for the appropriate editor. Newspapers have their own styles, requirements, and deadlines.

ELECTRONIC MANNERS

More and more of our lives are conducted electronically, whether it's by telephone, E-mail, or other means. As new as some of these technologies seem, old-fashioned common consideration should still be paid to the people at the other end of the line.

THE TELEPHONE

By far the most pervasive and integrated electronic tool in our lives today is the telephone. Myriad aspects of our lives are now conducted via telephone, and, as with every tool of modern life that affects other people, there are ways to use the telephone that are efficient, effective, and life-enhancing. And others that are abrupt, careless, and downright discourteous. The same basic principles hold true for personal calls as well as business calling (for more on the latter, see Chapter 9, Office Etiquette, page 242).

Basics of Telephoning. We've all been using the phone since we were children, but brushing up on the basics of good phone behavior can't hurt. Americans answer the telephone by saying "Hello" and waiting for the caller to respond. We end calls by saying "Goodbye." Try not to sound abrupt when speaking on the phone because it translates to the other person as impatience or annoyance. Your body language may be saying something pleasant but it plays to a piece of plastic.

Identify yourself as the caller. Close friends and intimates will know your voice but anyone outside your immediate circle may not place it at first. Don't assume that people beyond your nearest and dearest will automatically know you by first name alone, either. I once knew a family in which every woman identified herself merely by saying "Hi," expecting anyone who answered to know which of the four sisters was calling. The presumption that they were always at the top of one's mind became annoying.

Make sure to identify yourself even when someone else answers. You can say, "Hello, is Mary home? This is Betsy Smith calling," or some such simple greeting. If you recognize the person at the other end, greet him or her by name, perhaps exchange a pleasantry, and then ask for the person with whom you wish to speak.

Be sensitive to the hour. Sometimes it's difficult to know when is a good time to reach someone, particularly as people lead busy and fragmented lives. If you can avoid the dinner hour, do so, as we all find calls during meals annoying. When you can't, try to keep the conversation as brief as possible.

Try not to call late at night or early in the morning. I try not to call people after 9:30 P.M. or before 9:00 A.M. If I know someone never retires until midnight and welcomes calls until then, I'll make an exception. On weekends I try not to call before 10 A.M. unless there are young children in the house, in which case I know people are up and about earlier.

Similarly, people who work at home are often busy working. You may find yourself with extra time, but don't assume they are on your schedule. Keep conversations brief unless the other person indicates it's a good time to visit.

As the recipient of a call at an inconvenient time, you have responsibilities, too. It is your duty to let the caller know if he or she is interrupting something important. Ask if you can call back at a time convenient to the caller and explain briefly but politely why you can't talk. You can simply say, "I'm sorry, I'm getting the kids to bed right now. May I call you in half an hour?" or some such honest and polite remark.

Some people have a hard time telling others that they are busy. In that case, turn on your answering machine during that busy time and return calls when it's quieter.

Telephone Solicitations. I don't know one person who enjoys someone trying to sell to him something over the phone. The kindest thing to do to end such a call, though it may not seem so at first, is to say politely but firmly at the outset something like, "I'm sorry, I'm not interested in buying anything over the phone. I won't waste your time. Good day." Remember, being rude to the caller is not a good solution.

Wrong Numbers. We all occasionally get the wrong number. When you realize something is amiss, apologize to the person who answers and repeat the number you were trying to reach. This way you are less likely to dial it incorrectly again. Don't just hang up, that's plain discourteous.

Call-Waiting. The sophistication of phones has come a long way, and call-waiting, in which a call rings through while you're on the phone, is here to stay. When a call comes through you have two choices. You can ignore it and the caller will have to ring back. Or you can ask the person you are speaking with to please hold, saying something like, "I'm sorry, I've got another call coming through which I'd better take. Can you hold a moment, or shall I call you back?" If your first caller holds on, make sure you keep the second call brief, asking if you can call that person back. Never leave a caller on hold for more than a minute, if you can possibly avoid it.

Speakerphones. Sometimes it would be so much more convenient to have your hands—and neck—free when talking on the phone. That's when speakerphones can come in handy. It is just for this reason, however, that you need to be careful. People really don't like the notion that you are not paying full attention to the conversation. They also may not like the idea that other people might be listening to what's said. Also, the sound quality is usually substandard, making it difficult to hear and always obvious. If you use a speakerphone, ask the other party's permission before getting into the conversation.

Dialing Away from Home. When using someone else's phone, always ask permission first. Ask permission before giving out another person's number for the forwarding of calls. If making a long-distance call, use your own phone card or ask the operator to have the calls charged to your home phone.

The Electronic Answerer. The answering machine and voice mail have become a ubiquitous and useful part of American life. No longer do you have to sit by the telephone and dial a number every few minutes waiting for a person to return, or perhaps worse, try to remember to call back later.

Not surprisingly, there are a few basic rules for using these helpful devices. First, in taping your greeting, don't try to be too clever, as it wastes the caller's time. A simple, straightforward message on the machine is usually best. You can say something like, "You've reached Jane and Paul Lawrence [you may use your phone number if you don't want to use your name]. We can't take your call right now, but if you'll leave your name and number one of us will call you back as soon as we can."

As the caller, your message should be succinct, too. You should give your name, the time you called, and a brief message. You probably won't want to leave bad news on a machine but deliver the news on the returned call instead.

Eavesdropping on a caller leaving you a message is impolite, especially if you decide to pick up partway through. Screening calls implies you are making high-handed judgments about whom you want to talk to and who isn't worth your time. If you should happen not to make it to the phone before the machine picks up, explain the circumstances.

Cellular Phones. The ultimate portable phone also seems here to stay. Cell phones can be very convenient but don't be confused: Unlike your home phone, they are rarely private. Anyone near you on the street, in a restaurant, or in the same train car cannot help but overhear part of what you are saying. And it isn't solely a matter of your privacy—your full-voiced conversation can be irritating and intrusive to others. Therefore, try not to inconvenience those around you. Never use cell phones in a public place, such as a theater or restaurant, unless you excuse yourself to a private spot. Besides the noise and distraction, it sends a message that you'd rather be somewhere else.

When in an enclosed space, such as a train, try not to use them at all unless you are seated alone. If you must, keep your calls brief and your voice low. Make sure you turn off your phone's ringer before a show or performance.

Some new cellular phones and beepers can use lights or vibration instead of a ringer to alert the owner of a call. These can be useful for those times when you truly need to be available to take a call. If you know you must take an emergency call during a social event, consider skipping the event.

When you give out your cellular or beeper number, be sure to mention how you would like it used: only in an emergency (and define an emergency), whenever there is news, whatever. Remember, too, that, contrary to what some people seem to think, cellular phones are not a badge of importance; using them ostentatiously isn't gracious or polite.

Children and the Telephone. Small children love telephones. Very small children do not usually know how to speak on a real telephone, so until they are old enough to answer the phone properly, they should not be allowed to toy with the phone. Answering the phone properly consists of "Hello. May I ask who's calling? Just a moment please while I get my mom (or dad or babysitter)." Don't let small children call adults during the workday unless you have checked it out ahead of time.

E-MAIL AND THE INTERNET

Computers, once the domain of business, have entered our homes and become essential tools of communication and entertainment for millions of people. We send messages to friends and relations via electronic mail. We meet people, play games, do research, and even shop over the Internet and World Wide Web. Friends of mine say that they stay in much closer touch with members of their families through E-mail than they did before they had it. For those wired in, these tools can open a world of opportunities when used responsibly.

Discussion groups are available on almost any topic that you can imagine. Not everything available in cyberspace is appropriate for everyone, especially children. Most parents are aware that they bear some responsibility for their children's choice of entertainment, and cyberspace is no exception. (For more information on the do's and don'ts of cyberspace, see Chapter 9, Office Etiquette, page 240.)

PERSONAL ELECTRONICS

There was a time not long ago when people who wore pagers needed to be reached in an emergency. Today, people wear them for convenience as much as necessity. When a caller needs to reach someone else who is away from home or office, he or she can call the number and it will alert the wearer, who will return the call. This can be quite handy, but care must also be taken when using pagers, especially in public or in a social setting. There are few things more rude than having a lovely lunch or dinner repeatedly interrupted by someone's pager. A friend of mine recently counted seven interruptions while lunching with a friend. Completing a discussion on any topic was impossible. And none of the calls was so important that it couldn't have been dealt with after lunch at the office.

Pagers also present a problem when people leave them on at public functions. Everyone is disturbed when one goes off, first by the sound, and then by the person having to get up and leave the row, usually disturbing everyone along the way. So, if you use a pager, please consider your neighbors and friends. Turn it off when in public unless it really is a matter of life and death. If you know you will have to take a specific call, arrange for it in advance and excuse yourself to make the call.

Electronic watches that beep at regular intervals can be a problem, too, especially in a public place. How many of us have been at a movie or a concert when, during a quiet moment, someone's watch sounds off, *Beep, beep.* It is unnecessary. In fact, it's quite common these days for audiences to be asked to turn off all pagers and watches before a performance.

Many people don't seem to know how to turn them off, but it seems to me that if you wear one it is your duty to figure out how the equipment works. After all, communicating to people around you that you don't care about them is not a message you want to send. It's well worth the time to learn what's required in order to be courteous. At bottom, we all want to communicate clearly that we do care about and pay proper consideration to the people with whom we share our world.

2

MODERN TABLE MANNERS

One of the things that people often worry about when confronted with the prospect of a new social situation involving a meal is how to behave at the table. They ask themselves, "Which fork will I use?" "How should I act?" "What can I talk about?" People are often concerned that they will embarrass themselves, their hosts, or their partners.

Since all manners arise from the instinct to treat others kindly, table manners will actually benefit those who use them and those who view them. Simple consideration is the bedrock of all good behavior, table manners included, and once you understand that, you can eat at any table with confidence. Basic good manners will carry you through situations from a simple supper at home to the most formal of dinners. That's not to say, however, that there aren't a few extra elements that will help polish your manners.

What I desire most at my table is that my guests feel relaxed. I also enjoy seeing elegant table manners in use—*and* I find they contribute to a sense of ease, actually making it simpler for people to have a good time. On the other hand, I'm the first to admit that correct but stiff manners are almost as bad as slovenly behavior since exaggerated formality calls attention to itself just as loudly as does rudeness. Neither one will do.

Elegant manners are understated, natural seeming, and straightforward, too. For instance, you sit up at the table in order that you can see and speak to the people around you. You look at *them,* not down at the table or your plate. Again, though, sitting so straight as to look stuffed will look uncomfortable and may make everyone else aware of your (possible) discomfort or, at least, your rigid posture.

Don't lean on your elbows while eating because it makes you appear tired or bored; such a position can also get in the way of eating. On the other hand, casually resting the elbows on the table in the relaxed interlude between courses shouldn't interfere with anyone else's space or send your tablemates the message you are exhausted or lazy.

You don't stuff your mouth or chew with your mouth open because these habits are most unpleasant to behold. They make you look greedy, too, and can even give you indigestion.

You wait to start eating until everyone has been served (unless urged to begin by the hostess) so that you don't appear gluttonous. When you finish eating well before everyone else, it suggests you are hurried, impatient, and inconsiderate.

We want our fellow diners to be comfortable. To achieve this, they need to have the elements of the meal easily accessible, be made to feel a part of the group, have pleasant conversation available, and not be distracted by rude personal habits. Sharing a meal, after all, is a cooperative venture: Hostesses and hosts appreciate guests who lend the proceedings an air of ease and civility, and guests value a considerate and well-prepared welcome.

TWELVE BASIC RULES OF TABLE BEHAVIOR

You probably already obey these simple rules. But if you don't, you may be sending messages you don't intend to those who have invited you to dine with them. To make everyone feel comfortable—including yourself—try to adopt these as basic to your table behavior:

1. Sit up straight—not too rigidly, but not slouched.

2. Chew quietly, with your mouth closed, and avoid slurping or making other unattractive noises.

3. Cut food into bite-size pieces, one piece at a time.

4. Do not stuff your mouth.

5. Eat slowly. Do not inhale food but instead chew it.

6. Once you have put food on a utensil, eat it. Do not wave it or hold it in midair while talking or listening.

7. Keep your elbows off the table when eating. You can't sit up if you are leaning on your arms.

8. Do not speak with your mouth full of food.

9. Help yourself to foods that are near you; ask your dining companions to pass you those that would require awkward reaching.

10. Always say "please" and "thank you" when foods are passed and when accepting and declining food.

11. If you must leave the table during the meal, excuse yourself.

12. Compliment the cook for the effort of preparing the meal, whether in your own home or someone else's.

YOUR TABLE HABITS

Nowhere else in your day-to-day life is basic consideration as important as at the table. Rude habits distract other diners and may even detract from their appetites.

EATING AND DRINKING

This can't be emphasized too much: Never chew with your mouth open. Slurping your soup makes a most irritating sound, no matter how good it may feel in the mouth. Stuffing one's mouth distorts the shape of the face and tells your tablemates you are disregarding them altogether.

Things we do in preparing to eat can interfere with other people's dining pleasure, too. Reaching across the table obstructs other people, makes you seem greedy, and risks upsetting elements on the table. It's also unnecessary: A simple request—"Please pass the butter"— is more efficient and a demonstration of politeness.

Piling large quantities of food on your plate before others have had a chance at the food sends the wrong message, namely, "I'm more important than you and I deserve as much as I want." Talking while poking the air with a fork for emphasis invades other people's space, risks bits of food flying, and has the effect of directing all attention to you whether appropriate or not.

Cutting up all the food on your plate, as you would for a child, makes it appear as though you are preparing for a race. Instead, make individual portions for each bite, showing that you are enjoying the meal and its pace.

There are a few other things we shouldn't do at the table. I have heard it said that in some cultures it is good manners to release a good burp at the table after a meal, as a compliment to the hostess. That's simply not so here. No one should make rude noises while anyone is eating. If you must burp, do it as discreetly as possible. If you need to sneeze, cover your nose and mouth with your napkin. In both cases, a simple "excuse me" follows. If you feel an attack of gas coming on, excuse yourself from the table and go to the lavatory.

BODY LANGUAGE

What you do with your body while at the dining table can communicate clearly your attitude to your hosts and fellow diners. Lounging at the table shows a lack of interest toward your fellow diners. Tipping your chair back as though it were a rocking chair does more than suggest you are relaxed. To the hosts, it reveals an insensitivity to them and their belongings. I know of one fellow who had the unfortunate habit of abusing his hosts' furniture in this way and finally was rewarded by one of the weakened chairs collapsing beneath him at the table. He never did it again, although he still complains about his hosts having weak chairs!

Just as there are some behaviors to avoid at the table, there are several good ones to remember. When the person next to you is speaking, slow your eating—or stop briefly—and turn slightly toward him or her while listening. This small courtesy suggests you are interested in what's being said. Just sitting up straight, in a relaxed manner, shows everyone that you are alert and pleased to be there.

GROOMING AT THE TABLE

A dinner table is not the place to practice personal grooming. Never pick your teeth, clean your nails, comb your hair, or put on lipstick. Don't blow your nose unnecessarily; if you must, use a tissue and blow your nose discreetly or even excuse yourself and go to the bathroom for a moment. The same holds true for sniffling or repeatedly clearing your throat.

CONVERSATION

I find that the best table conversations, whether for a family dinner or a formal one, are those that are of interest to most or all the people at the table and that have elements of humor or surprise. I try to avoid subjects that are unpleasant and likely to cause distress or argument. Detailed recountings of the mundane events of the day probably won't add much to a meal, but amusing stories and bits of news will.

When children are dining with you, try to get them to talk about what has been fun or interesting that day; their candor and insights can make for an informative and fun meal for all. In general, matters of business and household minutiae are probably better reserved for another time. No matter what the situation, one should try to avoid arguments and heated discussions while people are eating.

HANDLING UTENSILS

An area of great concern for many people is how to handle utensils at the table. I think one of the reasons for this lies with our increasingly casual ways; rules that a generation or two ago were generally accepted are no longer a given in many households. Another explanation might be the custom of setting a family table with the fork on the left, knife on the right, and teaspoon outside the knife. Some find this arrangement confusing, because the spoon often goes unused.

With the exception of the unused spoon, however, proper table settings are quite logical, as they reflect the order in which the utensils are to be used. We start with the outermost fork or spoon in the setting and work our way in, usually using one utensil per course. If you are served a first course of soup, for instance, the properly set table will offer a soup spoon on the outside right of your place setting. (For more on utensils and their arrangements, see Chapter 3, The Tools of the Table, page 86.)

If you find yourself faced with a question of which utensil to use, just wait until your host or hostess takes the first bite (that's the considerate thing to do anyway) and observe which utensil he or she uses. If you don't know how to eat something, again, watch your hosts and proceed from there.

Once you've used a utensil, never put it back on the table; put it on the side of your plate. The exception to this is in a restaurant where patrons are encouraged to retain their forks for the next course. This is a practice I dislike. It's discomfiting to be left with an awkward choice: You can sit there with your fork in hand, waiting for the next course to arrive; or, alternatively, you can set the used fork down, perhaps on a clean tablecloth or, worse yet, on a not-so-clean bare table.

When you are resting between bites of food and joining in the lively and interesting conversation, you can place your knife and fork across one another in the middle of your plate. When you are finished with the course, place them parallel to one another and on one side of your plate. The latter is a signal to a waiter, should you be in a restaurant, that you are finished.

SERVING FOOD

At casual dinners food is often served family style, which means that it comes to the table in serving bowls and on platters from which the hosts serve or people help themselves. Your obligation as a diner is to serve yourself, then pass the bowl or platter, perhaps holding it for the person next to you.

Usually food is passed to the right because most people are right-handed and it is easier to reach the food. Food may be passed in either direction; however, it makes sense to pass the various dishes in the same direction to avoid awkward crossing over.

Usually the hostess or host will start the passing of food or ask someone seated near a particular dish to start it. The central element of the meal, often meat or fish, will typically be circulated first, followed by vegetable and other dishes.

Meat passed on a platter is usually accompanied by a meat fork. Each diner spears a piece or two, at an angle, or slides the fork under the food and moves it to his or her plate. Vegetables are served with large spoons.

The trickiest utensils to use are the serving spoon and fork together. The correct approach is to use one hand, with the spoon lifting the food and the fork steadying the serving from above as the food is transferred to the plate.

When a portion of food is discrete, say, served on a lettuce leaf or toast, take the entire portion onto your plate. If there is a garnish on the platter, you may take a little of the garnish as well.

If there is a gravy or sauce, use the ladle or spoon provided. If a small pitcher resting on a plate is used and there is no ladle or spoon, you are expected to pour from it. Gravy may be poured over meat and potatoes but not over vegetables. Spoon a portion of a thick sauce next to the food it is to accompany.

INFORMAL DINING

Local, regional, and ethnic customs range widely for informal meals. However, the general order of courses and serving, from a simple supper in the kitchen to more elaborate events, typically share a number of characteristics.

At a family meal, people take their accustomed seats upon entering the dining room. If there are guests, the visitors usually are placed by the hosts. A woman guest is traditionally seated next to the host, a man next to the hostess. There is no hard-and-fast rule about this, however, and if people would be most comfortable elsewhere, seating can be flexible.

As you approach the table you will see an array of china, silver, and glassware. You may notice that some elements don't match. For instance, all the first course plates will match one another, but may not match the dinner plates, which will be brought in later. Similarly, a fish fork used for a first course may not match the dinner fork, but all the fish forks will be alike, unless the hosts are showing off their rare collection of fish forks.

Upon sitting down, the diners should find a napkin either between the utensils, under the fork, or to the left of the fork. At a truly formal dinner the napkin will be placed in the center of the service plate. If a blessing or grace is offered, wait to place the napkin in your lap until it is over. If not, the first thing you do when sitting is to put the napkin in your lap, where it will stay until the meal is over, except for the moments when you gently wipe your mouth with it. It's also appropriate to use the napkin before taking a sip of a drink, so you don't leave a smudge on the edge of the glass. When you wipe your mouth, place your utensils on the plate.

If you are wearing lipstick, try to dab your mouth gingerly and drink carefully to avoid leaving large smudges on the napkin and glass. Blotting your lipstick on a tissue before sitting down is also a good practice.

If you leave the table during the meal, place the napkin on the table beside your plate, not on your chair. At the end of the meal, place your napkin to the right of your plate. Unless it is a family dinner and you plan to use it again, do not refold the napkin but drape it loosely. Don't wad it up.

At the beginning of the meal, wait for the person who prepared the meal to sit and begin before beginning yourself. This is both basic courtesy and consistent with the tried-and-true custom of waiting for the hostess to raise her fork. Even children should be taught at a young age to wait for everyone to be present before beginning. The host or hostess should also not linger in the kitchen unless necessary. Should there be a delay, they should encourage diners to begin.

Often bread is served at the beginning of a meal. At a formal or fancy informal dinner it may be placed on the bread-and-butter plate before guests are seated. The French custom is to put bread directly on the table. If your host or hostess does this, you may follow, otherwise put it on your dinner plate. If butter is passed, use the butter knife (if one is provided) to transfer a pat of butter to the edge of your plate, then return the butter knife to the butter plate. The butter knife is there is keep the butter clean of food. Use your dinner knife to butter your bread unless a butter plate and spreader are at your place.

At a family meal, diners usually aren't shy about asking for second servings. When guests are present, however, the considerate host or hostess should try to be alert to the guests' needs since, traditionally, they are not supposed to ask for seconds. As a guest, you needn't feel shy about asking for condiments; you can request that salt and pepper, butter, or any other seasoning on the table be passed to you.

At an informal meal, food may be handled in several ways. Meat and poultry can be carved in the kitchen, at the table, or at a sideboard, depending on the inclination and skill of the carver. It can then be placed on a platter and brought to the table. A stew or soup can be served in the kitchen and portions brought to the diners, or a tureen or big pot may be placed directly on the table and the soup served from it.

Salad may be served as a first course or after the entrée. The salad should be dressed shortly before the meal or at a sideboard just before serving. Avoid putting bottles of dressing on the table. I think the nicest way of serving salad is to bring the fresh greens to the table in a beautiful bowl. I often decorate the bowl with tasty and edible flowers. When serving, I can adjust the amount of salad to my guests' wishes and even compose it a little as I serve, perhaps placing a flower at the edge of each portion.

Dessert may, like the other courses, be served in the kitchen or at the table. Cakes, pies, and soufflés are often best served at the table, since they are attractive to behold before serving. Again, the host or hostess may tailor the amount served to individual diners. Wet desserts, such as puddings and ice-cream concoctions, are usually composed in the kitchen and brought to the table looking their best.

In America it is considered good manners to praise the meal and the person who prepared it, though without gushing too much. I know that when I've worked hard to prepare a meal, it makes me feel warm and happy to hear that friends and family have enjoyed it.

FORMAL DINING

As you enter the dining room, dinner having been announced by the hosts, look for a place card that indicates where you are to sit. Stand by your chair until everyone has reached the table. If you are a man, it is still considered polite for you to pull out the chair of the woman on your right.

When you sit, you will be faced with an array of glasses and silver, but there should be no more than three of each utensil. If more are required, they will be brought with the course that requires them. As at an informal dinner, the china and silver may not match completely but again will match within each course.

Food at a formal dinner is usually put on plates in the kitchen and served to seated guests by a server, not the host or hostess. As always, food is served counterclockwise around the table, on the guest's left. When a person bearing a bowl or platter appears at your elbow, you turn slightly and take no more than a moderate-sized portion of food onto your plate using the utensils provided. If the server serves you, lean slightly out of the way so that the person can reach in to place food on your plate discreetly. (See also the section on formal dining, page 89.)

Once everyone has been served, wait for the sign from the hosts for the meal to begin. From then on, remember to use the utensils on the outside first, working your way in for each course. When in doubt, check the behavior of your hosts.

When offered bread at a formal meal, check to see if bread-and-butter plates are on the table. If you have one, use it. If butter is passed, take a serving using the butter knife, transfer it to the edge of your bread-and-butter plate (or dinner plate in the absence of a bread-and-butter plate), and return the butter knife to the butter plate. Again, the butter knife is intended to keep the butter clean of food. Butter your bread with the butter spreader on your bread-and-butter plate; if you don't have one, use your dinner knife.

There is one element that you may see at a formal dinner that you would never see anywhere else. The finger bowl is a small glass bowl served after a messy course. It saves the napkins from being hope-lessly stained. When presented with one, you dip your fingers in the water, which may have a slice of lemon floating in it, and blot them on your napkin. The finger bowl is not for rinsing grapes or drinking (though I've seen both done!).

You may also be served a small quantity of sorbet, in a flavor such as lemon or champagne, between courses. This is meant to cleanse the palate. It is not dessert and you need not eat all of it.

Keep in mind that there is a logic to dining, formal or informal. The purpose is to enhance the enjoyment of the food and the company. Use your good sense, follow your hosts' lead, and you'll find the conventions relaxing and reassuring.

STYLES OF EATING

When faced with a plate of food, the basic goal of the considerate diner is to transport the food to the mouth as unobtrusively as possible. This means there are to be no grand displays of imagined notions of propriety nor, conversely, careless exhibitions of slovenly habits.

There are two basic styles of eating in this country, the American and the Continental. The American method, which could also be called the zigzag style of eating, is the one most of us use. It is not as efficient as the Continental method, but both are correct and acceptable.

The American method goes this way:

• In preparing a bite-size morsel for eating, hold the fork in the left hand, tines down, to secure the food.

• Cut with the knife, holding the handle in the palm of your right hand.

• Once a piece of food is cut (no more than one bite should be cut at a time), the knife is placed on the edge of the plate and the fork transferred to the right hand with the tines up.

• The food is scooped or speared and placed in the mouth.

• The American method calls for placing a hand at rest in the lap when you are eating with only a fork or spoon. If you are left-handed, all of the above hand positions are reversed.

The Continental or European method of eating is even simpler:

• Secure the food by holding the fork handle in the palm of your left hand, tines down, index finger pointed along its length. Cut with the knife held in the right hand.

• No switching of hands and placement of the knife is required. Once the meat has been cut, it is pushed onto the fork using the knife held in the right hand. Then the fork is moved, tines down, directly to your mouth. You may also use the knife to pile a small amount of food on the back of the fork's tines.

1. *Hold the knife and fork to cut meat.*

2. *Place the knife (blade toward the inside) on the plate after you have cut the food.*

3. *Bring the food to your mouth with the fork tines up.*

Fig. 2.1 Styles of eating: The American method

• While you are putting the food in your mouth, keep the knife in your hand, ready for the next cut. Alternatively, you may also return the knife to the edge of the plate until you are ready to use it again.

• The Continental method also calls for a hand at rest to be placed lightly at the edge of the table, rather than in the lap. If you travel to Europe you may eat in either manner, as most Europeans are aware of the American zigzag style.

A third acceptable approach is the Combination method, and as you might expect, it uses a little of each technique. Meat is cut and conveyed to the mouth as in the Continental style, while vegetables and other fork foods are eaten with the fork in the right hand, tines up.

With any of these methods of eating, food may be pushed onto the fork using the knife or a piece of bread.

1. *After cutting the meat, continue to hold the knife and keep the fork in your left hand.*

2. *Take the food into your mouth in your left hand, with the fork tines down. You may keep the knife in your hand or return it to the plate until you are ready to use it again.*

3. *Your knife may be used to pile a small amount of food on the back of the fork's tines.*

Continental style of eating for right-handed people (left-handed people reverse the process).

Fig. 2.2 Styles of eating: The Continental method

Regardless of the method you choose, there are a few dos and don'ts to remember:

• Always hold the utensils properly. Never grab a fork and hold it as if it were a shovel. Never hold the knife and fork vertically, as a small child does when first learning. Avoid arching your wrists— it's tiring and looks awkward.

• Keep your elbows from flapping, holding them fairly close to the body.

• Keep flatware balanced on the edge of the plate during the meal. Once a utensil has been used, no part should touch the table again.

• When passing your plate for seconds, place the knife and fork slightly on the right of the plate, aligned with each other, so there is room for food. Make sure to keep the plate level when passing it.

• A gentle reminder: All food should be eaten in manageable bites without overfilling the mouth; chewing is to be done with the mouth closed. Wolfing down food aggressively does not denote enthusiasm but greed.

EATING TRICKY FOODS

Considerate hosts at a formal or informal dinner make sure that the dishes served pose no difficulties for diners. That said, you may still find yourself on unfamiliar territory when it comes to certain foods, so here are a few handy guidelines for dealing with some likely dining challenges.

Artichokes. Whole artichokes are finger food. Begin at the outside and work your way, leaf by leaf, into the flower. Pull off each leaf, then dip the meatier end into butter or a sauce if one is provided. Place the end between your teeth and pull it forward. Then set the inedible portion of the leaf on the edge of your plate.

The leaves become smaller and more tender as you work your way in. When the leaves become too small to eat comfortably, or when you see the fuzzy choke, remove the last leaves and choke using the knife or spoon, and set them aside. You've reached the prize: the cup-shaped heart or bottom. Decorum usually dictates that you switch from finger eating to using your knife and fork. Quarter the heart before dipping it in the butter or sauce.

Asparagus. Firm stalks of asparagus may be picked up in your fingers, the tips dipped in any sauce that may be served, and eaten from the tips down. Limp asparagus should always be eaten with a fork or knife and fork.

Avocado. If a half is served filled with dressing, use a spoon to scoop out the flesh. If served filled, use a salad fork to eat the filling. If served in slices, eat them with a knife and fork.

Bacon. If crisp, eat with the fingers; if limp, cut the bacon with a knife and fork and eat with the fork.

Shellfish Stew. For bouillabaisse and other shellfish soups, use your knife and fork to eat pieces of fish and lobster. You may eat any shellfish in the shell with a fork. Use a soup spoon for the broth.

Baked Potato. Slit the tuber with your knife or with a fork. If you wish, you may use your fingers to open the potato a little to allow steam to escape. Do not scoop the flesh onto your plate, but eat it from the skin. You also may cut up the entire potato, skin and all, and eat the skin.

Caviar. Should you be lucky enough to be served caviar, take a small portion on your plate with toast and garnishes. Spread caviar on the toast, top with lemon juice and garnishes if you wish, and eat in several bites.

Chicken. If you are at a very casual party, such as a picnic or barbecue, you may assume that you can eat chicken with your hands. Otherwise, wait to see what your host or hostess does. If you are unsure, cut the meat from the bones with your knife and fork.

Corn on the Cob. This vegetable is to be eaten with the fingers, holding one hand at either end of the cob. Spread butter with a knife and sprinkle with salt only a few rows at a time. You will never be served this at a formal meal.

Small Fowl. The small scale of Cornish game hens and other small birds makes them a bit of a challenge to eat. Begin by separating the drumsticks from the body with your knife and fork. Carve a few slices of breast meat, place them on your plate, and cut with your knife and fork. If the bird is stuffed, scoop out the stuffing onto your plate before eating. Squab and other tiny birds are eaten with the fingers, although some meat may be cut off first.

Crudités. Pick up one piece of vegetable at a time and dip it gently into the dip or sauce. Take it to your mouth at once; avoid waving it around while talking. Don't dip a once-bitten piece into the communal dip or sauce, as that's unsanitary.

Egg in a Cup. Crack the shell gently with a knife or spoon and lift it off the top. Steady the cup with one hand while eating the contents with a spoon.

Espresso. This strong coffee is served after dessert. If an accompanying lemon peel is served, twist it before dropping it into the coffee, or place it at the edge of the saucer if you do not care for it. Generally it is left in the cup when the coffee is finished.

Fajitas, Pitas, and Other Stuffed Finger Foods. The rolled tortilla or bread, complete with contents, is eaten with the fingers. Anything that falls out is consumed using a fork.

Whole Fish. Cut off the head. Make a slice with the fish knife along the center back. Lift one side of the fish from the bones. Using a fish knife and fork, carefully remove the spine and accompanying bones and set aside. If you wish, flake off the skin. Use a fish fork and knife to pick up small pieces of fish. (Fish should always be eaten in small bites in order to avoid taking in a bone.) Remove any bone that does make it to your mouth with your fingers and place it on the side of the plate.

French Fries. These are finger food when served in a casual setting. Pour ketchup to the side, not over the fries, and dip them in. In a less than casual setting, cut into bite-sized pieces and eat with a fork.

Fruit. When served at a seated meal, apples and pears should be quartered with a fruit knife, cored, and eaten with the fingers. If you prefer, you may peel each piece individually.

Cherries and grapes are eaten out of hand, unless they are served in a sauce, in which case they are to be eaten with a spoon. Drop any pits and seeds into your fist and put them discreetly on the side of your plate.

Fruit compotes are eaten with a spoon. Remove any pits from your mouth using the spoon and, again, place them at the side of the plate that lines the bowl.

Melon wedges are eaten with a spoon or cut from the rind and into pieces with a knife and fork. Melon balls are eaten with a fork. When eating watermelon, pick out as many seeds as you can using a fork before eating the meat of the melon.

Peel oranges with a sharp knife and eat in sections with a fork or fingers.

Papaya is usually served halved. Scoop out the flesh and seeds with a spoon.

Cut peaches and plums in half with a fruit knife, remove the stone, and eat with the fingers.

Garnish. If it's edible, you may eat it with your fingers. Feel free to eat appealing herbs such as parsley, as well as fruit and flower garnishes.

Gravy. It's preferable to use a ladle or a spoon, but if none is present you may pour from the boat.

Ice Cream. When served as an accompaniment to cake or pie, eat with a dessert spoon or fork. When served alone in a dish, use a dessert spoon or teaspoon.

Lemon. Squeeze lemon juice with one hand while shielding fellow diners with the other.

Pasta. Twist a few strands of thin pasta on the fork pressed against the plate. Big flat shapes, such as lasagna, may be cut with a fork.

Paté. Spread on bread, toast, or cracker and eat with the fingers in several small bites.

Pizza. Eat as a finger food unless the consistency is so soft or soggy that it would be difficult to hold and a knife and fork seems a better approach.

Clams, Mussels, and Oysters. When these are served in their shells, hold the shellfish with one hand and pry it open with the other. If it doesn't open easily, set it aside; it probably isn't good. Break off the half shell or open it wide like a book. Reach inside with your fingers and pick up the clam, mussel, or oyster by the neck. Put it in your mouth and swallow. When shellfish is served on the half shell, eat with a seafood fork.

Crab. Steamed crab is another food you will never see at a formal meal. To eat it, remove the legs with your fingers and gently suck the meat out of them. Break the back open and remove the meat with a small fork. With soft-shell crabs, the entire crab, shell and all, is edible. It is to be eaten using knife and fork.

Lobster. Lobster is eaten like any other seafood when it is served out of the shell, often with a seafood fork. Steamed whole lobster is another matter altogether. You won't encounter it at a formal dinner, since it's eaten with the hands. Lobster can be so messy, in fact, that it's often served with a bib.

To eat a lobster, start by twisting off the claws. Crack each with a nutcracker. Remove the meat using a fork or pick. Next, break the tail off the body. Its meat can be removed using your hands to straighten the tail and your fork to release the meat.

Twist off the legs and suck out the meat gently. Break the body in half lengthwise. Use a fork to reach small pieces of meat in the body and, if you wish, to eat the tomalley (the liver) and roe.

Shrimp. Eat shrimp cocktail with an oyster (seafood) fork. If the shrimp are too large to eat in one respectable bite, eat from the fork in two or three bites. Large shrimp that have been butterflied are usually eaten with the fingers, held by the tail.

Snails. If served in the shell, pick up by the tongs and place in one hand. Remove the snail with the oyster fork using your other hand. You may drink the juices from the shell if you wish. If served out of the shell, just use the oyster fork.

EATING CUSTOMS AROUND THE WORLD

The key to eating anywhere in the world is to keep in mind that graciousness almost never fails. If you can mime what those around you do, you will most likely be deemed a good guest even when the foods and utensils are unfamiliar. When in doubt, look to your hosts to see what they are doing. Also keep in mind that everyone likes to have his or her efforts acknowledged in some way, so be sure to compliment the hosts on the meal. You need not be quite as effusive as you might be in this country, but express your appreciation. Another courtesy is to try at least a small amount of everything that is offered.

EATING IN EUROPE

Since most American notions of table manners came originally from Europe, you will find that the dining conventions aren't all that different there from those you see in the United States. You may, however, find that manners abroad are slightly more decorous than here, where behavior has become rather informal in recent years.

One difference you may notice is that a diner's hand, when at rest, is placed lightly on the table next to the plate. Only in America is a hand at rest placed in the lap. While you needn't feel you must adopt the hand-on-the-table approach, it is a good idea to make it a point of leaving your elbow off the table at all times.

In Europe, even simple meals tend to be served in courses. Salad is served after the main course and before dessert. Coffee or tea is served as a last course, after dessert, not with it.

Europeans eat using the Continental method—with the tines of the fork pointed down, knife pushing the food onto the fork, and no switching from left to right. Again, though, they are usually familiar with the American switch-off method and won't dismiss you as a boor if you eat in this customary American manner. (For more on styles of eating, see page 53.)

EATING IN LATIN AMERICA

Again, most accepted table manners in Latin America originally came from Europe, and you will again feel comfortable at the table.

In some instances, you, as the guest, will be expected to take the first bite. At other times the hostess will do so. Take your cue from your hosts.

EATING IN ASIA

The most striking difference in food customs in Asian countries is the use of chopsticks instead of a fork and knife. There probably won't be an array of silver and crystal like that we are accustomed to seeing. Don't be aghast if you don't see napkins, as in some countries hot moist towels are passed between courses to clean the fingers.

As a foreigner, you may be served with Western utensils, and you may not. It's good to be prepared so that you will not appear ignorant and Eurocentric. Mastering the art of eating with chopsticks isn't hard, and practice does help perfect the technique.

If you are eating in China, it helps to know a few things about Chinese customs. When you arrive you may be offered a Western-style cocktail. You may also be offered a cup of tea as a sign of hospitality. Tea is also drunk throughout the meal and at its conclusion. Chinese wines may also be served during the meal. A festive party usually includes many toasts during which tea or wine is sipped.

Before reaching the table you should know that it is considered polite to appear reluctant to enter the dining room. Hosts often have to announce dinner twice, and then guests slowly make their way in. Guests are shown to the choicest seats.

Once seated, the host may apologize for the poor meal. This is merely a formality, but one that is countered with equally polite protests that the host is being modest. Guests are expected to take the first bites.

Chinese banquets are known for the large number of courses served, eight or ten being quite common. Make sure you take a taste of each course, and don't fill up early.

You may find, during the course of the meal, that the host honors you or another guest in particular. This is done by the host taking a morsel of food from his plate and placing it on the guest's plate. We are always brought up to reciprocate, but in this instance you do not. You accept the morsel gracefully.

USING CHOPSTICKS

The following method of using chopsticks is one among many:

Step 1. The narrow end of the chopsticks always holds the food. Pick up one chopstick and hold it about one-third of the way from the top. Rest it between your thumb and fourth finger.

Step 2. Pick up the second chopstick and rest it between your second and third fingers, using the thumb for support. Your second and third fingers control the movement of the top stick that is used to pick up and hold food.

Step 3. To pick up food, hold the chopsticks so that the narrow ends act like pincers. Grasp a piece of food with the chopsticks and guide it to the mouth. Most foods are eaten from the plate or bowl in this manner. When eating rice, the bowl may be picked up and the rice essentially shoveled into your mouth using the chopsticks.

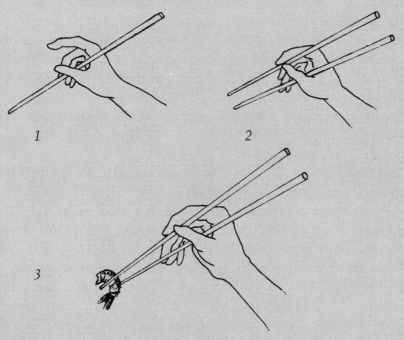

Fig. 2.3 Eating with chopsticks

At the end of the meal, the host may again protest about the poor meal. Here again, you will be able to insist heartily and truthfully that the meal and hospitality have surely been the best in China.

If you find yourself in Japan, you will find that meals are slightly more ritualized and even less familiar than those of some other countries. You may be seated on the floor at a low table. Since we are used to chairs, you may find that getting and remaining comfortable is a challenge. Move around as little and as unobtrusively as possible.

The meal starts when the guest makes a slight bow to the hosts after sitting down. The main guest always starts the meal, after which others begin eating.

Rice is the mainstay of the Japanese meal and is served first. You will find a covered empty rice bowl at your place. You remove the cover and place the bowl on the offered serving tray. It will be filled for you. You return the bowl to its original position on the table, pick up your chopsticks, and begin eating.

Rice is usually followed by soup. Soup is considered the test of a Japanese cook and should be praised appropriately. Drink a little of the soup first directly from the bowl and then eat some using the ladlelike spoon provided.

As other foods are passed or offered, use the serving chopsticks. If there are no serving chopsticks, use the large ends of your own chopsticks to serve.

An empty rice bowl signals that you are through. If you would like seconds, leave a little rice in the bottom of the bowl.

Tea is served at the end of the meal. It is customary to dip the chopsticks lightly in the tea to clean them. Lay your chopsticks on the table when finished. After tea, replace the lids on your bowls. Thank your hosts for the lovely meal and bow slightly once again.

EATING IN AFRICA

Africa is such a large continent and has so many cultures with varied customs that it is hard to generalize on manners. Formal European manners are used in some places, while in others you may find that eating with your fingers from a communal pot is the rule. In countries where food is eaten with the fingers, it is usually only done with the right hand. In some countries guests are expected to take the first bite, in others, the host starts the meal. Rest assured that you will be given a sign or gesture to help you understand your duties.

EATING IN INDIA

Like Africa, India is so large and has so many customs and table manners stemming from geography and history that it is hard to generalize. In large cities you are most likely to encounter familiar dining customs, especially in restaurants. In people's homes and in rural areas customs vary. Eating with the fingers is common, and again, only the right hand is used for eating (unless you are left-handed). In the north of India, people eat only with the fingertips, never dirtying the fingers below the first knuckle. In the south, food is often piled onto a banana leaf and eaten with the whole hand. Whatever method is used, clean hands are of the utmost importance, so a finger bowl may be passed. The meal usually ends with dessert and coffee.

EATING IN THE MIDDLE EAST

Customs vary from country to country in the region, and many places use European methods, especially in urban areas. One thing to know about dining in people's homes: An invitation to dinner does not necessarily mean that both husband and wife are included. If the meal is in any way related to business, the spouse is not usually expected. In Arab households a man's wife is introduced only to very close friends. However, given today's changes in business practices, if both members of a couple are invited to dinner, the host's wife will often be present, too.

Food is usually served communally or passed by a servant. It is polite to heap your plate and to eat as much as you can. The host takes the first bite, to show that he is eating the food with his guest, not merely giving it to him. The meal may begin with a prayer and will end with coffee or tea.

TEACHING CHILDREN TABLE MANNERS

As a parent, one of your most important tasks is to provide your children with an environment and the tools to become strong, healthy, smart, and educated so that they can succeed in a world of ever-changing challenges. One of the gifts you can give your children is good manners that can ease their way into the adult world.

Until a child reaches the age of five or so, many of the niceties of table manners will fall on deaf ears, and meals in general may be somewhat chaotic. However, some of the groundwork for good table behavior begins very early.

The best way to teach good table manners is to use them at home every day, grown-ups and children alike. Training should begin for children as soon as they are big enough to eat with a spoon. Children learning to speak can be taught to say "please" and "thank you" as part of the everyday give-and-take of conversation. A child who learns to say "More juice, please" at two is already halfway to the six-year-old equivalent, "May I please have some more juice?"

Teaching basic table manners early doesn't mean you try to require a toddler or preschooler to sit completely still and handle knife and fork, never speak out of turn, and be patient throughout a long meal. That's not reasonable.

It does mean that you should treat children as members of the family, not as a foreign species. A baby can't be taught to wait to eat until everyone is served, but she may well notice if you and your partner treat each other with respect. In coming years, as you actively teach a child a little patience at the table, the insistence upon age-appropriate discipline and eating habits won't come as a surprise if the youngster has been mastering elements of it all along.

Children notice everything. If you eat with your mouth open, they see it. They notice if you talk with a full mouth. If you keep your napkin in your lap and use it to wipe your mouth, it may not seem a great hardship when you ask a child to do the same. If you take turns speaking to one another, the youngsters will learn the same lesson more gracefully. Psychologists call this *modeling*: If you demonstrate good manners in action, your children are more likely to adopt them.

The best way to start teaching basic table manners is to have a family meal, preferably dinner. If you can, sit together at a regular time at a table that has been set. A table that is pleasing to look at when everyone arrives at dinner conveys an important message: "This is a special time, different from cooking, playtime, or work time."

Set the table simply with silverware, napkins, and plates. Children often find the simple ritual of setting the table for dinner enchanting, especially if you include a pair of candles or a few flowers. Let them help by putting out silverware—even toddlers can take the spoons to the table. Don't worry if the setting doesn't mimic exactly the conventional arrangement—it deserves to be praised just for the effort.

The meal itself won't always be relaxing and sometimes will be far from it. Small children are messy, noisy, and prone to interrupt. Parents have to master many things, and one of them is how to eat in these adverse situations. This does not mean, however, that family meals must be loathsome. It's a time to see one another, discuss the day, and little by little instill good behavior.

There may be years of interrupted stories and conversation when children just have to blurt out what's on their minds. By setting a good example of waiting your turn to talk and gently correcting them now and again, they will gradually learn. And a child who has been encouraged to relate the events of the day from age four on will probably have an easier time later in life keeping up dinner conversation.

Some basic manners can be taught with relative ease. Three-year-olds can be taught to take small bites, chew and swallow before talking, and eat with their mouths closed. Getting a three-year-old to use a fork and spoon instead of fingers may take longer. Preschoolers also can learn to ask politely for additional portions of food or for condiments to be passed to them.

There are some things small ones just can't do, such as sit still through a meal. However, as toddlers they can be taught to ask to be excused. They also can be made to understand that if they leave the table they may not come back to eat seriatim. This is a basic courtesy to the person who has prepared a meal and to the others who are eating it—even those who are children.

Some parents prefer to feed small children first and then relax with a quiet, civilized adult meal after the children have been put to bed or while they are playing. But even if children are fed first, an adult should supervise them and begin to instill the basics of good behavior for when they do graduate to the adults' table.

You can use play to teach manners, too. Most children by the age of three play Make-Believe. Many, especially little girls from age two on, love to have tea parties. Boys and girls both will often play restaurant, where one person is the waiter or waitress and the others are patrons. Listen in on one of these, and you will observe that they always use what they perceive to be perfect manners. You can encourage this behavior by participating in the game when asked, offering gentle suggestions as to procedure and speech, and, of course by setting a good example.

When your child reaches age six, you may want to begin seriously teaching table manners. One method that works and that can be fun is to prepare your child for a special event such as a meal with grown-ups, if you don't normally eat with your children. You might make the goal a meal in a nice restaurant. By making it a game of achievement, you give the child something to look forward to or work for, and the small steps make learning easy. You can use the following four steps at home:

Step 1. Talk about the desirability of learning proper table manners with your child. Make a date with your child for a meal, just the two of you, during which you will begin to teach the finer points of table manners.

Step 2. Prepare an elaborate meal for the two of you. Put away the plastic and the stainless, and bring out your best. You don't have to make fancy food, just serve your child's favorite foods as separate courses. At this meal you will explain table manners step by step, from placing the napkin in the lap to leaving the table.

Step 3. Prepare a more formal dinner for your child and your spouse or another honored guest. This meal is for your child to show off the newly learned table manners.

Step 4. Take your child to dinner in a nice restaurant. It need not be an especially expensive restaurant, but one where the service is good. If possible, reward your child with a special treat after the meal such as a movie, play, or a trip to a special ice-cream shop for dessert.

Manners should never be a source of worry. On the contrary, knowing how to go about the business of eating and entertaining properly can provide a sense of confidence—for children and adults alike—that makes life easier.

3

THE TOOLS OF THE TABLE

A beautifully set table is a joy to behold. It invites you to enjoy yourself, almost saying, "Come, sit with me awhile." Yet elaborate table settings can intimidate the novice diner. Perhaps it's fear of facing an implement we don't know how to use. Is it a sardine fork, corn scraper, or ice-cream knife? As our world becomes ever more casual, however, most of us can relax, secure in the knowledge that we will in all likelihood never have to ask ourselves such a question.

Unlike so many things in life, table settings are based on sweet reason. This is not to say that it's always clear what to use, even if you don't have a corn scraper at your place. Even the most sophisticated eater can be faced with a piece of equipment whose use is not apparent. The basics of table setting, however, from a casual supper with friends to a formal dinner, should be logical and sensible. They consist of the same basic elements, which include flatware (knives, forks, and spoons), china (plates, bowls, cups, and serving pieces), glassware, and linens. In the pages that follow, we'll consider each of them in their familiar and sometimes unfamiliar forms. I've included information useful to both hosts and guests, since after all, we will all be on both sides of the table, so to speak, as both the inviter and the invited, as well as diners at simple family dinners.

FLATWARE

Whether you use sterling-silver or stainless-steel cutlery, flatware remains basic to every table. Beyond the standard issue knife, fork, and spoon, however, there lies a world of variation.

Sometimes a new food is served and a guest is at a loss about which utensil to use. If the host or hostess is at the table, you can discreetly watch to see what she or he uses, but sometimes this isn't practical, such as when the hosts are serving, have urged guests to begin, or are seated at another table.

A little knowledge is the solution to the problem. Eating implements are divided into three basic categories: fork, knife, and spoon. Does the challenging food require stabbing, cutting, or scooping? Remember that it doesn't really matter in the grand scheme of things if you use the wrong utensil. If you realize you've put the wrong piece to use, ignore the error. Don't put it down and start again—just continue eating. You may occasionally find that you have a piece or two left over at the end of the meal. Again, ignore it. Perhaps a course was meant to be served that didn't make it to the table. Or an extra knife might have been put out for those who needed it and you didn't. Or you might have made a mistake. At worst, these are minor faux pas that will probably go unnoticed or, if detected, will be ignored by the good host and hostess. And don't forget that your fellow diners, graceful as they may appear, might be improvising as well.

For your part, give missing silver the same treatment. If you are missing something that you can manage without, make no mention. If you drop a piece of silver, leave it and ask for a new piece. The exception to this is if you drop a loaded utensil onto the host's rug. Then you must retrieve it inconspicuously, and if necessary, alert the host that the matter requires clean-up attention. (A stain averted is infinitely preferable to an awkward moment avoided because you were too embarrassed to speak up.)

For ease of use, only three pieces of each utensil should be placed at a setting at one time. More than that would make your place setting look like an exhibit at a silverware convention. If more pieces are needed, they should be brought with each course. This means that as a guest you will never be faced with more than three each of forks,

A   B   C   D   E   F

Fig. 3.1 The six forks: *from left: A. Dinner fork, B. Salad fork, C. Oyster fork, D. Fish fork, E. Dessert fork, F. Fruit fork*

spoons, and knives. But let's talk about which of each of these utensils you may encounter.

FORKS

Today the fork is the workhorse of the table, but this has been true only for the last two hundred or so years. Before that fingers were used. During the Victorian era, when the pleasures of the table were taken very seriously, a complete service often contained ten forks. These days you will never be faced with more than six kinds of forks, and never all of those at one meal. In general practice, one usually encounters two or three. These are the six options:

Dinner Fork. This is the all-purpose eating utensil, used for main courses, vegetables, salad (if there is no salad fork), and fish (if there is no fish fork). It is also properly used for removing butter from your bread-and-butter plate for use on foods on your dinner plate.

Salad Fork. This fork is used for salad and first courses. It is smaller than a dinner fork and has one tine that is broader than the others. The salad fork also usually doubles as a dessert fork and often as a fish fork.

Oyster Fork. This is a very small fork with short tines. It is used for eating seafood on the half shell, lobster in the shell, and shrimp or seafood cocktails.

Fish Fork. About the same size as a salad fork, this utensil has slightly broader tines.

Dessert Fork. Smaller than a dinner fork, larger than a teaspoon, the dessert fork today is interchangeable with a salad fork.

Fruit Fork. A small, narrow fork used with a small fruit knife, this once common utensil is now rarely seen.

SPOONS

The indispensable spoon, used for thousands of years, is just as useful today as during the era of grand dining, when a complete set might contain ten or more different shapes and sizes. Today, you are most likely to encounter two or three spoons at a fancy meal. Over the course of a day, you might encounter up to seven. These include:

Teaspoon. This is the spoon that all others are measured against, the all-around spoon that is used for cereal, dessert, coffee, tea, and soup in cups. At a simple meal it is placed to the right of the knife to round out the setting, even when it is not used.

Soup Spoons. There are two shapes of soup spoons, distinguished by the bowls of the spoons. The round bowl is technically for clear soups, the oval for cream soups and other hearty soups. In today's practice, however, they are interchangeable. Clear soups traditionally were served in cups or deep-sided bowls, while hearty and cream soups were served in rimmed soup plates.

When using a soup spoon, it's polite to fill the spoon by pushing

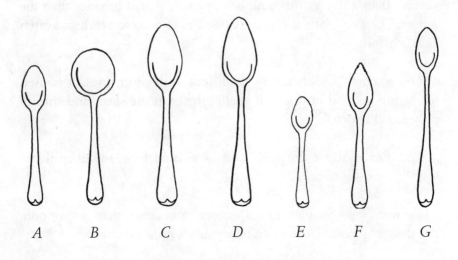

Fig. 3.2 The seven spoons: *from left: A. Teaspoon, B. Round soup spoon, C. Oval soup spoon, D. Dessert spoon, E. Demitasse spoon, F. Grapefruit spoon, G. Iced-tea spoon*

the utensil away from you, then sip from the rim of the spoon. When you get near the bottom of the bowl, tip the bowl slightly away from you before dipping the spoon. When at rest, the spoon may be positioned with its handle on the edge of the bowl or on the service plate under the bowl. Once you have finished with your soup, place the spoon on the service plate, if there is one, or in the empty bowl.

Dessert Spoon. Technically, this spoon is larger than a teaspoon, but in practice a teaspoon is often used instead. It may be placed above the dinner plate with the handle facing right, sometimes along with a dessert fork, or it may be laid with the dessert course.

Demitasse Spoon. This small spoon is used with after-dinner coffee served in small demitasse cups with saucers.

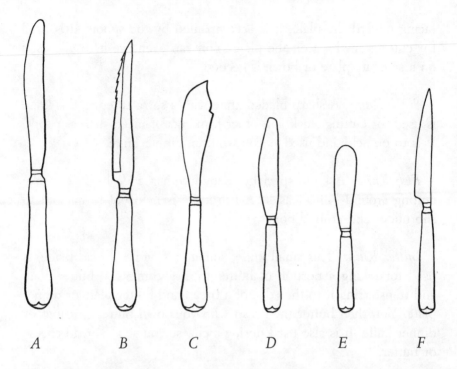

Fig. 3.3 The six knives: *from left: A. Dinner knife, B. Steak knife, C. Fish knife, D. Butter knife, E. Butter spreader, F. Fruit knife*

Grapefruit Spoon. A small, sharp spoon with a pointed bowl and sometimes a serrated tip, the grapefruit spoon, as its name indicates, is used for grapefruit, which usually is served at breakfast.

Iced-Tea Spoon. This spoon, essentially a long-handled teaspoon, is used for stirring iced tea. It's ubiquitous in some parts of the country, rarely seen in others.

KNIVES

An essential element at many meals, the knife is perhaps the oldest implement. When people were still using their fingers as forks, they were hacking off meat with a knife. In everyday life you are most likely to encounter three knives, but you should know about six:

Dinner Knife. Also called a place knife, it is the third element of the basic dinner setting. Resting on the right side of the plate, blade facing toward the plate, it is accompanied by the spoon. It is used for cutting anything on the plate. You can even use it to cut salad on a separate plate or bowl, if needed.

Steak Knife. A sharp-bladed knife with a serrated edge, this knife is used for cutting steak and other firm cuts of meat, such as chops. It is to be held and used as you would a dinner knife.

Fish Knife. A knife specially shaped with a wide blade to make cutting around bones easier. A fish knife is held not to cut but to slip under and around bones.

Butter Knife. This small knife, sometimes with a broad blade, is used for taking a portion of butter from a communal butter plate and transferring it to the edge of a bread-and-butter plate or dinner plate. You then butter the bread with your own butter spreader or dinner knife. It is also used during a cheese course to spread cheese or butter.

Butter Spreader. A very small blunt knife, the butter spreader is placed on the side or across the top of a bread-and-butter plate. It's used to spread butter, jam, or anything else on one's bread.

Fruit Knife. A small sharp knife used for cutting fruit at a formal meal. When used alone, this knife is useful for quartering the fruit and removing the core and seeds in preparation for eating the fruit with the fingers. When used with a fruit fork, the fruit is cut into small pieces using both knife and fork. Between cuts and bites, place the knife on the side of the plate in the rest position.

SERVING UTENSILS
If you've ever encountered antique silver you know that the range of serving utensils can seem mind-boggling, including such obscure items as pickle forks, olive forks, and sardine servers, among others. In essence, though, all serving utensils are simply variations on the familiar themes of the knife, fork. and spoon.

The more eccentric pieces are rarely seen today, although they can really add fun and surprise to a table. But at the very least, you will probably need large versions of spoons, forks, and knives for serving. One appealing aspect of the great variety in serving utensils is that the range can allow you to be especially creative, mixing and matching pieces with one another. They don't all have to match at each course. The basic categories are these:

Serving Spoons. The largest spoon in a service, substantially larger than a soup spoon, is the serving spoon. It is used to serve food from bowls, usually vegetables of various kinds. Naturally each different serving bowl needs its own spoon, so you'll need several for service at the table.

Anyone who serves a variety of foods with sauces and condiments also needs serving utensils smaller than a standard-size serving spoon. If you have them, ladles in a variety of sizes, from very small ones for sauces up to a large one for soup or punch, are very useful. If you don't have these, teaspoons and soup spoons work well. Soup spoons are generally used when a spoon, rather than a ladle, is called for, as when you serve a small bowl of vegetables. They may be used for sauces, too.

A salad spoon is essentially a very large serving spoon, with a stainless or chrome bowl and a silver handle. This is used for serving composed salads such as potato, pasta, and rice salad as well as those containing meat, fish, or other vegetables or grains. It may also be used for large puddings.

Serving Forks. A large fork called a cold-meat fork is very useful for serving from platters foods such as sliced meats, fish, and grilled vegetables. If a cold-meat fork is not available, meats may be served with a carving fork, the fork that accompanies a carving knife.

Serving Fork and Spoon. Sometimes a serving fork and serving spoon are used together when a portion is to be moved from a platter intact. The spoon is usually slipped under the serving and the fork is placed on top to balance the food. Both are then moved together to the plate.

Salad Servers. The standard salad set for a tossed green salad consists of a large spoon and fork. Most often you see salad sets in wood, since the corrosive nature of salad dressing leads to pits in silver. Sets made to match a silver service have silver handles. Salad servers are also found in stainless steel. Occasionally you will see a set of salad tongs—a salad fork and spoon or two spoons or scoops hinged together at the base of the handles.

Cake and Pie Servers. Cake and pie knives are both wedge-shaped, the difference being that a cake knife is straight, while a pie server is curved near the base to allow a piece to be scooped out. Wedding cakes and other sturdy confections sometimes require a cake knife that resembles a serrated bread knife.

Luncheon Service

You may encounter a service of flatware which at first seems like a simple dinner service but is actually a luncheon set. The main fork and knife are slightly smaller than those for dinner, while the teaspoon remains the same. These days luncheon sets are most frequently used for dinner.

Will you have stainless or silver? If you are setting out to buy a set of flatware, consider your needs for now and for the future. If you are just starting out on your own, you will need a set of stainless cutlery at a minimum. It doesn't have to be expensive, although the heavier the better, especially if you think your needs might change in the future.

If you are getting married or have an established household that you are thinking of upgrading, consider investing in sterling silver. This is a wise choice if you think you will ever entertain. Nothing looks better on a table than softly gleaming silver. It can serve for casual dinners as well as fancy ones. Sterling silver takes any meal, from a family dinner with the kids to a seated business dinner for a dozen, from merely eating to dining.

Many people automatically assume that silver is too expensive. However, when you consider what good-quality stainless cutlery costs, a standard place setting of silver is not much more. One economical way to buy silver is to buy at auction. At estate auctions complete sets of sterling silver, often in open-stock patterns, routinely sell for much less than a set of high-quality stainless at retail.

Some people think that keeping silver free of tarnish is a lot of work. It need not be, for the more you use it the less you have to polish it. One time-saving trick is to keep it in a tarnish-resistant silver box or bags between uses.

CHINA

Plates, bowls, cups, and their variations are essential to almost all meals. You probably won't need an example of every known shape at any one meal, but you will be faced with at least a plate or a bowl at almost any one. Usually there are no more than four plates to deal with at a moderately elaborate dinner.

PLATES

In medieval Europe before the advent of plates, feasts were eaten off hard, flat loaves of bread called trenchers. At the end of the meal, people either ate the bread, gave it to the poor, or fed it to the dogs. Disposable plates, you see, have been around longer than you might have thought!

Dinner Plate. This is the workhorse plate, the one you eat the main part of the meal from. The largest of the main plates, it holds the entrée, the vegetables, and the salad if no salad plate is used. Dinner plates usually measure about ten inches in size, although the diameter varies.

Luncheon Plate. These are slightly smaller (roughly nine inches in diameter) than dinner plates and are often used for dinners as well as lunches. That practice is perfectly acceptable, as long as you don't try to put too much food on them. The same is true, by the way, for any plate: If the plate is so loaded it spills over the edges, you have too much food on it.

Service Plate. Also called a charger, this is a decorative plate used at formal dinners and in fancy restaurants. Its purpose is to hold the place setting until the first course arrives, at which point it is whisked away. Sometimes a plate for the first course is placed on top of the service plate and both are removed at the end of the course. Service plates are usually more elaborately decorated than dinner plates and sometimes are a little larger, too.

Salad Plate. This plate, around eight inches in size, is smaller than a dinner or luncheon plate. Its principal purpose is to hold salad, but it can also be used for serving a first course, dessert, breakfast, or as a liner for a bowl of soup.

Bread-and-Butter Plate. At about six inches in diameter, this is the smallest plate in a standard setting. It is used for bread, butter, rolls, and passed finger foods, such as olives. It is also useful for serving hors d'oeuvres or as a liner for a small bowl of soup.

When the table is set with a bread-and-butter plate, a serving of butter is always placed on the rim of the plate, never on the dinner plate. The bread is broken over the small plate and buttered on the plate, not over the dinner plate.

BOWLS

Perhaps the oldest food vessels, bowls are used in every culture the world over, and have been since the dawn of civilization. They may be made of gourds, wood, metal, plastic, or, for most of us, ceramic.

Soup Bowl. Soup bowls come in two styles: rimmed and not. Traditionally, rimmed soup bowls were used primarily for cream-based soups. Deeper, smaller bowls, often with handles, were for consommé. The distinctions are not rigidly held today. Both are served with a plate underneath to catch drips and provide a place to rest the spoon.

Cereal Bowl. This round, usually deep bowl is used to hold cereal and soups.

Sauce Bowl. A small shallow bowl, the sauce bowl is used for sauces and small servings. These bowls are sometimes used in casual meals to keep separate servings of foods that don't mingle well with other foods (stewed tomatoes and greens with vinegar are two that come to mind).

CUPS AND SAUCERS
A proper informal place setting for dinner used to always include a cup and saucer, but today you are more likely to have coffee or tea served after the meal.

Coffee or Tea Cup and Saucer. Coffee and tea cups vary in size and style. Should you wish to set a place with a cup and saucer, place it on the right of the setting with the handle of the cup placed at about four o'clock. When handling a cup and saucer, always hold the cup with one hand, by the handle, fingers in. Wagging a little finger remains a sign of false gentility.

Demitasse Cup and Saucer. Demitasse, which means half cup in French, is much smaller than a normal coffee cup and is used to serve espresso or other strong coffee after dinner. It never appears as part of a place setting.

SERVING PIECES
The most common serving pieces are bowls, which may vary in size from larger than a soup bowl to large enough for a salad or family-size servings of pasta. They may be used to hold vegetables and other side dishes. Most china services have at least three. These days people use a wide variety of sizes which need not all match a service. Nor must they match each other, so long as they are pleasing and coordinate with the meal served.

Salad Bowl. Salad is frequently served from a large wooden bowl, usually with wooden servers. Sizes vary widely, from those that contain lettuce for two people to ones big enough to hold greens for ten or more. Salad may also be served from a large china bowl. Sometimes salad is served into individual wooden bowls, but only at casual dinners.

Soup Tureen. A tureen is a large and often footed bowl that is fitted with a top. Soup is ladled from the tureen into individual bowls.

Platters. Large plates range in size from around twelve inches long to over two feet or larger. They can be almost any shape but usually are oval or rectangular, to accommodate food easily.

GLASSWARE

When you sit down to a formal dinner you will be faced with an array of glassware that on first glance might bring to mind images of dinner at the court at Versailles. Most dinners, of course, feature a much simpler setting consisting of a water glass or goblet and one or two wine glasses. Regardless of their number, glasses are simply managed.

One of the great things about glasses is that you are never in doubt about which to use, since liquid is poured in them for you and at the right time—which is to say, immediately before the course for which the beverage is intended.

Water Glass. Whether a stemmed goblet, proper for informal as well as formal dinners, or a plain tumbler, suitable for informal dinners only, the water glass is generally the largest glass on the table. The exception to this is the iced-tea glass or goblet, which appears on tables in hot climates of America when wine is not being served. It takes the place of the water glass.

Red Wine Goblet. The largest of the wine glasses, and increasingly the all-purpose glass for white as well as red wines, the red wine goblet generally holds about six fluid ounces. When wine is poured, the glass is never filled to the top but should reach about one-half to two-thirds of the way to the top of the glass, depending on its size. All stemmed glasses are held by the stem, in some cases to keep the

Fig. 3.4 Glassware: *from left: A. White wine goblet, B. Champagne flute, C. Champagne coupe, D. Sherry glass, E. Cordial glass, F. Brandy snifter, G. Cocktail glass, H. Old-fashioned glass, I. Pilsner glass*

beverage from warming to your body temperature as well as to maintain the elegant look of the glass.

White Wine Goblet. This stemmed glass is smaller than the red wine goblet. At a meal with many courses you might find yourself served different glasses of white wine with different courses. Each will have a slightly different shape.

Champagne Glass. Champagne, that most festive of wines, has two shapes to call its own. The first, the champagne flute, is the most popular today. It is tall and narrow, the better to hold the bubbles and keep the wine cold. The traditional champagne coupe is wide and shallow and can be used for serving sherbet or desserts such as mousses and puddings.

In most informal or formal table settings, the water goblet is placed just above the point of the knife, on the right. Continuing to the right and slightly above the water goblet is the red wine glass (often an all-purpose wine glass) and to the right of that, and often slightly in front, is the white wine glass.

There are other glasses that may also have occasional uses, in some cases at the table but more often before or after a meal.

Sherry Glass. There was a time when a formal dinner often included a first course of consommé, and sherry was always served with it. Today, sherry is more often served as an aperitif. Since sherry is a fortified wine, it is usually served in its own stemmed glass which is smaller than a white wine glass.

Cordial Glass. Cordials were once served as a standard end-of-the-evening drink, and they may yet make a comeback. Cordials are highly fortified and usually quite sweet, and so they are served in very small stemmed glasses, holding only an ounce or two of fluid.

Brandy Snifter. Brandy is often served in a balloon-shaped glass with a short stem. An ounce or so of wine is poured and the enclosing shape of the glass traps the wine's aroma as it escapes. Many people savor the aroma almost as much as the drink. Unlike other wine glasses, which are held by the stem to maintain the wine's temperature, a brandy snifter is cradled in the palm of the hand, stem extending between fingers.

Cocktail Glass. Once a staple of the well-stocked glass case, these are used less frequently today, as the fashion for mixed cocktails has largely given way to serving wine as an aperitif. These, too, may be making a comeback, however. A cocktail glass looks like a short-stemmed white wine glass.

Old-Fashioned Glass. A short glass, holding about six ounces of fluid, used for mixed drinks. A double old-fashioned glass is the same shape but taller, holding twice the amount.

Pilsner Glass. If you are serving beer as an aperitif, this is the elegant approach. The glass is tall, and flute-shaped.

LINENS

One of the ways to create atmosphere in the dining room is with linens. The choices are broad, from crisp and formal to relaxed and colorful to coolly elegant to warm and cozy, and all manner of in-betweens.

Tablecloth. Tablecloths serve a useful purpose in protecting the table from the ravages of dinner. A cloth can also provide a background for the decorations of the table as well as cover up any imperfections that might be underneath. You don't have to have a gorgeous table if you have a smashing cloth.

Place Mats. Used to protect a particular area of each setting, place mats come in a wide variety of styles. Some are made of elegant linen and lace, others are more informal and easier to care for.

Table Runner. A runner is a long strip of fabric, usually coordinated with place mats, that covers the center of the table. A runner is primarily decorative, but can help protect the table, too.

Except for the most formal of occasions, it is proper to forgo all coverings and let a handsome wooden table speak for itself.

Napkin. This is a practical must, even if you have to resort to a folded paper towel. For the most informal of meals it makes sense to use paper napkins, but for any kind of gracious entertaining you will want to use cloth. The most formal napkins are white linen damask and measure twenty-four inches square. Other dinner napkins range in size, starting at about one foot square. The larger the napkin, the more protected the lap. Attractive linen dish towels can also be folded and used as large napkins. Luncheon-size napkins, about twelve to fourteen inches square, can be used for breakfast, lunch, or dinner.

Cocktail Napkin. When serving cocktails and passed hors d'oeuvres, a small napkin (about four inches square when folded) is useful. Little linen napkins are especially nice served with a drink, but paper ones are perfectly acceptable. Paper cocktail napkins are especially well suited to hors d'oeuvres, as they often get quite soiled and are used in large quantity. (See pages 89–90 for napkin folding.)

SETTING THE TABLE

Once you know how to set a table, you'll always know what to do when faced with even the most elaborate or unusual event. We'll start small at a very casual dinner. As we work up, you will see that the whole scheme of things is nothing more than an elaboration on a few simple principles.

CASUAL DINNER

To start, you may want to spread a tablecloth or use place mats, or leave the table bare if you have a nice table that is not easily marred.

Next comes the setting. Casual table settings at home usually consist of a knife, fork, teaspoon, and sometimes salad fork, placed on either side of a plate or to the left and right of where a plate will be placed when it arrives full of food. A glass (wine or water) is placed above the plate to the right, above the tip of the knife. The napkin is either in the center of the place, holding it until the diners are seated, under the fork, or next to it if a plate is already in place.

An everyday setting can be even simpler. If you are serving a meal consisting of soup and salad to family, you may put out only the utensils you know will be needed, such as a soup spoon and salad fork.

Even a very casual table can look most inviting and festive with a set of low candles, a vase of flowers, or a pleasing decoration as a centerpiece. Candles should always be either higher or lower than the sight line of those seated, no matter how formal or informal the meal. Too often we find candles burning right in the middle, making it difficult to see our dining companions.

THE INFORMAL DINNER

One step up in formal dining from a casual dinner, the informal dinner table contains the elements most of us are likely to see at all

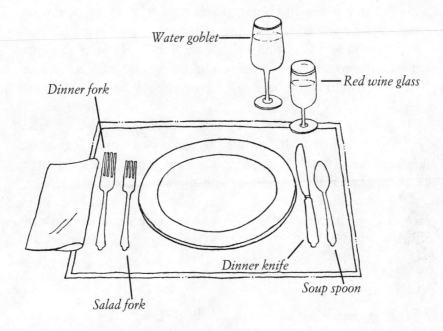

Fig. 3.5 Place setting for the informal dinner

but the most formal of dinners. Informal dinners run the range from truly informal to quite elaborate.

The table for an informal dinner may be spread with a tablecloth that is colorful and patterned, white or ecru lace, or white damask, depending on the event.

At each setting you will find the elements appropriate to the meal. The elements in the setting should be symmetrically and evenly positioned. The center is usually anchored by the napkin, unless you use a service plate or dinner plate (for a very informal meal). To the left are the dinner fork closest to the plate, to its left a salad fork for a first course requiring a fork. On the right, the dinner knife is closest to the plate, blade pointing in, with an optional dessert spoon or soup spoon, if that is your first course.

If you serve salad along with the main course, place the salad plate, if using one, to the left of the forks. If you serve salad in the European style after the main course, place the fork closest to the dinner plate, and bring in the salad plates with the course.

If you use a bread-and-butter plate, place it above the forks, the butter spreader resting across it.

You may also choose to place a dessert fork and spoon above the center of the setting. Or you may bring them out with the dessert (especially helpful if you have to wash up the salad forks for the last course).

The water glass or goblet once again sits above the knife, with a wine glass to its right. If you plan to serve two wines, the second wine glass will sit to the right of the first. The glasses appear in descending order of size, starting with the water glass.

If the party is large, say, more than eight, you may find that using place cards simplifies seating. A place card is a small card, usually folded, written with the guest's name and placed above a place setting.

THE BUFFET TABLE

For large parties, or where space is limited, serving a meal buffet-style is practical. A buffet table is usually arranged with plates and cutlery at the end of the table where people begin. Since a buffet meal is by definition one of limited space, the settings are usually simple. Often the cutlery—fork, knife, and spoon or just fork and knife—are rolled into a napkin. The napkin can be cloth or paper, depending on the formality of the meal.

Dishes of food are arranged on the table in logical order, usually with the main elements of the meal—main course and vegetables—where the guests will begin loading their plates. Breads and salads usually come at the other end of the table, since breads are easy to balance and salads can fit in small spaces or be served on a subsequent visit.

If there is room, the table may be decorated with candles, flowers, or arrangements of decorations. Often, the placement and arrangement of food on platters provides most of the decoration.

Two important notes: If guests will have to stand or perch to eat, make sure to serve only foods that need little or no cutting, and then set out only forks. If at all possible, be sure to provide large plates. Small plates tend to get overloaded with food, making it difficult to keep foods from sliding off the plate onto the floor or lap. Since people often eat off their laps at a buffet meal, a large plate helps, since it's easier to balance.

You may also set up a buffet to coordinate with a set table. Plates may be stacked on the buffet table or set at each guest's place. Guests then find their place cards and proceed to the buffet line.

THE FORMAL DINNER

A formal dinner includes all of the elements of a fancy informal dinner, with a few added elements, primarily more courses, understated decorations, and fancier dress.

A formal dinner traditionally included seven courses. Today, the most you are likely to encounter will be five. They include any of these three variations:

Appetizer	Appetizer	Soup
Soup	Fish	Fish
Meat	Meat	Meat
Salad	Salad	Salad
Dessert	Dessert	Dessert

Sometimes fruit and cheese replace the dessert; occasionally they are served after the dessert.

A few elements are different at a truly formal dinner table from an informal dinner. The table will look a little more conservative, for one thing. Tablecloth and napkins are always white. The tablecloth should hang down about eighteen inches from the edge of the table (a good general gauge for any tablecloth). Formal napkins are generous in size, measuring twenty-four inches square. They are folded simply in one of two ways, either into a rectangle, or diagonally into a rectangle with a point, as shown on the next page.

The napkin is placed in the center of the service plate or charger. A decorative service plate holds the place until the food arrives. When the first course is served before the guests are seated, the napkin is positioned to the left of the setting but not beneath the forks.

Standard place cards, whether plain or bordered in gold or silver, measure three-quarters of an inch high by two and a half inches long

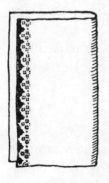 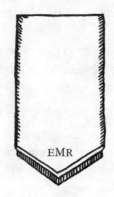

Napkin folded to form a loosely rolled rectangle (left).

Napkin folded diagonally allowing monogram to show in the center point (right).

Fig. 3.6 Napkin folds

when folded. They are placed in the center of the napkin, or just above the service plate at the center of the setting.

The centerpiece, as the name implies, is in the center of the table. It must be low enough that people, when seated, can see one another unobstructed. A centerpiece consisting of flowers is always appropriate, just be sure that no one flower has an especially pungent scent, as it can interfere with the enjoyment of the food and may irritate the allergies of some of your guests.

Candles on a formally set table are always white and should be brand-new. Again, candles placed in sticks or candelabra should not obstruct the guests' view of one another, which typically means they are tall enough to be above the diners' sight lines.

The number of candles to use depends on the lighting of the room and the number of guests. If the room is well lit and the candles serve only as decoration, one or two pairs should be enough for a table of eight. If the room is to be lit with candles, allow one candle per person. Candlesticks or candelabra should be in balance with respect to the centerpiece (for example, three candles on one side should be matched by three on the other).

Candles should be lighted before guests enter the dining room and should be extinguished after they leave.

There should be enough saltcellars and pepper pots to be within easy reach of everyone at the table. Very small individual sets may be placed at each setting or between every two settings. If using open saltcellars, these must be accompanied by tiny salt spoons—

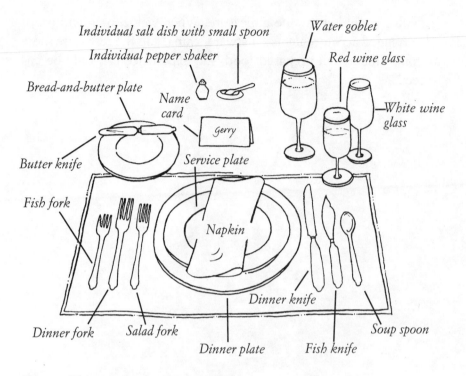

Fig. 3.7 Place setting for the formal dinner

gone are the days when diners dipped their fingers in for a pinch of salt!

A formal table may be set with little extras, too. Dishes or compotes filled with thin chocolate mints, candied fruit, or nuts may be in evidence. Mints and candied fruits are placed wherever there are symmetrical vacancies at the table. They are not for nibbling on during the meal but are left throughout and sometimes passed at the end. Nuts are sometimes placed on the table in large silver dishes or in individual dishes at each place. They are removed along with the salt and pepper shakers after the salad course.

A menu card may be used at a formal dinner. A menu card is exactly what it sounds like—a card with the evening's menu written on it. If used, the card is placed in front of the host, although occasionally one is placed between every two guests. The menu card only lists the courses of the meal and their accompanying wines, never the extras such as bread, relishes, candies, or nuts.

Dining should always be a pleasure. When well-chosen and properly arranged accoutrements—flatware, china, and the rest—are there to complement well-prepared food, the experience can only be enhanced.

4

ENTERTAINING AT HOME

Humans are programmed to party. Since time immemorial people have gathered to feast and celebrate. Just about anything is worthy of making a party, whether it's to say, "It's great to be together," or for a more formal purpose, such as marking one of the various holidays of the year. You can make a party for two or two thousand or any number of guests in between. You can entertain almost anywhere. For really large special events, such as weddings, major anniversaries, charity functions and such, people often choose to entertain in restaurants, rented spaces, and other venues.

But the vast majority of parties take place at home.

Parties serve a variety of purposes. Social gatherings in which you get together with a few close friends or family members are often the easiest. Other kinds of events serve specific purposes beyond just having fun. Large parties, such as open houses and cocktail parties, provide an opportunity to bring together a wide circle of acquaintances, sometimes carefully mixing business and social friends. A dinner for office associates becomes an opportunity to socialize in an out-of-the-office context.

If you're just learning how to entertain, the prospect of organizing a party beyond merely ordering in take-out can seem daunting. But I like to turn that around and think of just starting out as a time full of prospects and opportunities to have fun.

It doesn't matter if you don't have much equipment. You can tailor the event to what you do have, or borrow from friends. You don't have to be a well-trained cook, though it does help to have a few dishes that are sure to please you and your friends (trying them out beforehand is recommended!). You don't need a large and beautifully decorated home—I know one young couple who became known for their warm hospitality and delicious meals while in the middle of rebuilding their house. More than one meal was served on sawhorses amid the silvery glow of bare insulation. All you really need is a generous spirit, a desire to share a good time, and the confidence to say, "Let's have a party!"

As always, the primary goal of the host or hostess is to see that the guests enjoy themselves. We generally do this by offering good food and drink, lively conversation, and a friendly, welcoming atmosphere. You don't have to own the finest crystal and silver or serve intricately prepared food worthy of a four-star chef, and you don't have to—and indeed should not—require stiff properness in the deportment of your guests.

It does help to know your own unique style of entertaining. How do you know what you like if you haven't done much? It may take some trial and error, but thinking through the kinds of gatherings you like best will help you hone your personal style. Maybe you love elaborate multicourse dinners for twenty. Maybe you like casual dinners for the dearest of friends. Perhaps brunch or afternoon tea is your thing. Perhaps you have a shady deck that helps beat the heat of summer, or a cozy dining room that feels most welcoming when glittering snow is on the ground outside.

Whatever kind of gathering you feel most comfortable planning is the kind you should have. This doesn't mean, however, that you must always create the same kind of party over and over. Like wardrobe options, you can try on different kinds of entertaining, expanding the scope of your parties as you gain confidence.

PLANNING A PARTY

Entertaining easily and well takes practice, but with good planning and a relaxed attitude, anyone can make an event memorable. Once you've chosen the kind of party to give, it's time to begin the preparations. You'll need to know whom to invite, what to serve, and how much time it will take, both before the event and at the event.

CREATING A GUEST LIST

If you have to think more than a split second about the people you would like to entertain, perhaps you should think through the purpose and style of the gathering. If the party is for neighbors, perhaps you might want to include a new neighbor to get to know old friends. If it's a business dinner, you probably want to eschew social friends, as they might feel left out of business discussions while the business guests might be perplexed by gossip about a neighborhood cat or character.

Try to invite some friends whose personalities and conversational skills you know can help the party flow smoothly. This lets newcomers find their own comfortable niche and lessens the burden on the hosts as they see to last-minute details. Just as you don't want a party made of up total strangers, parties made up of the same people over and over again benefit from new blood. Include a few new faces if you can.

If possible, invite people from different generations. You will find that conversation is almost always more interesting when differing views and perspectives are represented. Try to balance your guests' personalities. If one of your guests has a personality that thrives on an appreciative audience, you will probably want to invite a few good listeners. Don't fuss about the old-fashioned rule of having a table equally balanced by gender. More important is to anticipate which friends will get along best.

INVITING YOUR GUESTS

Once you've created a guest list, it's time to invite them. For a large party or a party celebrating a special event, you will probably want to use a written invitation. (For more on these, see the section on formal invitations, page 26).

For casual dinner parties of eight or ten, you can issue invitations by telephone. By taking this direct approach, you can usually get a fairly quick reading of who will be able to attend. For a large party or event you may wish to issue the invitation a month or so in advance, but for casual dinners a week or so notice is usually adequate. (The occasional last-minute get-together can be fun too, so don't think of a week's notice as an absolute deadline that must prevent you from following through on an impromptu notion.)

If you receive a written invitation that reads R.S.V.P. (*Repondez s'il vous plaît*) with an accompanying telephone number, call as soon as you know whether you can attend. As an invited guest, you (or those you've invited) should respond as soon as possible. Plans for seating, food, and beverages are to be made, and the hosts need to know before the last minute. It is simply not acceptable not to respond at all. This goes for a large party as well as a small dinner. If no number appears on the invitation, call or write a simple reply.

Sometimes, even considerate people don't get around to responding to invitations in a timely way. You may find yourself now and again having to jog your friends. You can do this nicely. You might try something along the lines of "Hi, we've been pretty busy lately, and I'm afraid we might have missed your call regarding dinner on Saturday. We so hope you are free to come." Chances are good that the person's failure to call is no more than oversight, but there is also a chance that a mailed invitation hasn't been received.

When an invitation reads "Regrets only," the hosts only expect people who cannot attend to respond. As a host, this can make your preparations a bit of a gamble, however, because you never really know who—and how many—will be coming. No response is required to an invitation to an open house. Typically, such invitations state the starting and ending times, so that guests know how to time their arrival and exit. Any party that takes place during standard mealtimes should include a corresponding meal, even if it is only a light one.

PLANNING THE MENU

Every party has a menu, even if it consists only of cocktails and peanuts or cocoa and cookies. That means, however, that some advance thought is required as to what you will serve your guests.

In general, it's a good idea to serve dishes you already know how to prepare, since preparation mistakes or miscalculations of quantity or scheduling are less likely to happen with familiar foods. Of course, serving your house speciality isn't always the answer. (I for one would never get around to serving anything new if I didn't occasionally take a chance and branch out when guests are coming.) There's the issue of party food, too: How often do we make elaborate dinners or hors d'oeuvres for just family? At some point you have to take some chances and leap into the unknown—at least a little.

However simple or complex the food and beverages at your party, the meal must suit the event. Balance is the key element in menu planning. At its most basic, lunch or dinner is composed of elements from the basic food groups: protein, vegetable or fruit, and grains. This is not rocket science for anyone who has ever made a few meals.

Balance is also subjective, involving complementary flavors, colors, and textures. Meals that consist of too many similar elements tend to be rather boring. A cheese soufflé served with pureed vegetables and a pudding for desert has no variation in texture. A veal stew served with steamed cauliflower and white rice is bland in color.

Don't opt for meals with too many jarring elements. A meal in which every dish is highly seasoned leaves no room for the palate to taste them fully. Some dishes need to take center stage, others need to support them. A little diversity in a menu makes a meal memorable. Too much makes it a mess.

Think back to the food of the most successful parties you have attended. Were sweet dishes balanced with savory ones? Were crisp and chewy textures set off by smooth or soft ones? Was there variety in the color of the foods on the assembled plates? Was the soup hot and the ice cream softened? Was there a reasonable rhythm to the arrival of the courses, or were there great delays? Or a sense of being rushed from one to the next? The goal of planning a meal is to achieve perfect balance and timing, and even though meals don't always unfold the way we would hope, the rate of success is higher with careful planning.

America has experienced a revolution in food over the last few decades. Today almost everyone is familiar with cuisines from around the world that only a generation ago were seen as exotic. We are also far more aware of healthful eating, and that very consciousness often goes well with the explosion of new flavors being used even in everyday cooking. All these changes make creative menu planning much more fun than it used to be.

If you don't know where to start, I suggest doing a little homework.

There are cookbooks and food magazines published for just about every taste and temperament. Consult a few if you are at a loss about what to make. If you are inexperienced or lack kitchen confidence, don't tackle especially complicated or time-consuming recipes for your first party. Find dishes that won't leave you feeling intimidated and panicked in the hours just prior to your guests' arrival.

Another element to consider when planning a meal is the tastes and needs of your guests. It's easy to avoid serving a dreaded dish to a good friend if you know his food phobias or sensitivities; you can delight another by serving her a favorite. You can keep a cook's notebook and, when you hear of a friend's particular taste, jot it down. It can save unnecessary embarrassment and win you accolades. Most of all, it shows your guests courtesy and respect.

You can't anticipate everything, however, so there will be times when you unwittingly serve a guest something he or she cannot eat or doesn't care for no matter how attuned you are to people's tastes. I once knew a person who became unhappy in her life and one of the ways she chose to show it was to begin eliminating food groups from her diet. She began by dieting to lose weight, but after a while it seemed as if she were determined not to eat all. One side effect of this was that the more foods she cut out, the more difficult it became for her to socialize (and for her friends to invite her for dinner). Luckily, after a few hungry years, she made a change in her life and was able to eat in public again. You can't make every guest (or host) happy all the time.

Don't underestimate the importance of timing in planning and giv-ing a party. There's no one formula for getting it done right and at the right time: Your own work methods will dictate what works for you (are you a do-it-all-yesterday person or a last-minute Lou?). For many people, though, the most efficient way to create a meal for company is to work in stages as much in advance as possible. Other people prefer concentrated time in the kitchen on the day of the party.

Unless you have a kitchen staff, I find it is generally better to make dishes that do not require too much last-minute preparation. If you are the kind of host or hostess who loves to work surrounded by guests, by all means serve soufflés; otherwise leave such preparations to the restaurant chefs. As you think about your menu, remember that one of your primary jobs is to be with your guests.

WHAT TO SERVE

The most formal dinner you are likely to encounter in someone's home will consist of four or perhaps five courses. Such a meal is likely to consist of a first course, entrée, salad, and dessert or cheese course.

A first course may consist of almost anything, from vegetables and pasta dishes to meats and fish. Whatever you choose, it shouldn't be more powerful in flavor or density than the entrée. The first course should entice the taste buds, not completely satisfy the appetite.

Often soup serves as a first course. It may be a heavy cream-based soup or a lighter broth-based soup. One rule of thumb to follow is, the heavier the first course, the lighter the entrée should be.

A second course prior to the entrée, which is rarely seen these days, can be a dish of fish, shellfish, or game. It, too, should entice the appetite toward the main course.

The entrée, or main course, is the centerpiece of the meal. It usually consists of a portion of meat, fish, a stew, or a substantial vegetable dish. At a really casual meal, it could be a pasta dish or a casserole.

Many people serve salad as a first course. I prefer to serve it as a separate salad course after the entrée as a palate cleanser. I like a fairly simple salad of greens with a light dressing.

For many people, the success of the meal is defined by dessert. Like all the courses, the dessert course should be planned to balance the rest of the meal. If you serve a particularly hearty first course and entrée, you might want to choose a light fruit dessert to keep your guests from feeling uncomfortably heavy. A light meal can accommodate a rich dessert.

Occasionally you will see a cheese course served after or in place of dessert. A cheese course includes a selection of fine cheeses, high-quality crackers and/or small slices of delicious bread, and perhaps slices of fruit, such as apple or pear. Port is the wine of choice for a cheese course.

For a casual meal you may elect to serve almost everything at once. For example, if you're having a chili party, you don't need a first course unless you want one. Just put the pot on the table, along with the corn bread, salad, and any vegetable you might want to serve. In general, dessert should come later, presented after the table has been cleared of the main portion of the meal.

FIVE BASIC RULES FOR ENTERTAINING

In planning your party, these touchstone rules may help to guide you:

1. Invite congenial guests who you think will enjoy one another's company.

2. Plan the party thoroughly, including a timetable of what food items will need to be prepared and when.

3. Be ready to serve plenty of well-prepared food and beverages.

4. Set a pretty table, taking care to arrange your china, cutlery, glassware, and linens to best advantage.

5. Be confident and expect to have fun.

THE WORK PLAN

Once you have your menu decided, make yourself a work plan. Note what needs to be done in advance. Assemble a shopping list. Schedule the preparation of the entire meal so that you won't be caught short, slaving away while your guests drink their fifth aperitif, gnaw on their fingers, lose interest in dinner, and fall asleep.

One way to make a plan is to gather all the recipes and plot out their preparation, at least in your own mind. Then make a list of what each requires in the few hours preceding and during the party. This may seem awkward, but after a few parties some of it will come naturally and you will be able to abbreviate your lists.

When you get ready to cook, approach the meal systematically. Professional chefs set out every piece of equipment and every ingredient needed before beginning to cook. Few of us civilians do this regularly because of our need to rush along and get everything done. How many times have you become engaged in conversation with a guest, then lost your place in the recipe because you didn't have everything measured in advance?

A NOTE ON POTLUCKS

One popular and easy-to-plan party is one in which the guests contribute dishes. Such gatherings can be as simple as one guest bringing a salad and another bringing dessert, or a large function for which, say, thirty people bring dishes.

When planning a potluck party, try to direct the dishes people bring. You may not be able to ask for specific dishes, but you can give guidelines so that you don't end up with a table of desserts and only one savory item. As the planner, be prepared to bring a dish or two that can round out the meal, but which might be less popular to make, such as a couple of vegetable side dishes.

PLAN THE TABLE SETTINGS

Just as you plan a meal in advance, plan your table settings and decorations. Make sure you have the linens you need and that they are pressed and ready to go. Check to see that the silver is shiny, and that you have all the china and glassware you need. If you are having a cocktail party for fifty, will you use plastic cups, or might you consider renting the glasses?

On the day of the party, plan some time for set up. Set the table a few hours before guests arrive (see Chapter 3, The Tools of the Table, page 86, for information on setting a table). Set up the bar, but add the ice at the last minute. Assemble any platters or other serving dishes you will need. Decide where to put coats. Check your lists, keeping in mind the steps required and the timing of each dish of the meal. In short, take a little time and think through every element of the party and plan how it will be carried out.

STAFF

Say you're having a cocktail party for fifty to celebrate your new home. It's too much to do alone, so you decide to hire a bartender and two waitstaff to make drinks, pass hors d'oeuvres, bus dirty dishes to the kitchen, and clean up. You've found them through word of mouth or the notice board at the local college or the Yellow Pages.

You've interviewed them and they all seem professional and pleasant. Maybe you've interviewed a number and have narrowed it down to the final three available for the night of your party.

Before you hire your staff, make sure you have a clear understanding of the duties involved, the hours you expect them to work, and the fee you will pay. The best way to do this is in writing. You don't necessarily have to create a contract; a letter of understanding will usually be sufficient. Make sure you ask them to come an hour or so ahead if you would like help with last-minute preparations. Also make sure you tell them how you would like them to dress. The most standard dress is a white shirt and black trousers or skirt. If you want them to wear something out of the ordinary, you should plan to provide it.

After the party, when they are ready to leave, you pay by check or cash, as prearranged. If you have been pleased with their efforts, feel free to tip them about 10 percent, and up to 20 percent of their fee for extraordinary service.

WHAT TO LOOK FOR WHEN HIRING WAITSTAFF

In interviewing candidates to help serve at your party, you want a person who will make your guests feel welcome but not intrude into their conversations or otherwise act inappropriately. That means you should look for someone who will be:

- Attentive but not pushy
- Well-spoken but reserved
- Neatly groomed
- Ready to anticipate needs for food and drink
- Pleasant to you and your guests
- Willing to pitch in and help beyond serving food and drink.

There will be lots of jobs such as helping with coats, cleaning up, and minor food prep and presentation.

When hiring a bartender, all of the above qualities help, as does a knowledge of mixed drinks, should you elect to have a full bar.

Hiring a Caterer

Some parties are too much for one person, either because you don't enjoy cooking for days ahead or because you are too busy. That doesn't mean you can't have a party at home—you can hire a caterer!

There is a caterer for just about every kind of food, event, and budget you can imagine. They also vary widely in the amount of services they provide. Full-service caterers can provide everything from food to table settings to staff. Some caterers will prepare food (all or part of a meal) and drop it off. Home chefs, known technically as food service accommodators, can come to your home and just cook the food.

The best advertising for caterers, like most services, is word of mouth. Ask around and think back to catered meals you've enjoyed. (For more information, see the section on choosing the caterer, page 150.)

BASIC DUTIES OF A HOST OR HOSTESS

These may seem obvious, but keep in mind that you should be available to ensure that:

- Your guests are welcomed warmly and they find the heart of the party as well as the bar.
- Your guests have been introduced to one another.
- Their plates and glasses are filled.
- The food is plentiful and tasty.
- The conversation flows.

Last but not least, remember to relax and enjoy your guests. After all, they've come to see you and you organized this party so you should enjoy their company, too.

LET THE PARTY BEGIN!

So it's five minutes to six and your first guests will be arriving at the top of the hour. The snacks or hors d'oeuvres are nicely presented and ready to go. The bar is set up, the table set, the house is presentable (too late now if it isn't), and you are dressed and ready. Relax, soon the game begins. And you know what? It'll be fun.

The Hosts' Role

The first guests arrive.

You greet them at the door. The host usually greets women he knows with a peck on the cheek and shakes the right hand of the men and the women to whom he is being introduced. The hostess usually greets everyone she knows with a peck on the cheek and offers a handshake to those she does not. After greetings and introductions are made, you take the guests' coats and hang them up or place them in their designated spot.

Perhaps your guests hand you a house gift—maybe a thoughtfully chosen bottle of wine, some homemade goodies, an interesting book, a bouquet of flowers. The flowers are arranged and tied with a bow or are already in their own vase, so you can display them without having to do major flower arranging. If you are presented with wine, your guest may say something like, "This is a little something for your cellar." If another food is brought the guest might say, "I thought you might enjoy these for breakfast one day," or "For your family dessert tomorrow," or something else to indicate that they don't expect you to serve it at the party.

You usher your guests in and offer them something to drink. If you are having a party of more than ten or a dozen guests and you entertain alone, you might want to have a bartender (or a willing friend) serve drinks. These can be poured individually or passed on a tray (especially useful when serving a limited variety of drinks). Whoever does the serving always provides a napkin with each glass.

You settle your first guests in, making light conversation. If there are two hosts one stays with the guests while the other attends to new arrivals. You switch roles occasionally. If you are entertaining alone, your guests will have to amuse each other when you are called to welcome new ones. Newly arrived guests are introduced to anyone they don't know (see the section on meeting and greeting, page 19) and general pleasantries are exchanged.

You can use an introduction as a conversation opener. For instance, you can identify a person's occupation or interests. For a housewarming party, you might say something like, "I'd like you to meet Robbie Haldane. He coordinated our landscape design and made our small ideas much better." When introducing people to one another, make sure to mention both first and last names. If you are a guest, feel free to introduce yourself to other guests you don't know.

As your guests get comfortable, you pass hors d'oeuvres, and conversation flourishes. When serving appetizers, make sure that you provide napkins (paper cocktail napkins are fine) for finger food and small plates if you serve anything with a sauce. When serving cheese and crackers or other appetizers assembled on the spot, be sure to assemble enough to serve each guest before passing.

If you serve appetizers at a buffet, make sure to provide small plates as well as napkins so guests can take several items, leave the table, and circulate, making room for others. Guests tend to congregate around the table and bar, and providing portable tools may help avoid congestion.

Hosts come and go as needed to put the finishing touches on the meal and to facilitate conversation. Try to have at least one of the hosts with the guests at all times. It's best if both hosts spend time with their guests lest their friends think the cook does nothing but slave in the kitchen for them. Watchful hosts keep an eye on their guests' glasses and refill them as needed.

Watchful hosts also monitor the conversation. By that I mean they watch to see that people are talking freely, having a good time, getting a chance to participate. Occasionally a host may need to direct or redirect conversations, open up new topics, or include a left-out guest. In large groups hosts should try to bring together people they believe would enjoy talking with one another or, if the talk begins to be overheated, maneuver a guest from one conversation to another ("John, I've always wanted you to meet my brother-in-law Frank. . . .").

THE GUESTS' ROLE

The hosts of a party have obligations, and so do the guests. When you are invited out, you too have an obligation to help make the party run. Hosts reasonably expect their guests to mingle and talk, get to know each other, and find areas of common interest.

Not everyone is expected to stand out as a conversational star. Who would all those stars talk to? But it does help if you are happily open to pleasant conversation and able to respond intelligently. This shows courtesy not just to your fellow guests but to the host as well.

Take a little time before you arrive at the party to think through the event. Who will be there? Are you likely to meet any people that you've met before? What are their names—first and last? What did you talk about the last time you saw them? Do you share any interests? What news of the week is likely to be discussed? Have you any insights to share on the subject?

When should you arrive at a party? That depends on where you are and what kind of party it is. In most cities, no one is expected to arrive until at least ten minutes or up to half an hour after the stated time. In certain parts of the country and outside of cities, people tend to arrive on time or up to twenty minutes later. If you find yourself early, kill some time driving or walking about the neighborhood until the appointed hour. People are rarely ready for guests early, and it wouldn't be considerate to expect them to be.

If the party is an open house, you may come an hour or so into the event, depending on how long it runs. Don't, however, show up fifteen minutes before the end and expect the party to carry on just for you.

If you are unavoidably delayed, call your hosts if you possibly can. If you know you will be more than an hour late, be sure that you will still be welcome and don't be angered or disappointed if the hosts offer to give you a rain check for another time.

Once at the party, be alert. Don't sit like a lump, waiting to be entertained. Join in and mingle. If it's obvious that the hosts could use a little help, volunteer to assist. Generally speaking, stay in the rooms you are directed toward. The exception to this is the bathroom. You may feel free to ask directions to it if you are unfamiliar with the layout of the home.

Make sure you thank your hosts when leaving the party.

And, please, I know it's old-fashioned, but it's the proper thing: Call or even send a note of thanks within a day or two of the party. Hosts really appreciate it, and it's always rewarding to be thoughtful to someone who has opened his or her home to you.

Dinner Is Served

About an hour after the first guest has arrived you should be ready to eat, if you are serving a meal. Should some of your guests still not have arrived, you may hold the meal fifteen or twenty minutes and start when they arrive. Anyone who is that late shouldn't expect a long conversation period. Lead your guests into the dining room or otherwise direct them to the food. (For more information, see Chapter 2, Modern Table Manners, page 49.)

When seating people for dinner, try to create combinations of people that will make for interesting conversations. Should there be guests of honor, they are seated next to the hosts, who are seated at the ends of the table. Should there be only one host, seat a guest of honor at the other end of the table. Try not to seat couples together. If you have an even number of people of both genders, alternate them female-male, female-male around the table. If the numbers are uneven, don't worry about it. Left-handed people should be seated at the ends where they are most comfortable.

Table Conversation

Perhaps the most important element of a dinner party is the atmosphere and conversation at the table. Delicious and beautifully served foods are certainly important, but few dinner parties can be deemed successful without pleasant, lively conversation. Upsetting or unpleasant discussions can destroy the atmosphere quicker than burned vegetables. This applies at home with the family as well as in public or someone else's home.

You need not stick to discussing the weather, dull indeed after a short while, but try to avoid risky subjects. If you talk politics, it helps to know where everyone else stands in relation to general issues. If you discuss events of the day, try to listen to other opinions and let others talk without feeling you must convert everyone to your philosophy. If others aren't able to do this, try to steer the conversation to another topic. This is one of the duties of hosts, but guests can help out, too.

Lively conversation is desirable, being dominated by a bore is not. Try not to hold center stage too long, no matter how interesting you think you sound. Try not to interrupt and then dominate a going conversation, as it declares to all that you feel yourself to be the most interesting and most important person present.

At a large dinner party, group conversation often isn't possible, but individual talk is most welcome. Try to engage the person next to you in conversation. If you don't know the person, you may start with general observations about the meal or the event. If that goes well you can move on to more personal subjects, such as the nature of the relationship with the hosts, other guests, and topics of the day. Try not to speak over the person next to you in order to converse with someone else.

Be sure to speak to each person seated next to you. There used to be a moment at formal dinners at which the hostess "turned the table," moving from speaking with the person on her left to the person on her right. Every person dropped their conversation and turned to the other side. Those who persisted in their conversation kept the table blocked, leaving at least two people with no one to talk to. Even though we don't formally see the table turned as often these days, it's useful to keep an eye out as conversation does tend to turn from neighbor to neighbor. Move your conversation as the need becomes apparent, and include your neighbor in the current conversation, if one of your neighbors appears to have no one to talk to.

Once the meal is completed, clear the table or tables and enjoy your guests. At really informal meals guests may offer to help clear and hosts may accept. Never stack plates at the table: That would make your guests feel as if they were in the kitchen about to do the washing up themselves.

Resist the temptation to do the dishes between courses. You should be enjoying your company, not leaving them to talk while you clank away in the kitchen. If you have help, they will clear the table and take care of the dishes.

THE PARTY WINDS DOWN

After the meal you may wish to usher your guests to the living room for entertainment, coffee, after-dinner drinks, or just conversation. For some people this provides an opportunity to slip out, for others it's an opportunity for some real visiting. Often people are especially relaxed or mellow after a good meal. As a guest, however, resist the temptation to settle in for hours of conversation, especially if it is already rather late. Depending on the time, guests should stay no more than an additional hour—two if the meal ended early, say, before nine o'clock. If you are being entertained on a weeknight at a family-style meal, try to leave after half an hour or so.

If entertainment is offered, guests should be attentive to the program, not each other. This is an instance when a real visit with friends will need to be postponed.

When leaving, thank your hosts for the evening and feel free to praise something in particular. I know I always like it when I get feedback on a special dish, piece of entertainment, or a particularly good conversation. Guests should remember to take any party favors that were at their places.

As a final note, guests should call to thank their hosts for the party within a day or two. For a very formal meal, you should write a note of thanks for the evening.

ENTERTAINING FOR BUSINESS

Hosting a dinner for business associates or fellow workers is exactly the same as entertaining friends, except that everyone must be especially sure to be on good behavior. I don't mean stiff behavior; in fact the more relaxed you feel, the better you will come off. I mean good behavior such as being considerate of your fellow guests in conversation and table manners. This graciousness makes everyone comfortable.

Business associates who gather for a meal can feel slightly more vulnerable than when with social friends. Inflammatory topics are to be avoided at all costs, since all conversation may be evaluated from a business perspective. Conversation should be lively but circumspect. Do you really want business associates to know your political opinions, youthful indiscretions, or family secrets?

Seating guests for a business meal may follow protocol more than at a social event. The most important guests sit closest to the hosts, who are placed at the ends of the table. The highest-ranking woman sits to the right of the host, the highest-ranking man to the right of the hostess. The second-most important guests, should there be any, sit to the left of the host and hostess. Other guests should not be seated by importance, unless protocol is being observed, but rather to enhance conviviality and make your guests comfortable.

HOSTING WEEKEND VISITORS

Many of us enjoy entertaining friends overnight in our homes. During an extended stay, you get to visit in a leisurely manner that is not possible during the course of a single evening. As with all entertaining, there is an art to making the overnight guest feel welcome.

One of the first obligations of the host is to make guests feel at home. We do this in a number of ways. We make sure that the house is clean, the guests' room is pleasant, and that guests have the privacy they need. The hosts should pay attention to the guests' wishes and provide good wholesome food. Most important, we provide company and entertainment that will show our guests a good time. It probably wouldn't be much fun for a houseguest to just sit around and watch you and your family go about your daily routine.

This doesn't mean you have to turn everything topsy-turvy (although sometimes you might want to), throw your schedule to the wind, and exhaust everyone with round-the-clock sightseeing and entertaining. It does mean providing options for activities your guests might enjoy and going out of your way at least a little to show them that you are glad they have come. This might mean preparing a special meal, inviting congenial friends in, or taking your guests out.

The exception to the rule of putting yourself out for guests is when they come for an extended stay. After a couple of days of entertaining them, you may confidently expect them to entertain themselves for a large portion of each day.

When guests arrive, try to be there to greet them. Nothing provides as warm a welcome as a live person. If you can't be there, let them know in advance and leave a note at least, welcoming them and explaining any household peculiarities they should know (the dog in the family room, the fresh paint on the deck, the wine chilling in the refrigerator).

Once greeted and settled, you might want to consider running your guests through the itinerary for the stay. Guests often like to know what is on the agenda so they can prepare themselves and schedule their time. If you have no specific agenda, you can discuss options of things to do and let them help choose. If you are really organized, you might even write out the itinerary and place it in the guest room for easy reference.

THE GUEST ROOM

Not everyone is lucky enough to have space for a guest room, but if you do, entertaining will be easier for you and your friends and relations. There are a few things you can provide to make your guests' stay more enjoyable. These include a good reading light, a comfortable chair or sofa on which to sit, a comfortable bed with plenty of pillows and blankets, places to hang and put away clothes, clear surfaces on which to put belongings, perhaps a television or radio, and varied reading material. Other touches geared to your particular guests are often most appreciated, too. These might include an arrangement of fresh garden flowers, the daily newspaper, or a carafe of fresh water with glasses.

The thoughtful host will also provide a supply of fresh towels for guests, as well as toiletries that might have been forgotten such as a toothbrush, toothpaste, deodorant, shampoo, and conditioner. It often helps to have a hair dryer and an iron available, too. If your house is spacious enough that your guests will be using a separate bathroom, you might put in plain sight indulgences such as bath salts, body washes, lotions, and powders. Basics such as soap, tissues, and extra toilet paper should be a given. Remember, the idea is to make them feel at home.

Sometimes a special little service done for a houseguest is most appreciated, too. A pot of tea brewed and ready with a plate of cookies when a guest arrives sends a special welcome message. I remember one special time when I visited my sister. She knew mine had been a long journey, so when I arrived she handed me a delicious glass of wine, disappeared, and drew me a scented, warm bath. She had laid out fresh towels and soap. A small table in the bathroom held a bouquet of fresh flowers and a coaster for my wineglass; the room was lit with candles. On the steamy mirror she had written "Welcome, Sis." I *did* feel welcome.

How to Make Sure You Get Asked Back

The thoughtful guest tries to anticipate how he or she can enhance the visit so that everyone has a wonderful time and wants to do it again. To that end the first rule to remember is that when you are a guest in someone's home, you are not at a hotel. Visiting is a cooperative effort, and anything you can do that will be helpful to your hosts without getting in their way will more than likely be appreciated. Offer to pitch in whenever it appears you could be useful.

Try not to expect to be constantly entertained. During what is obviously busy family time, fend for yourself—go for a walk, take a nap, offer to go get the newspaper or do errands. If you are visiting for more than a day or two, plan a day of sightseeing by yourself, offering to take the hosts. Offer to make a meal or take your hosts out.

Be neat. Your room shouldn't be a shambles. If you offer to make lunch for everyone, don't then leave a mess for your hosts to clean up. When you leave, ask the hosts if you can strip the bed for them.

Be sure you bring your hosts a token of your appreciation. You can bring some nice wine (more than one bottle), a basket of food goodies, an unusual plant for the avid gardener, or something that relates to their interests or passions. (See also the section on house gifts, page 214.)

Once home, be sure to write a brief note of thanks, or at the very least call to thank your hosts. You might also send a gift along, one suited to their house or interests. This is most appropriate if you didn't bring them a house gift at the outset of the visit, if your gift seems small given their hospitality, or if you happened to come across something that you know your hosts would particularly like and you wish to express further thanks for a wonderful time.

When Children Are Hosts and Guests

The day a child has a first play date at home is the day he or she becomes a host or hostess. When they are quite small, the visit may be closely monitored by a parent or two, but by the time they reach the age of five or so, they begin to entertain more in their play, and thus they can assume a few duties.

Before a friend comes over to play, you might want to ask your child what activities he or she has in mind. Make sure your child understands that the visitor should be given a choice of things to do and should be allowed to pick and choose from among the list.

A child who has friends over very often will soon develop a facility for the all-important skill of negotiating. When confronted with a friend who doesn't want to do what your child wants to do, your child should be able to compromise. If, for instance, one youngster wants to play Frisbee outside and the other child to play a board game, your child can suggest, "How about if we play one round of your game, and then go outside for twenty minutes of Frisbee?" Such compromise takes practice, of course, and it is not something that a three-year-old can often do. You may be called in to help on occasion.

Children should be taught to treat their friends as guests. They should let the friend go first most of the time, have the best seat in the kitchen, and sometimes choose the activity. This doesn't mean that your child must let the other child rule the day. If your child is really getting taken advantage of, you will need to step in to even things out.

One of the things that parents try hard to hammer home from babyhood on is that in play everyone shares. This is especially true when a friend comes over to play. You may need to remind all children—yours and visitors—of this rule every now and then. Older children should be able to serve refreshments to their friends—another form of sharing—without an adult's supervision.

Children need to be taught how to be good guests as well as good hosts. Good guests share and compromise and try not to be bossy. I will never forget the little girl who came to visit my daughter who demanded everything her way—"Because," she explained, "I'm the guest." The good guest doesn't demand, nor does she let the host or hostess be overbearing and bossy. If needed, even a guest can appeal to the fairness of a grown-up, but only after trying to work things out. Kids often resolve their differences much better together than do grown-ups who step in.

When things go really wrong, a child should know how to get out of the situation by saying something like, "My mom asked me to call; I think I had better do it now." When you get such a call, try to be sensitive to what's going on, offering advice or a summons (and if necessary a ride home).

When it comes to food, the polite guest takes what is offered and eats it if at all possible. If what's on offer is really unpalatable, a child should politely decline and try not to make comments on how it's not like that at home.

All children should be taught from a very early age to respect the needs and wishes of other people and their property. Just as you don't break toys at home, you don't do it at someone else's house.

They also need to be taught how to be courteous to those outside their own home. The best way to do this is, of course, through example at home. Children who learn the skills of being good hosts and guests are developing skills that will last their whole lives, helping to make them gracious adults at ease in the world.

When teens host parties at your house, an adult must be on the premises, preferably at a discreet distance from the main goings-on but within close enough proximity that he or she can occasionally check on the party and manage any situations that get out of control. Few teens know how to handle a situation such as uninvited peers showing up. An adult should be prepared to deal with such an event.

Entertaining at home should be a pleasure for hosts and guests, and good planning and common consideration can help ensure an agreeable—and even delightful—time is had by all.

5

DINING OUT

As the revolution in American food has progressed, Americans have gotten in the habit of going out to eat regularly. Perhaps this is because people have more disposable income or because more women work outside the home and have less time and inclination to cook. Whatever the reason, increasing numbers of people dine out, visiting not only fast-food eateries but also enjoying the true restaurant experience at full, seated meals.

Whatever the restaurant situation, there are guidelines that can help make the experience of eating out more enjoyable for everyone. Knowing what's expected of you and the members of your family in a restaurant can be a great comfort in a new place. We'll start at the simpler venues and move up to more formal settings.

FAST-FOOD AND SIMPLE RESTAURANTS

Basic courtesy to staff and fellow diners is the rule. When ordering, decide on your choices expeditiously in order not to hold up the line. Treat the person behind the counter with respect, asking politely for items. If the service is slow, do not take out your frustration on the server. You may ask if there is a problem, but criticizing the person's competence, directly or indirectly, won't speed up service. It may raise tempers and lower other people's assessment of you.

Once you have your food, use basic good table manners. All those seated nearby may observe you struggling with your sloppy hamburger, too, so try to keep the mess to a reasonable minimum and chew with your mouth closed. Rude sounds detract from the appetite and enjoyment of those around you. This goes for children as well as adults.

There is nothing worse when looking for a seat in a fast-food restaurant than a sea of tables piled with empty wrappers and cartons. Yes, the staff is there to clean up, but they often can't keep up with the volume. So give the next customer a break and bus your own table.

Simple restaurants are a good training ground for teaching children how to eat in public. A child of four or five can generally remain in his or her seat for most of a fast-food lunch (a child of six or so may be ready to remain at the table during the course of a more formal seated meal). At simple eateries, children can learn some of the basics of ordering, eating, and behaving properly in public. Many six-year-olds are mature enough to make an informed menu choice or two, without too much parental input. Children of around five can usually be expected to speak directly to waitstaff when ordering. Eating with utensils properly may still elude the skills of the six- and even seven-year-old, but practicing in casual restaurants may speed them along.

FINE RESTAURANTS

Dining out in a fine restaurant is a special experience. The evening can take on almost any form, from a romantic dinner for you and your spouse to a celebratory dinner with friends, to a working meal with business colleagues. How relaxed you are and how much fun you have will vary with the event, the restaurant, and mood, but the steps to having a fine meal are always the same.

When you arrive for a meal for which you have a reservation, be on time. Expecting a restaurant to hold a table for more than fifteen minutes, at the most, is unreasonable. Don't be surprised or offended if a popular spot in your area is even less accommodating.

In expensive restaurants, you will usually be greeted by a maître d'hôtel (referred to simply as the maître d', manager, or hostess). This person is responsible for seating diners. Inexpensive restaurants often let diners seat themselves. If no one is in the front to greet you and you are unsure, ask a staff member about the seating policy.

In expensive restaurants, the responsibility of the maître d'hôtel often carries beyond seating the guests. He may take your order, supervise the service, sometimes prepare a dish at the table, and at some point during the meal discreetly inquire of diners if everything is satisfactory.

Some people feel that by tipping the maître d'hôtel in advance they guarantee themselves a better table and service. This is not necessarily so, and few maîtres d'hôtel wish to be seen taking "bribes." If you do want to tip the maître d' in advance, in an effort to get better service, do so discreetly. Five to ten dollars should be ample, depending on the community and how fancy the restaurant is. Again, keep it discreet.

When you arrive you may wait for others to join you or be seated right away. It's never polite to order food before your fellow diners arrive, but you may order a cocktail, should your dinner companions be running late.

SEATING

When determining where to sit at the table, consider your fellow diners. Anyone with special needs such as long legs or left-handedness or a disability should be given the seat that suits him or her best. In general, the host of the meal, should there be one, takes the head of the table.

It used to be axiomatic that the host, a man, let a woman sit inside on a banquette so she could see out. These days the rule is less practical, as women are often the hosts themselves, and more women dine together.

ORDERING FOOD

Once you are seated, a waiter or the maître d'hôtel will bring menus and list the specials of the day. You may then study the menu in preparation for ordering your meal. You may ask the waiter about foods or dishes with which you are unfamiliar. A good waiter or waitress should be able to tell you simply how each dish is prepared.

Also, feel free to ask the price of specials that were described but do not appear on the menu.

Waiters and waitresses should never condescend to diners. They may correct the pronunciation of a dish only if the diner appears to be having a hard time with the word. Similarly, the diner treats all the staff members with consideration and a quiet understanding that the waitstaff are providing a gracious and efficient service.

If the menu is in courses, also known as table d'hôte, you will need to decide which of them you want. If you are paying for the meal yourself, this is easy—just order what you wish. If you are someone else's guest, it is polite to confine your meal to two courses, the entrée and dessert. You might want to have an appetizer course in mind, however, should it become obvious that others are having one and you are expected to order one, too.

The sensitive host with deep pockets can discreetly encourage guests to order three courses. He or she might say something on the order of: "My, the appetizers look inviting. I'm going to have one. Do you see anything that appeals to you?"

In many restaurants here and abroad, the waiter waits for diners to close their menus as a sign that the diners are ready to order. Such discreet waiters can really help make a meal flow smoothly. Less happy situations result from overeager waitstaff who continually return before you are ready to order. If this happens, politely ask your waiter to give you a few more minutes.

A good waiter or waitress will magically appear at a lull in the conversation to take your order and answer any questions you might have. Dishes should be described in enough detail to let you know what you are ordering, but not so much that you get confused.

It is perfectly acceptable to let your waiter or waitress know if you have a particular schedule to which you must adhere. If, for instance, you have tickets for a show, you can mention that fact as you are seated, or when ordering, saying something like, "We have an eight o'clock curtain. Would the grilled fish come fairly quickly, or would you recommend something else?" Similarly, if you would like to stretch out your meal, when the waiter appears to take your order you could say something along the lines of: "We're so enjoying our evening that we would like to wait a few more minutes."

ORDERING DRINKS

The waiter or waitress will usually ask if you would like to order a drink at the time that the menus are brought. You may order a beverage at this time if you wish. You may also ask to wait a few minutes. Many people prefer to order wine with dinner and thus may wait until they know what they and others will be eating. If you mention you will be drinking wine with dinner, the wine steward, should there be one, will be dispatched to discuss the selection.

You need never be embarrassed to ask the price of a wine from the wine steward or waiter. The markup is so high on a bottle of wine—300 percent is not unusual—that it can add significantly to the cost of a meal.

When ordering cocktails, be aware of your fellow diners. If no one else at your table orders an aperitif, you might want to rethink your choice or keep your drink to one, so as not to hold up the meal for others.

When your dining group is small, you may wish to coordinate entrées so that everyone's main course goes well with the wine. Generally speaking, heavy dishes including meats such as beef, lamb, and pork take a red wine, while fish and chicken often go best with a white wine. There is a wide variation in the body of white and red wines, however, so ask the wine steward to recommend a choice that might suit everyone at the table. If your group is large, you can order a bottle of red and a bottle of white if that makes entrée ordering easier.

If you are someone's guest, let the host suggest and order the wine.

SERVICE

In most restaurants, food is brought to the table in courses. Food is generally served at your left and empty dishes are cleared from your right, just like at home. Exceptions are of course made when it is inconvenient to serve conventionally. When it is difficult for a waiter or waitress to get access to your place setting, you may volunteer to handle a dish. Waiters should always avoid reaching in front of a diner.

Once the food has been served, the waiter may have some additional services to offer. If a food is served with a separate sauce, the waiter may serve it, and you should signal when you have enough. Often a waiter will offer to grind fresh pepper on a dish or sprinkle fresh Parmesan cheese. Again, indicate when you have enough. If you would like something that has not been brought, make your request to the waiter.

Similarly, if food is unacceptable in some way, such as overcooked or undercooked, discreetly summon the waiter to your table and explain the problem. Always speak in a pleasant tone of voice. It is not the waitstaff's fault the food is unacceptable, but your waiter or waitress is in a position to help. If something you have asked for has not been brought, feel free to ask for it in a friendly manner.

Once you have finished a course, you may signal the waiter that you are finished by placing your knife and fork parallel to one another on the right side of your plate. If you are merely resting between bites, you may cross your knife and fork over one another. Dishes should be cleared only after everyone at the table is finished with the course.

After the table has been cleared of the entrée, the waiter or waitress will bring the dessert menu and offer coffee and tea. You may choose a dessert or you may share one if you wish. If you mention you will be sharing, usually an extra fork or spoon will be brought, often along with an extra plate. Sometimes the dessert is split in the kitchen.

Sometimes coffee and tea are served in their own little pots. Usually the tea bag sits on the plate next to the pot. You place the bag into the pot (not your cup) to brew the tea. When the tea bag arrives at the side of a cup of hot water, you have no choice but to place the bag directly into the cup. Once the tea is brewed to your satisfaction, you may remove the bag from the pot or the cup with your spoon, wrap the string around your spoon to squeeze out the excess, if you wish, and place it on the service plate or saucer.

Once the meal is finished, usually the bill will appear. If you wish to linger over your coffee or dessert, and the restaurant is not full, feel free. In a high-quality restaurant, the staff expect this, and the timing of the turns of the tables is based on a leisurely meal. This should not be abused, however. If you are the last people in the restaurant it is definitely time to go. If people are waiting to be seated, vacate as soon as you can. If the manager has asked you three times since the meal ended if everything is okay, it's past time for you to leave. However, hurrying you out before you've finished your meal is also inappropriate.

When the bill is presented, check it over carefully. Examining a bill is perfectly acceptable behavior—it is not considered miserly, just careful. If a mistake has been made, quietly point it out to the waiter or manager.

When paying the bill it is customary in this country to add a tip or gratuity. The standard amount is 15 to 20 percent of the bill before tax and the tip is usually divided among the waitstaff. Particularly with large groups, check to be sure that a tip hasn't already been added to the bill. The menu often states the house policy as well (often for large groups a fixed percentage is automatically calculated). If the tip has been added in, you need not add anything more unless the service has been extraordinarily good.

You may add the tip to the credit card receipt or leave it in cash on the table or in the folder or the tray on which the bill was presented. You may tip the maître d'hôtel (5 percent of the bill is appropriate) if you wish to express your satisfaction to him personally. In a fine restaurant, a wine steward who has helped you choose a wine is often tipped 15 percent of the cost of the wine. He or she will come over to you as you prepare to leave.

A meal with poor service should not be rewarded with a full tip. Reduce the tip by 5 percent or more or, in the event of terrible service, tip nothing at all. However, don't reduce the tip for things the waitstaff has no control over, since the tip makes up a large portion of their pay.

SERVING STAFF

People who serve you should always be treated with courtesy. Their job is to serve each diner's needs efficiently and pleasantly. Waitstaff work very hard in the course of a busy evening attending to a variety of wishes, requests, and personalities.

When addressing a waiter or waitress you may use his or her name should you know it. Otherwise, you may say, "Waiter," "Waitress," or "Miss." Mrs. and Mr. are not used.

To catch a waiter's attention, you may signal by catching his eye as he moves nearby or by raising a hand or finger discreetly. Never snap your fingers, clap your hands, tap an implement on a glass, whistle, or shout across the room. An efficient and courteous server will circulate and keep an eye out for your signal.

When a serving person arrives to take your order, be pleasant, ask any questions you need, and order as swiftly as you can. Try not to become overly friendly or take up too much of the person's time.

Try not to make too many out-of-the-ordinary or off-the-menu requests. A simple off-the-menu request, such as a bowl of plain noodles in an Italian restaurant, is fine, but combining items from different dishes is not.

As with anyone you encounter, be polite, especially when asking for a service. "Please" and "thank you" should be second nature. Do not argue with waitstaff about house rules. They do not set policy. It is not their fault that the wonderful braised lamb shanks are not on the menu this week. They do not compose the plate presentation, so if they say they cannot substitute spaetzle for the potato pancake, accept it.

On the other hand, you need not be bullied by a waiter. If the service is sloppy or slow or you face a person with an unpleasant attitude, you may let him or her know that you expect better service. Be polite but firm in your requests.

Should you encounter a serious problem, politely make your complaints known to the waiter or waitress first. If you don't receive satisfaction, ask to see the manager or the owner.

Problems that can be corrected along the way should be dealt with, those that cannot should be left alone, if possible. If you must complain after the meal is finished, consider whether it will do any good. If it is an exercise that your ego demands, think of another way to let off steam. What is the point of complaining purely for its own sake? In addition to criticizing the kitchen and the server, you will almost surely make the rest of your party uncomfortable. Your best revenge is never to go back.

SPLITTING THE BILL

It is perfectly acceptable to share the cost of a meal in a restaurant. Often, the easiest way to do this is to split the bill down the middle (for two people or two couples). Often a waiter or waitress will divide the check evenly between two or more credit cards if requested. If you need separate checks, tell the waiter when you order. If you are in a large party, say, ten people, individual checks may be very cumbersome and time consuming. It would be better to divide the check ten ways.

Two pieces of advice when eating with a group and paying individually. First, if you order the prime rib at fourteen dollars while everyone else has a chicken sandwich for six dollars, make sure you pay your extra share. You don't want to be eating at your friends' expense—nor do you want them to have to *ask* you to chip in more. Second, don't split pennies to make sure you pay only your exact share and not a cent more. This will waste time, irritate your fellow diners, and put a damper on the meal.

BUSINESS MEALS

Never underestimate the power of a meal, especially when it's in the context of conducting business. Maybe you hammer out multimillion dollar deals over lunch every day; perhaps you're still working at building business relationships. Whatever the purpose of a business meal, confidently going about the rituals of eating can keep you from the potentially devastating effects of looking like it's your first time out of the house.

Eating out for business, whether it be breakfast, lunch, or dinner, thus entails its own set of stresses. In addition to minding table manners and understanding restaurant etiquette, you must appear confident, relaxed, and prepared to discuss business—a tall order at, say, a seven o'clock breakfast meeting!

A business meal actually brings together almost all of one's social skills. Among the elements one juggles are table manners, one's abilities as a host or hostess, the ability to speak well, and the knack of thinking quickly while effectively dealing with other people.

THE PURPOSE OF A BUSINESS MEAL

We tend to think of business meals as exercises in power or as crucial to the success of a deal. In actuality, the business conducted during a meal is usually minor. The meal may serve an important purpose, but it is rarely the heavy lifting of deal making. More often, it is an intangible, but still invaluable, chance to cement the human side of the deal.

Broadly speaking, there are two kinds of business meals. One appears on the surface to be entirely social. Its purpose is to establish or strengthen informal business bonds or even to woo a client or prospective employee to give you a favorable nod when the time comes. At these meals, most often lunch, the parties scope one another out, scrutinizing each other for warning signs of trouble ahead, evaluating each other for clues to a good working relationship.

The second kind of meal is set up to discuss a specific piece of business and is known as a working meal. At these meals, which sometimes even have an agenda, everyone arrives ready to discuss a project in detail.

PLANNING A MEAL

Planning a business meal in a restaurant is relatively easy. First, make a short list of the restaurants that you like to frequent. Generally speaking, the more important the meeting, the fancier the restaurant. Of course, there is also the issue of how much money your company allows employees to spend on entertaining.

Next, call the person you wish to invite. By making the call, it is clear that you will act as host. You can say something like, "I've been hoping we could get together over lunch to discuss the new project. How does Wednesday of next week look on your calendar?" You coordinate calendars, agree upon a time, and then suggest your restaurant choice. This further clarifies that you will be acting as host. At the end of the conversation, confirm the date, time, and location.

Once you have the date and time, call the restaurant for a reservation. At a busy restaurant this is a necessity. Even if the restaurant is not likely to be busy but the business is important, it's best to call to alert them that you will be having a special lunch. This saves not just yourself but also your guest the inconvenience of being turned away.

THE ADVANTAGE OF BEING A REGULAR

It can be a great business asset to frequent a restaurant regularly. You may well get better service, especially if you have cultivated the staff with your charm and courteous treatment—and generous tipping. Nothing makes a better subtle impression on a business acquaintance than being greeted and known in your favorite neighborhood establishment. There is something ineffably powerful about having the maître d' ask if you would like your usual drink, your usual meal, or to ask if he could prepare something special for you.

ARRIVING AT THE RESTAURANT

If you are acting as the host for the meal, you will want to arrive before your guest or guests. If for some reason you are late, apologize briefly. No one wants to listen to a litany of excuses, even legitimate ones.

If you meet outside the restaurant, ask your guests if they wish to check their coats, season permitting. Guests who arrive alone may check their coats if they wish to. Since you will be with them when they leave, you can retrieve them and pay the coat-check person.

Give your name to the maître d'hôtel or manager and let your guests precede you into the room. The restaurant staff will understand that you are the host of the meal. As the host, you may direct everyone where to sit. Generally, you try to give your guest or guests the best seats.

ORDERING

Your guests may look to you, as the host of the meal, for guidance, especially if they are junior to you. They may not ask but rather observe and take their cues from you.

Shortly after being seated, the waiter or waitress will ask if you would like a drink. You say, "Yes, I would," then turn to your guest and inquire, "What will you have?" The person may order his or her usual drink, and you can order yours. No one should feel pressure to either order an alcoholic drink, or not order one, and letting your guest order first is a courteous gesture.

These days, people drink alcoholic beverages less frequently at lunchtime than they used to. It is distinctly bad form in most quarters to have several cocktails at lunch, and a good strategy would be to keep drinking moderate at any sort of business function. Rarely does anything worthwhile get accomplished—nor are good impressions made—when tipsiness sets in.

If you are at lunch or dinner, you might suggest ordering a bottle of wine with the food, then choose one from the wine list in accordance with your and your guest's menu choices.

When the waiter comes to take the food orders, your guest or guests order first. If you sense a hesitation, you might order first. If your dining partner seems undecided on what to order, you might make suggestions, especially if the restaurant is known for a particular dish or if you know the menu well. When ordering, no one should mention their particular diet. That's private business.

THE HOST'S ROLE

The host's role does not end with the ordering of food. In addition to leading the conversation, the host should show the same concern for the comfort of guests that would be shown when entertaining guests at home. This means noticing things such as whether the food pleases your guests and doing something about it when it doesn't; whether the water glasses need to be filled; or extra utensils are required.

When the meal or your business discussions are through, ask the waiter or waitress to bring the check. The person who asks for it will be presented with the check. Sometimes the check is brought without asking and is given to the wrong person. If this is the case, reach for the check with a definite but gentle gesture. If your guest protests, you can say, "My company is picking this up." Some people find that avoiding the issue altogether works well. To do this they arrange payment with the headwaiter ahead of time, or during the course of the meal on a visit to the rest room.

When the bill arrives, the host looks over the check quickly but carefully. The host calculates the tip and places her credit card or money, with the check face down, on the tray or in the folder on which it was delivered. Never count out small coins for the tip, but you may leave those that are returned as change. Never let your guest pay the tip, but pay the standard 15 to 20 percent. Paying the bill should not appear to be an ordeal but should be swiftly and easily handled.

THE GUEST'S ROLE

As the guest at a business meal you have a few responsibilities, too. One is to have a pleasant time, or at least appear to. You don't need to gush with enthusiasm about the restaurant or the event but you may show appreciation and pleasure. Take no notice of the bill when it arrives, but do thank your host.

DISCUSSING BUSINESS

Even when a business meal is ostensibly social, there is always some kind of agenda in the host's mind. Even if you talk about hobbies and interests exclusively, it is with the aim of getting to know one another better as a key to doing business together. If you are the guest, you follow the lead. As the host, you initiate the business discussion. Business discussion, if it is not urgent, usually takes place after the entrée, to allow everyone time to eat.

If the meal by mutual agreement is a working meal, you can say something like, "Well, shall we discuss the new contract?" If the agenda is more subtle you can bring up the topic generally, saying something along the lines of: "While I think of it, what do you think of the proposed project?"

One piece of advice on topics to avoid: Never gossip about fellow employees or mutual business acquaintances, especially if it is to criticize their work performance. It will reflect badly on you and is likely to put your lunch mate in an awkward position. Don't talk politics unless you are sure of the views at the table.

Business meals should not go on all morning, afternoon, or night. Everyone has other things to do, and if it is during the day, this usually means work. The host should be aware of the time and when it is time to go, signal the waiter for the check, or if it has been paid, lay the napkin on the table and stand up. If you are the host, you see your guests out and to their transportation. Both guest and host thank one another for the time spent.

In the same way that entertaining at home is enhanced by an easy and graceful manner, restaurant eating is more pleasurable when the basic amenities and rituals are a natural part of the process.

RESTAURANT TIPPING

The following are good general guidelines for restaurant gratuities:

Headwaiter. For the maître d'hôtel or manager, a few dollars is appropriate, or up to 10 percent of the bill if a special service has been performed (for example, if you were given the best table in the house or seated without a reservation at a busy time).

Waiter or waitress. It is usual to leave 15 to 20 percent of the bill if the service has been satisfactory to excellent.

Bartender. Leave 10 to 15 percent of the bar bill if drinks are served at the bar.

Bus staff. The staff responsible for clearing the tables, keeping your water glass filled, and other duties usually share the tip of the waiter or waitress. You needn't tip them directly.

Coatroom attendant. One dollar per coat remains the usual rate.

Washroom attendant. If service is provided, fifty cents is the minimum tip.

Doorman. You needn't pay any tip for having a restaurant door opened for you, but fifty cents or more is appropriate for a doorman who hails you a cab, more if it is during rush hour or it's raining.

6

WEDDINGS

Love is in the air, life looks bright, you've met your true love, and the two of you have decided that you want to make it official. You are going to have a wedding! What could be better, for weddings are one of life's great celebrations. It will be your day to shine, the person you marry will be perfect and the celebration will usher you into a new and brighter world.

Given this pressure for perfection, there is probably no social event more weighted with expectation than a wedding. For many people it seems to be the event on which they lavish more time, energy, emotion, and money than any other as they try to create a perfect day to sum up all of their hopes for the future *and* repair the mistakes of the past. I've found that more people ask me how to create the perfect and correct wedding than anything else.

Often the intensity of the event is not confined to the couple getting married but radiates out to parents, siblings, other relations, and friends, not to mention the people involved in providing all the services for a wedding.

Expectation can build so that after a while it can all become overwhelming. Normally calm, balanced people can be reduced to control freaks—princesses and princes demanding total perfection as their due. Soon parents, siblings, other relations, friends, plus all the people involved in providing goods and services can get drawn into the psychodrama of creating a wedding.

Such upheaval need not be. All you really have to do is keep the most important things in perspective. After all, a wedding is a beginning. It is the formal recognition of the love and commitment of two people who want to create a life together. However, keep in mind that the lavishness or perfection of each element of your wedding will have little or no effect upon the eventual happiness of the marriage. All the glorious trappings are wonderful extras . . . if you can keep the main event in focus.

A wedding should be a celebration, not an ordeal. It can be lavish, simple, or a mix of both, but first and foremost it is about making a public statement of your long-lasting bond. If you can keep your perspective during this exciting, but also trying, time you will be able to look back on your wedding with only the fondest of memories.

GETTING ENGAGED

Electing to share your life is one of the biggest decisions you will ever make. It should be made between people who are in love, of course, but who are also mature enough to respect each other's needs and wishes. It should never be made because either of you feels pressure from others.

TELLING THE FAMILIES

Once you've decided upon this most exciting of events, you'll probably want to share it with the world. But start with your families, unless there is a compelling reason not to, then follow with close friends and relatives. These days, many people live great distances from one another. Your family and your intended may not be acquainted. If this is the case, try to schedule a trip to introduce your spouse-to-be to your family and vice versa. If the families don't know one another, it is customary for the groom's family to contact the bride's family, but no one needs to stand on ceremony when it comes to meeting each other. The important thing is to become acquainted, even over the telephone, before the wedding.

Announcing the Engagement

Some people choose to announce their intentions formally in the local newspaper months in advance of the wedding. In many newspapers these days, such announcements must be paid for. To find out how your newspaper handles announcements, call the office and ask for the society editor. The newspaper may have a form to complete, or you might be asked to write your own release stating the information. Traditionally, the bride's parents announce the engagement, although these days, engaged couples commonly do the announcing themselves. A typical announcement might look like this:

> Mr. and Mrs. John Smiley of 5420 Smith Lane announce the engagement of their daughter, Clarice Julia, to Ian Aaron Johnson, son of Mr. and Mrs. James Arnold Johnson, of Kewanee, Illinois.
>
> Ms. Smiley is a graduate of Taconic High School, the University of Vermont, and Tufts Medical School, and is a first-year resident at Johns Hopkins University Hospital in Baltimore, Maryland. Mr. Johnson graduated from Kewanee High School, the University of Illinois at Champaign-Urbana, and received a master's degree in electrical engineering from Tufts University. The couple plan to marry in August.

If you announce your own engagement, it might look like this:

> Clarice Julia Smiley and Ian Aaron Johnson announce their engagement to be married August 26th at her parents' home at 5420 Smith Lane. Dr. Smiley, a first-year resident at Johns Hopkins University Hospital in Baltimore, Maryland, is a graduate of Tufts Medical School, the University of Vermont, and Taconic High School. Mr. Johnson, an electrical engineer with the firm of Halley and Swanson, Baltimore, graduated from the Tufts School of Engineering, Tufts University, with a master's degree, the University of Illinois at Champaign-Urbana, and Kewanee High School, Kewanee, Illinois.

Any information you submit to a newspaper, whether a release or a completed form, should be typed and addressed to the society editor by name. A freshly typed release—not a copy—should be sent to each newspaper. If you choose to enclose a photo, send a good quality eight-by-ten-inch print. The newspaper may also want other details about your family, profession, or interests, which you may provide as you wish.

CHOOSING RINGS

For many people, an engagement is not official until the woman has an engagement ring. In our society, women usually wear the engagement ring and wedding ring on the third finger of the left hand. Many things in our society have changed, but this tradition has remained fairly intact.

Traditionally, the engagement ring is a gift from the groom to the bride. The days when a man asked for a woman's hand while bent on one knee, one hand outstretched with a velvet ring box in the palm are gone. Sometimes a man will choose a ring and surprise a woman with it as part of the asking process, but he should be fully prepared to return to the jeweler with his intended to choose an engagement ring together.

Although there are no rules as to what a woman should wear for an engagement ring, there are several considerations to keep in mind while purchasing one. First of all are the tastes of the person receiving the ring. If you don't know the sort of jewelry she likes, ask her or someone very close to her. Is her heart set on a modern diamond solitaire ring, an antique sapphire-set ring, or something handed down in your family (should you be so lucky)? Diamonds are the most popular choice, although colored stones are just as precious and beautiful.

Next, consider your budget. An engagement ring is a major purchase, something that will be worn for decades, so if you can only afford a diamond chip now, perhaps you might want to wait or consider a less expensive stone. On the other hand, because it will be worn for so long, you might want to stretch your budget a little, though not so much that you assume a significant debt.

Once you've established the kind of ring and the budget, visit a jeweler or two to scout out the possibilities. You might even discuss it with the jeweler and arrange to have the rings in your price range shown when you both come in.

When choosing an engagement ring, keep in mind that it is usually worn with a wedding band and should thus be coordinated. Wedding bands for both bride and groom are often chosen at this time. When choosing wedding bands, you will also want to consider having them engraved on the inside with both your initials and the wedding date or a simple message. The initials and date give the rings added significance both to you and succeeding generations.

PRELIMINARY WEDDING PLANS

A time frame of when to get married usually accompanies the initial decision. Typically, the period of engagement is a few months up to about a year. If you plan to wait more than a year, you might want to keep it to yourselves for a while, rather than let it become really old news among friends and relations.

My advice to anyone beginning to plan a wedding is to sit down and talk it through before you make decisions. When you are in love, or at any time for that matter, it is easy to assume that you know someone's opinion or preference. Even if you do, the best thing you can do for each other is to sit down and discuss your options. These include:

• When do you want to be married? Must it be June or is fall your favorite season?

• Do you both want a home wedding, a religious ceremony in a house of worship, a civil ceremony at city hall, or a nondenominational event, say, in a meadow?

• Do you want it small (say, up to 50 people), of moderate size (up to 150), or large?

• Will this be a social event for one or both families as well as for you?

• Will parents give you the wedding, or will you be paying for it partially or in full?

All of these questions and any others that come up should be discussed to establish an overall wedding plan that meets the expectations of both you and your intended. You might be surprised how often major disagreements arise later because basic understandings were not reached earlier.

Be prepared to listen to each other and make concessions. I know of one normally thoughtful woman who forgot even to ask her fiancé's wishes on several key matters. Amid the thousands of details, the bride chose the invitations with her mother and presented her fiancé with the tasteful and beautiful design as a fait accompli. She had no idea that he had kept a file of invitations over the years because he was looking forward to helping create his own wedding invitation.

THE ISSUE OF NAMES

It used to be that when a woman married she automatically dropped her own surname and took her husband's. Today some women keep their name, others take their husband's, and some do both, keeping their maiden name for business. Some women find that once they have children it is easier to use their husband's name, since children carry his name unless you blend the two last names, which can be unwieldy. There is no one "correct" way; the decision is entirely personal, but it is best to let family and friends know of your decision, to cut down on possible confusion.

SCHEDULING THE WEDDING

Planning a wedding does take time, especially if you want to have a large and elaborate ceremony and reception. A formal wedding usually takes about six months to organize, and if you live in a big city or want to be married in June, plan to schedule it at least a year ahead. If you know that a lot of people will be traveling considerable distances, you might want to consider scheduling the event for a three-day weekend. Remember, the convenience and enjoyment of your guests—and not just yourselves—is an integral part of a successful wedding.

Once you've chosen the date, contact the person you would like to perform the wedding and get the date on his or her calendar. Once the date has been chosen and the officiant secured, you are free to announce the upcoming event to the world. Even if you don't have an exact date, you can announce your wedding publicly.

WHAT KIND OF WEDDING WILL YOU HAVE?

Perhaps the most important choice to make after deciding to get married is how you want to marry. Much has changed in recent decades regarding almost every aspect of a wedding, but perhaps the most basic change has been to put more of the ceremony and party afterwards in the hands of the bride and groom.

Not so many years ago, the bride's mother, or both mothers together, made many of the decisions. The ceremony itself was usually ordained by the rites of the bride's family's house of worship. Occasionally, the groom's family was consulted and accommodated. Almost invariably, invitations followed standard forms. The reception was ruled by the customs of the community first, and then by the budget of the bride's family. The bride's dress was white (from the late nineteenth century on), the flowers were white and in season, the cake white. The bride chose her and her attendants' dresses. That's not to say that the bride didn't have decisions to make, but there were far fewer of them.

Today, many people wait until they are in their late twenties or thirties to marry. By then, their opinions are informed, as they've experienced a bit of the world and know what's available. Often the bride and groom have distinct notions of how they want each aspect of their wedding day. Very often, too, people marry more than once, and typically they take full responsibility for second and subsequent weddings.

The most traditional wedding takes place in a house of worship, using the standard wedding service for that congregation. Usually the bride and groom can choose readings and music of their own. The clergy may say a few words, or many, specifically to the bride and groom.

Sometimes the marriage ceremony is part of a larger religious service. Guests are expected to follow the order of the service as much as possible. That means they should stand and kneel along with everyone else and join in on hymns, where appropriate. If offered, guests at a Protestant wedding may or may not take communion, as they wish. At a Catholic wedding, only Catholics take communion.

Many lovely wedding ceremonies are held in places other than a house of worship. Outdoor weddings in homes, public spaces, rented estates or clubs, restaurants, or catering facilities are very popular. When weather is an issue, beautiful ceremonies can be held inside clubs, hotels, or restaurants. Under such circumstances, the actual wedding ceremony tends to be simple.

There are four basic wedding categories that can be useful in thinking about a wedding plan. The categories are formal; semiformal; informal; and intimate.

The Formal Wedding. This is the most expensive kind of wedding. It includes hundreds of guests, usually 200 to 500. The bride wears a traditional wedding dress with a train and a veil that reaches her fingertips or beyond. The men wear white tie or formal daywear (not tuxedos). Four or more people attend both the bride and groom. Invitations are formal and engraved. Flowers are elaborate. The reception, often held at a private club or exclusive hotel or restaurant, includes a seated meal and dancing to an orchestra or band.

The Semiformal Wedding. This is the most popular form of wedding. The guest list usually numbers between 100 and 250. The bride's dress is traditional but need not have a train or a long veil. The men wear black tie (or, in summer, white dinner jackets) or conservative dark suits. The invitations may be formal and engraved or less elaborate. The wedding party usually consists of three or fewer people attending both the bride and the groom, although the number is really a matter of preference. The reception, often held in a club, restaurant, hotel, at home, or in a wedding hall, may feature a full seated meal, buffet, afternoon tea, or elaborate hors d'oeuvre selection. Music may be provided by a small group, a single musician, or even a DJ who uses CDs or tapes.

The Informal Wedding. A guest list of 50 to 100 of your close friends and relatives usually defines an informal wedding. It may be held in a house of worship, hotel, wedding hall, at home—in short, almost anywhere. The reception may be held in the same location as the wedding or elsewhere, such as at home, a restaurant, hotel, club, or wedding hall. The bride may wear a traditional wedding gown, or long or short street dress. If she is wearing a veil, it is usually short. The bride is usually attended by one or two people and the groom by the same number. The men wear suits or black tie. Invitations may be formal or informal, engraved, printed, or handwritten. A meal—substantial or light—or tea is usually included as part of the reception.

The Intimate Wedding. This is the kind that often takes place on the beach at sunrise, at a city hall, or in the cleric's study. A handful of friends and immediate family usually attend. The reception can be anywhere—church, home, restaurant—and can include a full meal or not. The bride usually wears a street-length dress, although she may wear a formal wedding dress if she wishes. She can also wear a hat and gloves, unless she is being married at home, where they are not worn. The bride typically has one or no attendants. Invitations are handwritten or even telephoned.

While these descriptions can be regarded as general guidelines, there are few hard-and-fast rules these days. You may tailor many of the elements to suit your wishes and desires. Most people wouldn't want to handwrite a hundred or more invitations, but if you have a beautiful and tireless calligraphic hand, by all means go ahead and do it. The bride may wear any kind of dress she wants to her own wedding, although she may want to consider the appropriateness of certain styles for her dress and her attendants. If you have customs of heritage, by all means incorporate them into the plan if you wish.

PLANNING THE CEREMONY

The time is long gone when the bride and groom routinely followed a set service with little or no input. Today people contribute in all kinds of ways to make the ceremony especially meaningful to them. Careful planning and thoughtfulness can help make the event memorable, so when planning the ceremony yourselves, here are a few tips to keep in mind:

• If you write your vows yourselves, keep in mind that the wedding ceremony will be part of your public record. Write your thoughts down, set them aside, and read them again in a few days. Do they articulate what you really wish to convey? Don't be afraid to make revisions.

• Avoid topical references, for they will seem dated the moment they are spoken.

• Save any nicknames, in-jokes, and private language and references for private moments, unless you want all your friends and relatives to hear and remember you saying something like: "I, Pookie, love you bunches, Smidgie, and can't wait to be with you tootling down the inkadoo of life together." While this example may be a little overblown, I've heard similar ones, and believe me, it can be embarrassing out there in the audience. It can be embarrassing for you, too, if you have your wedding videotaped.

• If you ask a guest to read something, be sure you preview the selection. One person's idea of the perfect passage to celebrate a marriage just might not be yours. A friend of mine still shudders at the recollection of one of the guests at his wedding reading her own poem that told of a violent argument in which a couple threw crockery at each other.

• The same is true of music: Make sure that someone's selection is appropriate to a wedding and to your taste. Don't feel you have to do what everyone else does.

• Try to keep readings in a language the majority of your guests will understand, or provide a translation. I once went to a wedding in which the bride had kindly asked a friend to read a very long passage of a book in Portugese. The guests quickly lost focus and began to fidget. Again, remember your guests' experience as well as your own.

Duties of the Bride. When planning a wedding, it can seem as if the bride has the lion's share of the duties, that she must take the lead in preparations. That's often true, but when a woman has others to help, things usually go more smoothly. That's especially true when she can delegate responsibility for some tasks or at least take the counsel of others before making big decisions. Flexibility is important, too: Be prepared to rethink decisions should they prove impractical.

Your first duty as the bride is to make it down the aisle and have a wonderful time, along with your groom. That is the best thing you can do to start off your marriage well. You also need to do the most you can, within reason, to ensure that family and guests have a good time. That means working with people, treating them kindly and not trodding on their feelings and needs.

Try to keep the wishes of the groom in focus throughout the process. As the details of planning threaten to overwhelm you, try to keep a sense of humor. Plan for the details, but don't worry obsessively about them as the wedding nears. Finally, maintain a larger perspective: Again, your wedding day, as glorious as you wish it to be, is only one day out of your life.

A final note: The bride is responsible for her bridesmaids. Once you have asked someone to be a bridesmaid, it is up to you to decide in general what she will wear, though it's always a good idea to have her input as to style and cost. Try to choose dresses that will flatter each woman, a hard task, especially if you choose to have a number of attendants. You also need to arrange for housing for them, should any be traveling from out of town. It's also helpful if you can check out travel arrangements for them to find the best rates and schedules.

The bride should also buy each attendant a gift showing her appreciation. These tokens, often a piece of jewelry or other keepsake, are usually given at a bride's luncheon, the rehearsal dinner, or some other appropriate time when the bride and her attendants are together.

Duties of the Groom. Contrary to the way it occasionally appears, the groom does have responsibilities beyond just showing up for the wedding with a ring. If you are involved in the planning, so much the better, because you presumably are sharing some of the burden with the bride and her family. Indeed, the more you can feel that is your wedding, too, the better.

You need to be supportive of the bride while making sure that your own wishes and needs are considered. You also have the responsibility of paying for the rings; paying for the bride's flowers and those of the mothers and grandmothers of both bride and groom; organizing the ushers and their clothes for the wedding; applying for a wedding license; organizing and paying for transportation of the wedding party to and from the wedding and reception; planning the honeymoon; and paying the officiant. Oh, yes, and making sure that you and your bride enjoy yourselves at the wedding itself.

Duties of the Bridesmaids. While the bridesmaids have fewer specific duties than the groomsmen, they are expected to help the bride in any way they can in the days before and at the wedding and reception. They also will greet guests in the receiving line. Prior to the wedding, they may also entertain the bride by giving her a bridal shower.

Duties of Flower Girls and Ring Bearers: Children between the ages of three and eight often have roles in a wedding, with little girls acting as flower girls and little boys as ring bearers. You can have as many flower girls as you like, though typically a wedding requires only one ring bearer.

Flower girls walk down the aisle at the beginning of the procession, perhaps strewing flower petals along the way. The ring bearer's official job is to carry the rings, usually on a pillow—which can be tricky. Often the actual duties of the ring bearer and flower girls are dispensed with and the children just walk in the processional and recessional. Very young children usually join their parents for the ceremony and remain with them.

Duties of the Parents of the Bride and Groom. Often the parents of the bride are responsible for many of the practical aspects of the wedding and reception. In addition to shouldering the financial burden, they are often called to provide guidance and planning advice. Traditionally, the mother of the bride made most of the arrangements for the service, clothes, reception site, flowers, food and drink, invitations and mailing, music, entertainment, travel and accommodation, and anything else that needed organizing. Today, the mother of the bride often attends to many of these tasks, but usually in concert with the bride and groom and her own spouse.

The groom's mother, when not involved in the above tasks, has traditionally been involved in planning the rehearsal dinner and providing names and addresses for invitations. The father of the groom often doesn't have a specific role, except as needed in planning. The parents of the groom usually pay for the rehearsal dinner.

Obligations of the Wedding Guest. The duties of the bride and groom and the wedding party have been discussed, so why not the guests? The primary obligation of the guest is to enjoy the wedding and reception, and help the couple feel feted. You are not required to give toasts. You need not lead the conga line, unless you really want to. You certainly should not make yourself the center of attention, for it is the bride and groom's day, along with their families.

Tempting as it may be to celebrate your own wedding again, refrain from wearing your gown to another's wedding, unless it bears no relation to a standard wedding dress. Indeed, it is considered inappropriate to wear a white dress to someone else's wedding. Traditionally, it is also considered inappropriate to wear a black dress to a wedding, since it is the color of mourning.

You are obligated to give the couple a present, thoughtfully chosen and preferably sent or delivered ahead of time. It should be a present of significance, but in keeping with your means. Should your present not be sent prior to the wedding, there is a grace period of up to one year for giving the couple a wedding gift, to be used only under extraordinary circumstances. If the bride and groom have registered for gifts, you may choose an item from their registry, but you are not obligated to do so; you can always choose something else.

If you come from out of town and stay in a hotel room, you should expect to pay for it yourself, unless told otherwise.

DUTIES OF THE BEST MAN

The overall duty of the best man is to take care of the groom. To this end he may need to do all or some of the following (he and the groom should be clear on who is to handle what):

1. Help the groom dress for the wedding (after dressing himself, of course).

2. Receive the officiant's fee in a plain, sealed envelope from the groom and deliver it to him or her.

3. Be sure the groom has all necessary paperwork, including the marriage license, airline tickets and passports for the wedding trip, and so on.

(Duties of the Best Man, cont'd.)

4. Get the groom to the wedding site at least half an hour before the service and keep him occupied.

5. Keep the ring, ready to hand to the groom at the proper moment.

6. Sign the marriage certificate as the groom's witness.

7. Offer the first toast to the bride and groom at the rehearsal dinner and at the reception.

8. Be responsible for the going-away car.

9. Help the bride and groom leave the reception.

10. Return the groom's wedding clothes to his home or rental shop.

11. In general be as useful as possible to the family in the days before and at the wedding and reception.

DUTIES OF THE MAID OR MATRON OF HONOR

The primary duty of the maid or matron of honor is to help the bride in any way she needs. To this end she will do all or some of the following (she and the bride should be clear on who is to handle what):

1. Generally make herself as useful as she can during the days before the wedding and at the ceremony and reception.

2. Help the bride get dressed.

3. Help the bride with gloves, train, veil, flowers, prayer book, or anything else during the ceremony.

4. Hold the groom's wedding ring and give it to the bride or clergy when needed during the ceremony.

5. Sign the marriage certificate as the bride's witness.

6. Greet guests in the receiving line.

7. An emerging tradition calls for the primary attendant to offer a toast to the bride and groom at the reception and at the rehearsal dinner, if she wishes to do so.

DUTIES OF THE USHERS OR GROOMSMEN

In addition to being generally available and helpful before and after the wedding, the men who accompany the groom should be prepared to do the following:

1. Arrive at the church at the assigned time, dressed for the wedding.

2. Light candles fifteen minutes before the ceremony, should they be used.

3. Seat the guests.

4. Pull the aisle runner into position before the ceremony and put it back at the end of the ceremony, should one be used.

5. Walk in the processional and recessional.

6. Return to escort the bride's and the groom's parents out. Then return to take out the guests an aisle at a time by standing before the aisle to move out.

7. At the reception, take a turn dancing with the bride and bridesmaids.

WEDDING EXPENSES

Until recently, the parents of the bride were expected to shoulder all the expenses of a daughter's wedding, at least her first wedding. The bride's family has never been obligated to pay for a second wedding, although they may if everyone wishes it. The groom's responsibilities included the bride's engagement and wedding rings; the bride's bouquet as well as those of the mothers and grandmothers; and the wedding trip. The groom's family paid for the rehearsal dinner.

Many families still choose to pay for their daughters' weddings, but as with everything else, times have been changing. Brides with careers, cohabitating couples, couples marrying for a second time, and older couples now frequently share wedding expenses with their families or take full responsibility themselves. In some parts of the country and among some ethnic groups, the parents of the groom share the expenses with the bride's family, particularly when both families agree that they want an elaborate wedding.

Many working couples these days make more money than their parents, and it only makes sense for them to pay for at least part, if not all, of a wedding. One advantage to paying for your own wedding is that you have complete control and can make it exactly as you wish. People, even well-meaning loved ones, will be less likely to make weighted suggestions regarding the thousand and one details that go into making a wedding. On the other hand, paying yourself means you will bear the responsibility for each decision.

One of the many reasons couples choose to pay for their own weddings is based on distance. When couples live several hundred, or more, miles from their parents, they often want to marry where they live, and it makes sense for them to pay at least part of the expense. Parents may contribute, or if they prefer, they may give the couple a reception or party of their own when the couple visit them.

WHAT TO WEAR

The way we dress, especially at a major celebration such as a wedding, is indicative of the importance we place on the occasion. Everyone dresses in his or her best clothes, for in our society weddings are the most important of social celebrations. To wear everyday clothes would diminish the wedding to the status of the ordinary, like serving bologna for Thanksgiving dinner. The bride and groom often wear clothes that almost seem like a holdover from another era, but they are symbolic of the importance of the event, especially the bride's dress.

BRIDE'S GOWN
For many women, the wedding gown is the most important tangible element of the wedding. It's usually the most obvious symbol, and lots of women have fantasized about wedding dresses since they were little girls.

The traditional wedding dress since the late nineteenth century has been white or cream-colored and long. Even today, a white floor-length wedding gown is the choice made by most women, yet nowhere is it written that you have to wear a traditional wedding dress. So if you really don't care for traditional dress colors, choose a color most suited to you. If you prefer a tailored suit to a bouffant-style gown, wear one.

Do keep in mind, however, that what you wear to your wedding is a public statement that becomes a part of your history. The photos taken at the wedding will be pored over for decades to come. For instance, a slinky and suggestive dress may signal rebellion from convention for the bride, but for the guests it may look a little out of place at a sacramental event. I remember a few years ago there was a fad for brides to carry white parasols and wide-brimmed, turn-of-the-century hats. Today, you can peg the decade of marriage by those hats and parasols. Today's whim might look pretty dated in twenty years, but then again, so will much else. Do what you like—but keep in mind that today's event is tomorrow's memory.

For a formal wedding, the bride usually wears a long and often elaborate dress, perhaps with a train and a long veil held by a traditional headpiece.

The bride's dress for a semiformal wedding is essentially the same as for a formal wedding, although it may be less elaborate. The dress doesn't usually have a train and the bride may wear a veil if she wishes. The dress may be short or long.

At an informal wedding the bride usually wears a becoming dress or suit in a color or shade of white that suits her.

There used to be a rule that a woman who had been married previously never wore a formal white bridal gown to her second wedding. This is because white was a symbol of innocence and purity—virginity—and was thus reserved for women starting on married life for the first time. Today, the rules have relaxed, and if a woman really wants to wear a white wedding gown a second time, she may.

For many women, however, a white confection isn't really their style, and a second marriage provides a good opportunity to wear a gown in a style and color that really suits them.

Women over the age of forty or so usually forego the traditional wedding dress because it tends to be a costume best suited to younger women. However, the hard-and-fast rules of the past are gone, and a woman should wear what makes her feel best. After all, it's her wedding.

THE GROOM'S CLOTHES

In general, the groom's clothes are pretty simple to choose. At a formal daytime wedding he wears a morning suit that includes a gray or black cutaway coat, gray striped trousers, a wing- or turn-down collar shirt, and a gray vest (single- or double-breasted). A black (or gray)-and-white striped four-in-hand tie is worn.

At a formal evening wedding the groom may wear white tie or, less formally, black tie. White tie consists of a black tailcoat, satin-striped black trousers, a wing-collar shirt, a white single-breasted vest, and a white pique bow tie. Black patent leather shoes or dressy pumps are worn with thin black socks. Black-tie attire, which may also be worn at semiformal weddings, consists of a black dinner jacket worn with matching satin-striped trousers, a gray vest (single- or double-breasted) or cummerbund, a white pleated wing-collar shirt or a plain white turn-down collar shirt, and a black bow tie. Black shoes are worn with thin black socks. In summer and in hot climates a white dinner jacket may be worn.

For a semiformal daytime wedding the cutaway coat is replaced with a fitted black or gray jacket.

At an informal wedding, day or night, men wear solid-colored business suits, usually in a conservative gray, black, or navy. They wear white turn-down collar shirts with conservative ties and black dress shoes and socks. In summer the groom and his ushers may wear white suits or white flannel trousers with navy blazers or white jackets with gray trousers.

CLOTHES FOR BRIDESMAIDS AND USHERS

Generally speaking, the bridal attendants follow the lead of the bride and groom when it comes to clothes. If you have only one bridal attendant you might discuss with her what she will wear and let her choose. More than that and the bride usually chooses a gown that will be flattering for all her attendants. The attendants are usually expected to pay for the gowns themselves, and so it is especially important that the bride consult with her attendants and choose something in a price range appropriate to their means. If the bride has her heart set on something extravagant, she should be willing to pay for it herself. The attendants' gowns usually echo the length of the bride's.

As far as colors go, it used to be that black was a color never seen on women at a wedding, as it is the primary color of mourning and there was a time when mourning colors were taken seriously. Today, there seems to be a fashion for bridal attendants wearing black, as it is seen as the color of sophistication. Bright red was another color that attendants never wore, since it can attract attention away from the bride.

Groomsmen's clothes are quite simple, especially when compared to those of the bridal attendants. They wear whatever the groom wears. If the groom plans to wear black tie, the ushers do, too.

Occasionally colors become fashionable in men's formal wear. Avoid the temptation to color-coordinate the men's clothes with the color of the wedding because the result is to detract from the dignity of the occasion, and in a few years, those pictures will look dated indeed. Not many men would choose to wear a baby blue formal suit, and it usually shows in their look of discomfort.

Men's formal clothing is easily rented, and orders should be placed six to eight weeks before the wedding date. If possible, a week or so before the wedding, the groom and his ushers should go in to the store for a personal fitting.

CLOTHES FOR THE PARENTS

Mothers of the bride and groom often try to coordinate their outfits with the colors chosen for the wedding. This is so that they don't clash with the members of the wedding party. The mothers often consult with the bride and with each other about what they will wear.

If the wedding is in the daytime and informal, the mothers usually wear short dresses, even if the bride will be wearing a long dress. They wear short or long dresses to an evening semiformal wedding and long dresses to a formal evening wedding. Elegant pantsuits are an option these days, too. Generally speaking, the later in the day the wedding is scheduled, the dressier the gown can be, but these days mothers can wear pretty much what they want.

The father of the bride usually wears what the groom and usher wear, especially if he will be giving away the bride and standing in a receiving line. The father of the groom conforms to the groom's clothes if he will be standing in the receiving line, or as desired.

CLOTHES FOR THE GUESTS

Even as a guest, it's not always easy knowing what to wear. There are a few guidelines that can help lead you, however. What you wear largely depends on the time and location of the wedding. Formal clothes (long dresses for women, black or white tie for men) are not worn before five or six o'clock in the evening. If the wedding is during the day, women may wear anything from a suit (skirt or pants) to a pretty dress. If the wedding is at night, you will probably want to be a little dressier. Then you may choose a long or short dress or evening suit. You might also want to ask other guests what they plan to wear. If the ceremony takes place in a sanctuary and you plan to wear a low-cut dress or gown, you might want to wear a jacket or shawl until the reception.

Men usually wear suits to a wedding, unless they know for a fact that the wedding is very casual. When in doubt, wear a jacket and tie. After all, a man can always remove them if he finds the event less formal than he thought. For formal evening weddings, men usually wear dark suits or a dinner jacket. Sometimes the invitation will request black or white tie of all male guests. This is also a signal for a woman to get out her fancy evening attire.

FLOWERS

For most people, flowers are a key visual element. They're crucial to the look of a wedding ensemble, carried by the bride and her attendants and worn by the groom, the mothers of the bride and groom, and the ushers. Flowers can also provide a major decorating element for the sites of the ceremony and the reception. They are truly a complement to the proceedings.

To my mind, the most beautiful flowers are fresh and suited to the season, although brides who wish to keep their flowers after the wedding may choose silk or dried arrangements. A bridal bouquet often contains white flowers as the dominant color, but that is up to the bride and the florist. I have seen beautiful bouquets made from garden flowers, wildflowers, florist exotics, and a multitude of mixtures.

Traditionally, the bride's bouquet is the most elaborate of the wedding party; on the other hand, it can be as simple as a single stem. The bouquets carried by the attendants are usually color-coordinated to their dresses. The corsages for the mothers and grandmothers of the bride and groom usually coordinate with their dresses.

Flowers for the ceremony site, once again, may range widely. They should fit the style of the service, the site, or the family. When choosing a florist or designer, try to find someone who will listen to your ideas or guide you knowledgeably, and, of course, who can work within your budget. You should begin looking for a florist as soon as you know the date and site of the wedding and reception.

PLANNING THE WEDDING RECEPTION

Most weddings are followed by a party of some kind, whether it's a simple tea in a church parlor or an elaborate sit-down dinner. Customs vary from region to region and family to family. When a couple wishes to be married in the morning, a wedding breakfast, brunch, or lunch usually follows. If the wedding takes place in the afternoon, a reception may follow that features hors d'oeuvres or a light buffet. When the wedding takes place in the evening, it is usually followed by a seated dinner. No one of these approaches is more correct than another, and you should feel free to do what you want, given your means and taste.

Usually the reception is held immediately after the wedding, but it may be held days or weeks after the event. The bride may wear her wedding dress but usually wears another dress. You may also have two parties, as is often done when the wedding itself is very small but the bride and groom still want an opportunity to entertain their friends. Sometimes this is an expedient way to entertain family and friends who live far away; after the wedding, you go to them.

Reception Sites

As with a wedding, a reception can be held at any number of places. You can have the reception at home, in the garden, at a friend's or relative's, a club, hotel, restaurant, an historic site, a public hall, or in the social room of a church or temple.

Unless you plan to have the party at home, the reception site will need to be chosen and booked as soon as possible after you decide to get married. Certain times of year are especially popular for weddings—June, of course, but also September, October, and December. Sites for receptions, weddings, even clergy, get booked well in advance.

Catering halls, which often specialize in weddings, offer a range of meals—usually full sit-down dinners and buffets—and can provide everything from wine and cocktails to table linens, glasses, cutlery, and sometimes even flowers. You may have limited choices available, but they certainly make planning a reception easy. Other sites, such as party rooms attached to clubs, historical societies, social organizations, or community service groups provide the setting and often a kitchen, and you hire a caterer to provide the food.

Choosing the Caterer

In many areas there is a caterer to be found for just about every need. Some will cook on site, others will deliver finished food; some provide partial services, others full services including wine and cocktails, staff, linens, tables and chairs. A good way to approach the process is to ask around among friends, check advertisements and newspaper articles, then begin interviewing. If you know your budget in advance, you can discuss it at once. If you don't have an amount in mind, determine your budget based on your interviews and the number of people you feel you must invite to the wedding. The more you know about what kind of food and meal, as well as the services you require, the easier it is to determine the caterer best suited to you and your budget.

Just about any kind of meal can be prepared and served for a small wedding at home. If you are a talented cook and want to do it yourself you can, but be forewarned that it is a tremendous amount of work, especially on top of getting married. One woman I know, a professional caterer, created all the truly delicious and beautiful food for her own wedding, but afterward regretted it, for she had spent most of the week before and the day of the wedding in the kitchen. A better approach might be to hire a caterer or cook to provide most of the food and you contribute one or two signature items.

Before you award the contract for your reception—whether it's to a hotel, restaurant, catering hall, or private caterer—you should have a clear understanding in writing of schedule, services provided, menu, any extras such as decorations, and cost. Make sure the estimate and contract spell out the terms and the details as you've discussed them.

The Cake

The cake is often the centerpiece of the reception and is frequently on display as part of the decorations. Most catering halls and restaurants and many caterers can provide a cake, but if you have something specific in mind you might want to hire a particularly good cake baker or bakery to provide one.

Decorations

Decorating the reception site can be simple or complex, depending on how elaborate the wedding. Decorations range from beautiful bowls of wildflowers placed on tables to enchanted rooms of gauze flowers, fairy lights, trees, and flower arrangements costing thousands of dollars. It all depends on your budget and taste.

Many people find it helps to talk to floral designers for their ideas of effective decorating treatments. As always, budget is an issue, but some people like to choose a theme for their wedding—often a set of colors. Florists can work with you on this, too. Often the flowers used at the ceremony site can be brought and used for the reception as well.

Entertainment

Most wedding receptions have musical entertainment of one kind or another, and it is entirely up to you what to have. If you plan to have dancing you will probably want a band that can play a wide variety of dance music to suit the various ages present, or a disc jockey who has a wide selection of music available. If you prefer classical music, perhaps a string quartet would entertain your guests nicely.

When researching entertainment, ask around, check the phone book, and look in the newspaper or other local publications. Then interview the prospects. If you have favorite songs you want played, make sure you make your preferences known. Most will be happy to oblige, and those that aren't should be dropped from your list of candidates. Pros will have a tape you can listen to. Again, before hiring anyone, make sure you have a written understanding of the hours you have booked, the fee, and any extras or requirements.

PHOTOGRAPHY AND VIDEOGRAPHY

A visual record of a wedding is important to just about everybody. Over the years, those images often become an important means of remembering the event, keys to a wave of recollections. But getting good photos involves hiring a still photographer and, increasingly, a videographer to capture the event on videotape with sound. Whether you hire both a photographer and a videographer or just one, hiring a professional is usually the wisest course.

When hiring, it helps if you and your intended have a clear idea of what you want regarding photography and videography. Do you want the entire ceremony recorded, or just the wedding and the reception? Do you want candids, posed photos, or both?

Should you wish to have the ceremony recorded with photos or video, you will need to consult the person performing the ceremony. Some permit the entire wedding to be photographed or filmed, while others permit no photography or videography during the ceremony. Some permit flash; others don't.

Keep your guests in mind, too. There are few things more disruptive during a ceremony than to have an aggressive photographer or videographer shooting away, his camera clicking incessantly, his body constantly moving and blocking the view of the ceremony.

You will also need to have an understanding with the photographer or videographer about his or her role at the wedding and reception. You will probably want to meet with them a couple of weeks before the wedding to go over the shots needed and to make sure you each have an understanding of how much a part of the party you want him or her to be. Make sure the requirements for the ceremony as well as those for the party are understood. One good way to keep photographers unobtrusive at the reception is to have them set up a backdrop where guests can go to have candid portraits taken during the course of the party.

You should also keep the guests in mind when it comes to posed formal pictures taken just after the ceremony. Technically, the guests are not supposed to leave for the reception until the bride and groom have left. To have them wait around for an hour while pictures are being taken can be an imposition. Nor is it quite fair to send them along to the reception, since the party doesn't start until the bride and groom arrive, and so often refreshments aren't even served until key players are present. In short, the pictures should be taken expeditiously.

A popular method for getting candid wedding pictures is to have disposable cameras available for guests. They can be placed on individual tables or centrally located in a big basket (or two). However you choose to handle photography and videography, try to keep your guests' pleasure in mind. Being photographed can be part of the fun of the wedding, but endlessly waiting for the bridal party or feeling like an extra on a movie set is not.

INVITATIONS AND ANNOUNCEMENTS

Once you've chosen the kind of wedding, the place, and the date, it's time to think about preparing a guest list. If the wedding will be large enough for you to invite everyone you and your families know and like, that's terrific. If not, you will probably have to make some hard decisions.

Technically, the bride and the groom share the list equally, although there may be room for negotiation if the family of one or another lives far away. First on your list will probably be relatives, followed by close friends of your family. You will also want to include your dear friends, as will your parents. Your intended's parents will have a similar list of family and close friends. The person who will perform the ceremony, as well as his or her spouse, should be invited to the wedding and the reception; the husbands and wives of married attendants should also be on the guest list. If you can afford to, it's nice to let unmarried attendants invite a date, though this is a common candidate for cutting. The live-together partner of any key person should be invited, too. The parents of unmarried attendants (including flower girl and ring bearer) are to be invited, as well.

If your list is small, you may have to make decisions about groups of people, such as office, sports team, and social organizations of friends. Better to invite no one from the office than to invite three people and hurt the feelings of six others. If you have one especially close coworker you may wish to make an exception.

One way to handle the issue of letting a lot of out-of-town or in-town people know about the event without obligating them to send a present, which an invitation does, is to send an announcement just after the wedding.

INVITATIONS

Wedding invitations fall into two basic categories: traditional and nontraditional. Regardless of your choice, invitations should be mailed four to six weeks before the event, unless the wedding is so rushed that there isn't enough time. Sometimes people will also send out a "Save-the-Date" notice well in advance if they plan to be married at an especially busy time.

Formal Invitations. A formal invitation is one that follows simple wording and is printed or engraved in black ink on heavy white or cream stock. Such invitations come in two sizes. One measures about 5½ by 7½ inches and is folded once before being inserted into an envelope. The other, slightly smaller, measures about 4½ by 5½ and is not folded. Invitations are printed using a block or script type. The wording of this most standard invitation looks like this:

Mr. and Mrs. Hugh George
request the honor of your presence
at the marriage of their daughter
Sarah Miller
to
Mr. Frederick Allan Koussevitzky
Saturday, the tenth of November
at four o'clock
Stockbridge Congregational Church
Stockbridge, Massachusetts
and afterward
at 691 Stonewall Road
Red Rock, New York

Sometimes guests are invited only to the ceremony, and not the reception, in which case you leave off the last three lines alluding to the party afterward. For the guests who are invited to the reception, you enclose a card which looks like this:

Reception
immediately following the ceremony
691 Stonewall Road
Red Rock, New York
R.S.V.P.

If the reception is to be held several hours after the ceremony you would include a reception card giving the expected time.

A couple of things are worth noting about the formal invitation. You will notice that the only abbreviations that appear are for people's titles and the response request, R.S.V.P. (*repondez s'il vous plaît*—literally, "respond if you please"). The time of day is considered obvious without using A.M. or P.M. since weddings do not occur at ten in the evening or four in the morning. R.S.V.P. may not appear at all if you include a response card (see below). The year (spelled out) may be included on the invitation if you wish. If the wedding is to be held at a place other than a place of worship, the words "the pleasure of your company" are often used in place of "the honor of your presence."

Should the bride's parents be divorced, the invitation can be issued in both their names, if they wish, or it could contain the name of the parent (and stepparent, should that be the case) hosting the event. If the parents issue the invitation together, their names appear on separate lines. If the mother is not remarried she may use a combination of her maiden name and married name, if she wishes, such as: Mrs. Jones Smithton.

If either the bride's or the groom's mother is widowed she uses the name of her late husband, such as: Mrs. Paul Smithton.

If people other than the bride's parents are hosting the wedding, their names appear at the top of the invitation and then the last name of the bride is added to her line.

Increasingly, these days, couples give their own weddings. When this is the case, they may use their own names, as in the following example:

Susannah Leyton
and
Joseph Fox
request the pleasure of your company
to help celebrate our marriage
Saturday, the twelfth of May
Two thousand and two
at two o'clock
The Drysdale Club
New York, New York

Informal Invitations. Sometimes a formal invitation doesn't seem appropriate, such as when the wedding is very small, or there just isn't time to have one made. In this case invitations are written by hand or issued by telephone. You may respond with a telephone call or a note of reply.

Handwritten invitations may resemble a formal invitation, or they may be written in a paragraph such as the following:

Dear Elizabeth and Chet,

Sam and I are going to be married Friday, August fifteenth in the Church on the Green in Portland at noon. We do so hope you both can join us for the wedding and afterward for lunch at Antonio's.

Love,
Sarah

Nontraditional Invitations. Increasingly, we see invitations to otherwise formal or semiformal weddings that are worded more casually than the standard, are decorated, or use colored stock or ink. I sometimes think I'm being sent an overly sentimental greeting card when I see these. On the other hand, simple nontraditional wording can express much feeling without being sentimental. A lovely nontraditional invitation could say something like:

Please come and share with us our joy
as we celebrate the marriage of our daughter
Jeanne Marie
to
John Shepherd Rudin
son of
Harry and Louise Rudin
Sunday, the twenty-ninth of June
at two o'clock
Bethesda Presbyterian Church
and afterward at the Community Club
2850 River Road

Please respond   Linda and John Corning
5420 York Lane
Bethesda, Maryland

If you choose to use the names of both sets of parents, be sure to check with everyone first to make sure all wish to be included.

THE ENVELOPE

Each invitation is inserted into an envelope and addressed for mailing. In the case of a formal wedding invitation it traditionally goes into two envelopes. The outside envelope includes the name and address of the person being invited, handwritten in blue or black ink with the return address printed or engraved. The inner envelope is plain except for the handwritten name of the recipients. A sheet of tissue paper covers the front of the invitation—a throwback to when printer's ink tended to smudge nestled inside the envelope. The tradition of the inner envelope and tissue are on the wane, which seems fine to me, since they have outlived their practical usefulness.

If you choose to use the traditional envelopes there is a particular procedure to follow that minimizes the fuss. On the outer envelope, write the complete name and address of the guest, using no abbreviations. The name of every person invited should be in-

Fig. 6.1 The wedding envelope

cluded. If a family with children is invited, use a separate line for each child, unless there are too many to fit comfortably on the envelope in which case you write "and Family" after the parents' names. Adult children should be sent their own invitations, even if they still reside under the same roof with their parents. If you invite someone to bring a date and you don't know the person's name you may write "and Guest" following the name of the person you are inviting.

On the inside envelope, again write the names of those being invited, without abbreviations (except for Mr. and Mrs.). Another method for inviting a couple's children is to include their names after their parents' names on the inside envelope. If you get an invitation without your children's names at all, they are not invited. Never assume children are invited—people think through guest lists far too carefully to omit children accidentally. For an informal wedding you may be told in person to bring them.

Once addressed, insert the second envelope into the outer envelope, folded or not as indicated by size, tissue in place over the wording if used, wording toward the flap. You may include other enclosures before sealing the envelope. The filled envelope will be mailed first class, stamped not metered. I always like to see carefully chosen, beautiful commemorative stamps.

ENCLOSURES

Other elements to be inserted into the envelope with an invitation may include a response card, a pew card, map and directions, or an at-home card. Maps and directions may be photocopied, but any other enclosure should coordinate with the invitation.

Response Card. Until recently anyone who received a formal wedding invitation automatically knew what to do next: Write a formal reply. Today's relaxed standards, however, have demanded that people enclose a response card if they want to know how many people will be coming to their wedding. These cards have become so common that an etiquette has developed around them. The cards, which are considerably smaller than the invitation, should be printed with wording similar to this:

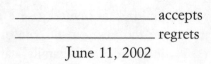

_____ accepts
_____ regrets

June 11, 2002

It's tempting to put "Number of guests," but this can be confusing, as it suggests that people can bring people other than those included on the invitation. It's also tempting to include a response date, but this should be avoided unless the caterer sets an extremely early deadline for ordering the food.

A response card should also include its own stamped envelope, printed on the front with the return address.

If you find that the response card seems a little cold, guests should feel free to write a few personal words on it—it's guaranteed to please the bride and groom. The card is there for convenience, not for formality. A message like "We can't wait to see you on your special day" is a nice touch.

Pew Card. Sometimes at a very large wedding, printed cards telling close family members and friends where to sit are included. Usually several pews are marked off with ribbons, thus reserving them for people with pew cards. The small cards are printed with the words "Within the ribbons" or with "Pew number _____" (filled in by hand). The card is handed to the usher as you enter the place of worship.

At-Home Cards. Occasionally couples include a small card announcing the bride and groom's new address and when they will reside there. They are only used by people who have not been living together. An at-home card should read:

Mr. and Mrs. John Rudin
will be at home
after the twentieth of August
15 Peabody Lane
Chatham, Illinois 12060

People who don't manage to get their presents to you will also know where to send them when you get back from your honeymoon.

RESPONDING TO AN INVITATION

When receiving an invitation with a response card, you may choose not to use it, but instead respond in writing. This is always correct and the most formal looks like this:

> Mr. and Mrs. Peter Haviland
> accept with pleasure
> the kind invitation
> of Mr. and Mrs. Smithson
> to the marriage of their daughter
> Samantha Jane
> to
> George Hawkman
> Saturday, the twelfth of June
> at three o'clock
> and afterward at
> the Westminster Club

Here is another appropriate, formal, but simple version:

> Mr. and Mrs. Peter Haviland
> accept with pleasure
> your kind invitation
> for
> Saturday, the twelfth of June
> at three o'clock

A formal regret looks like this:

> Mr. and Mrs. Peter Haviland
> regret that they are unable to accept
> the kind invitation of
> Mr. and Mrs. Smithson

You may vary it a little if you wish by saying, "the very kind invitation" or "your kind invitation" or "your very kind invitation" (thus leaving out the hosts' names).

Family members and really close friends who you know will be attending or will be in the wedding party need not respond formally, but should confirm at least by telephone.

Informal invitations may be responded to with a brief note or a telephone call.

WEDDING ANNOUNCEMENTS

An announcement of a wedding, sent a few days after the ceremony, is a good way to let people, especially those who live out of town, know of the event without appearing to ask for a gift. Announcements, similar in shape, size, and form to invitations, can be mailed after any kind of wedding. The year is always included, as are the city and state where the ceremony took place.

A standard announcement looks much like this:

> Mr. and Mrs. Peter Jones
> have the honor to announce
> the marriage of their daughter
> Samantha Jane
> to
> Mr. Maxwell X. Benvenuto
> on Saturday, the eleventh of June
> Two thousand and two
> Highland Park, Illinois

If you give yourselves the wedding, you may of course announce it yourselves, varying the wording as it suits you.

PREWEDDING PARTIES

One popular way to announce an engagement is to have a party. This can be a good way to introduce the prospective bride or groom to the other's family and friends.

ENGAGEMENT PARTY

Traditionally, such parties were given by the bride's parents, but today can be given by family members of either side or even by the

engaged couple themselves. When friends give the party sometimes
it substitutes for a bridal shower as a way to include men and women
together.

If a written invitation is issued it may contain wording such as
"honoring our daughter Sarah and her fiancé, Jake." Some people
prefer to keep the news a surprise until the announcement is made
at the party in the form of a toast proposed by the host of the party.
Gifts are not usually taken to an engagement party, unless it serves
as a shower.

WEDDING SHOWER

A shower is a party given to honor the bride, and sometimes the
groom, at which presents are given. These parties traditionally were
only for women, and more often than not, still are. Often a surprise
for the bride, a shower is usually given in the afternoon or early
evening and light refreshments are served. One does hear about lavish
luncheons given at clubs or in large halls, at which equally lavish gifts
are given. If planning such an event, great care should be given to
the expectations you place on your guests.

Showers should be given by friends of the bride—often bridesmaids or perhaps relatives—but not immediate members of either
family. This rule seems to be fading, but there is a good reason for
it. Since the immediate family has invited the wedding guests and a
present is expected from people attending, it was thought to make
the family look grasping to request a second present by throwing a
shower.

Invitations, which can be formal or informal depending on the
nature of the shower, should be issued two or three weeks in advance
of the party. The shower itself should be held a few weeks before the
wedding. Make sure that the people invited to the shower are also
invited to the wedding, as it would be embarrassing to invite someone
to a preliminary party without including them in the main event.

When it comes to shower presents, the hosts can handle them in
several ways. Sometimes it's helpful to select a theme. For people first
setting up house, presents for the kitchen or bath can be useful. More
personal showers can be fun, too, such as those with a theme of
lingerie or personal indulgence. Sometimes people chip in on a pres-

ent. At one bridal shower I know of, people pooled together to give the bride several gift certificates for a facial and massages, the latter for both the bride and groom. Whatever the theme, should there be one, wedding-shower guests should not feel compelled to spend a lot of money. A shower gift should not rival a wedding gift in expense.

If you are invited to a shower but either cannot or choose not to attend, you are not obligated to send a present. If you wish to, of course, feel free to send one along; you can be sure it will be appreciated.

BACHELOR PARTY

This is a party given by the groom's friends as a last wild gesture before settling down. Usually the groom has no say in what goes on, although his wishes may be heeded if he has considerate friends. The bachelor party should take place at least a few days before the wedding.

BACHELORETTE PARTY

This is a chance for the bride to kick back with best buddies and bridal attendants. There is no need to invite distant family members and the mothers to this one, unless you wish to.

BRIDE'S LUNCHEON

This party is given by the bride to honor her attendants. It gives everyone a chance to know one another if they don't already. The bride usually presents the attendants with a keepsake gift. Other family members and close friends may be invited to the party, and increasingly it has become an expanded party in which the bride and groom jointly give a party to honor all the attendants. The party, usually given a week or two before the wedding, may actually be a dinner or Sunday brunch.

REHEARSAL DINNER

It is traditional for the family of the groom to host a festive dinner the night before the wedding, directly after the rehearsal. The dinner is usually planned by the groom's family in consultation with the bride and her family. The party can be similar in formality to the wedding, or simpler and more casual, but never more lavish, as it might tend to overshadow the main event.

Invitations, formal, handwritten, or telephoned, depending on the formality of the evening and the wedding, are handled by the groom's family. All members of the wedding party, close family members, and out-of-town guests are invited. The officiant of the service and spouse, if you wish, may be invited, too.

Often, the wedding really seems to gather momentum at the rehearsal dinner, as toasts are given and people begin to celebrate the joy of the coming event. Everyone should be on good behavior, and the evening shouldn't run too long, since the next day, no matter what time of day the wedding takes place, will be a big one.

WEDDING GIFTS

Giving and receiving gifts is one of the pleasures of a wedding.

Such gifts should be chosen with care. If possible, they should please both the giver and the receiver. If you know what the bride and groom would like to have, your job will be made easier. Once you announce your wedding, you will find that people will begin asking what you might like as a present. As a bride or groom, you can make it easier by making up a list of things you both would like. Make sure to include items that are readily available and from a wide range of prices.

Give the list to close relatives who are likely to be asked your wishes and needs. Another good idea is to enter a wedding registry at a local store or two. You choose items in the store you would like, usually household items such as china and silver patterns, linens, glassware, kitchenware, and appliances and they are entered on their list. When people come in they ask for the list and can choose from it, knowing that they will be giving something you really want. You can even register at stores in another city, should you or your future spouse's family and friends live far away.

Young couples tend to need more things than people who have already set up households or been married before. For a second wedding or for people who already have established households, you might want to give something nontraditional, such as theater tickets, a subscription, wine, or a dinner voucher. You might want to check with the couple to determine what sort of things they might want, since such things often are not returnable.

Speaking of returnable items, it's most thoughtful to try to buy something that the bride and groom can return or exchange if they need to. This means including the name of the store with the present.

If possible, gifts should be sent or delivered in person before the wedding to the bride's home or to the couple's shared home. After the wedding, a gift may be sent or delivered to the couple's home. A wedding gift may be sent up to a year after the event, although if it drags on it's best to include a note of explanation.

It has become accepted in recent years to bring the present to the wedding reception. The couple should make arrangements for someone to look after the presents, collect them, and deliver them to their new home after the wedding.

It is also becoming accepted to give money as a gift. This can be done ahead of time or at the reception. If envelopes are given at the reception, a card or note should be included from the giver. The bride and groom never solicit the presents, but the groom merely accepts them with a warm smile and thank-you. Sometimes a box or bowl is provided for envelopes.

In some parts of the country it is customary to display first wedding gifts in advance of the wedding. This is usually done at the bride's parents' home. The gifts are arranged on a cloth-covered or decorated table. Gifts of similar value are grouped together. Checks are acknowledged by a card reading "Check, Mr. and Mrs. Samuel Peters." The amount is never revealed.

As a matter of safety, if presents are displayed and the engagement has been announced in the newspaper, you might want to add a floater to your insurance policy. Also, arrangements should be made for someone to keep a watchful eye on the presents during the wedding and reception when everyone else is out.

THANK-YOU NOTES

Yes, you must acknowledge the receipt of every wedding gift with a personal handwritten note. It can be a nuisance to do, especially if you have a large wedding, but it is just not acceptable ro receive a gift and not thank the guest in writing. The note doesn't have to be long, but it should be a personal acknowledgment of the specific item given. Writing thank-you notes may not be the most fun way to spend an evening, but they are not hard to do. They can even be a welcome chance to connect once again with your guests.

Thank-you notes can be written on notepaper imprinted with your name or initials, or plain notepaper. When men write thank-yous— and they should be encouraged to help out—they use plain white, beige, or gray notepaper. (If it's a matter of his refusing to help unless he chooses the stationery, let him use whatever he wants.)

Usually, it's not hard to find something to say about a present you like, though it's harder when you are struggling to find something to say about a duplicate or an item you don't care for. You may have to resort to a small white lie if you can't find a tactful way to describe the gift.

Truly, the hardest part of writing thank-you notes is getting around to doing it. Before the wedding it is so busy, and afterward one wants to settle in. The best thing is to set goals and work toward them. All givers should be thanked no more than three months after the wedding. I know of one bride who procrastinated so long that by the end (almost a year later!) she felt so guilty that she felt she had to write a two-page letter to each person, which made the task drag on much longer (and didn't exactly communicate an easy, gracious sense of gratitude).

COUNTDOWN TO THE BIG DAY

As the big day approaches, you will come to appreciate some of the well-established rituals and patterns of the wedding and the surrounding activities. One reason they've evolved is that, with the surprising stresses and demands of the occasion, it's comforting to have an established order of events to fall back on.

The Rehearsal

Rehearsing a wedding is a good idea, so that everyone in the wedding party knows what to expect. When a wedding is fairly large or formal, people often rehearse the wedding the evening before, kicking off the evening's entertainment, the rehearsal dinner.

The rehearsal need not be a big social event. Only the people participating in the wedding need be present: the person performing the ceremony, the wedding party, and the parents of the bride and groom. If an usher or bridesmaid can't be present, it doesn't much matter. Divorced parents and relatives who aren't in the wedding need not be present, unless it is important to help someone feel a part of things.

The participants will be charged with their duties and told what is expected of them and when. The person conducting the ceremony will lead the bride and groom in a walk-through of the ceremony. In the past, the maid or matron of honor stood in for the bride, as it was considered bad luck for her to be present, but this outmoded notion has fallen by the wayside.

Everyone will walk through the processional and recessional, with instructions on how to move and where to stand. The officiant walks everyone through the basics of the ceremony and gives the bride and groom a run-through of the vows. With luck, you should be out of the rehearsal in an hour or less.

Even if you don't have a formal rehearsal, a simple ten minute run-through is helpful to the participants. At the very least you need someone to tell everyone what to do and when to do it. Usually this task is taken on by the person performing the ceremony. If a clergy person performs the ceremony, he or she will discuss the protocol for the religion or denomination.

The Big Day Arrives

The duties of the ushers come first at the actual event, since they are responsible for the guests as they arrive. The bride and groom should give them a rough estimate of how many people attending will be friends of the bride and how many of the groom. Family members should be pointed out to them with their seat or row location.

When guests arrive, they are greeted at the door or the head of

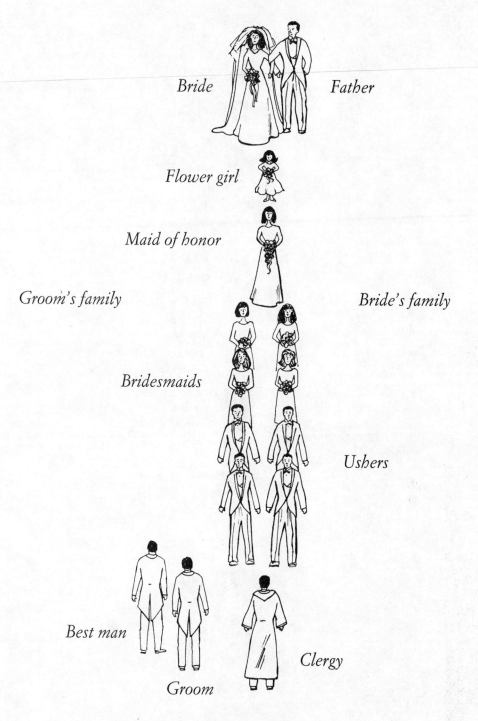

Fig. 6.2 The wedding processional

Fig. 6.3 The wedding recessional

the aisle by an usher. Each couple, family, or single guest should be asked whether they would like to sit on the bride's side or the groom's. The bride's side is on the left, where she will stand. The groom's is on the right, as you look down the aisle toward the ceremony. Traditionally, the usher offered his arm to the woman of a couple, or the oldest woman in a group, and escorted her to a pew or seat. Today, a less awkward approach is more usual, in which the usher will lead a couple or group to seats by walking in front of them. He should be prepared to offer his arm to a single woman or to an older woman who appears to expect the courtesy.

During the last few minutes before the ceremony, the grandparents are ushered in and seated in the second or third pew. This is a signal that the big event is nearing. Five minutes before the ceremony is to start, the parents of the groom are seated, unless they participate in the ceremony. Finally, the mother of the bride is seated by the head usher, and this is the signal that the wedding has begun. As soon as she is seated, unless she participates in the ceremony, the processional music begins and the procession starts.

Meanwhile, the bride and her attendants are waiting, ready to start in an anteroom or other out-of-the-way spot. Often the bride arrives very shortly before the ceremony, but she shouldn't be late. Once everyone has been seated, the signal will be given for the proceedings to start.

The groom and his best man will take their places at the front and stand looking back up the length of the aisle toward where the bride will appear.

The procession begins with the ushers walking down the aisle and standing to the outside of the groom on the right side. The bride's attendants follow the ushers, the maid or matron of honor the last one. Flower girls, if any, follow next, followed by the ring bearer. Finally, the bride appears, usually escorted by her father or other relative, holding his right arm, or in between both parents.

As the procession reaches the front, the bridesmaids take their places on the bride's side, in order of procession, the maid or matron of honor closest to the center aisle. When the bride reaches the front, she stops. In some ceremonies the officiant asks, "Who gives this woman in marriage?" and her father, or whoever is escorting her, replies, "Her mother and I do." If the bride's parents are divorced, this last step may be omitted in deference to the feelings of all concerned. In Catholic ceremonies the bride is escorted to the chancel steps and then her father retires to his pew. In Jewish ceremonies, the bride's and the groom's parents often follow them down the aisle and stand facing their guests.

The ceremony itself is in the hands of the person performing it, although the bride and groom usually have a role in the planning of readings and music.

Once the ceremony has concluded, the bridal party recesses down the aisle, much as they processed up, but in reverse order. This time, however, the bride and groom lead the way, followed by the maid or matron of honor escorted by the best man, and the bridesmaids escorted by the groomsmen. It does not matter if there are more bridesmaids than groomsmen, or vice versa. If there are extra bridesmaids, they should be escorted by groomsmen with a woman on each side. Extra groomsmen walk as pairs in the recessional. Flower girls and ring bearer may skip the recessional and accompany their parents or relatives out with the other guests.

The couple and their primary attendants usually then retire to an anteroom to sign the marriage certificate.

Once outside, the families may form a receiving line to greet guests or discreetly absent themselves to a back room until the guests have filed out. Often people take pictures once the guests have left the sanctuary. Try to keep the photography brief, as the guests will usually stay to see the couple off. If the photography will take a while, have someone encourage guests to leave for the reception, which can be instructed to begin without you. Frequently this is the time when people shower the leaving couple with rice, or the ecologically responsible birdseed, flower petals, or confetti. Sometimes this custom is reserved for when the couple leaves the reception.

LET THE PARTY BEGIN

Protocol often seems a paramount concern at the wedding reception. Will we, will everyone else, do the right thing? This is the part of the wedding at which I think people should be a bit more lenient. If you've created a meaningful and beautiful ceremony for the wedding itself, you should be able to relax and enjoy the party.

The most important thing to work toward is to make your family, friends, and other guests feel comfortable and happy—*and* to avoid hurting anyone's feelings. This can seem a tall order, given the inherently stressful nature of a wedding.

However, if the reception has been carefully planned so that you're not constantly dealing with crises, it shouldn't be too difficult. If, for instance, you know that certain relatives don't get along well, perhaps you can plan the seating such that they are placed far apart. Make sure you plan for the party's beginning and ending. Begin by getting the wedding party there expeditiously from the ceremony, and close by making sure it doesn't drag on all night. I would suggest, too, that you ask family members to circulate among the guests to make sure their glasses and plates are filled, that conversations keep moving, and that guests meet one another. Everyone is there to celebrate, and chances are very good that they will have a great time. But with good planning and care, you can help ensure they will.

INTRODUCING RELATIVES

If you've ever found yourself at the wedding of a relative constantly explaining your relationship to the bride or groom, you know that it can become tedious. Recently, I've seen people wearing charming name tags that cleverly state the relationship such as: "I'm the bride's aunt," or "I'm Buddy's uncle." By the end of the reception everyone knows who you are!

THE RECEIVING LINE

Once the ceremony is over or as soon as you get to the reception, it is customary to form a receiving line. The party doesn't begin officially until the guests have been greeted and welcomed by the hosts, but you can instruct the caterers to have hors d'oeuvres and drinks available when guests first arrive. Once they arrive, the bride and

groom should greet every one of their guests to thank them for coming; guests offer best wishes (to the bride) and congratulations (to
the groom).

It can be very tempting to skip the receiving line, as it can seem
tedious, but in the end it makes things much easier. I know of one
reception at which the bride and groom got separated just as they
arrived and they never managed to gather the wedding party to greet
their guests. They each spent the entire reception greeting and trying
to point out each other's parents in an effort to direct their guests,
and answering questions about members of the wedding party. At
one point the bride had a small line of people greeting her, the groom
had another, her parents a third, his parents a fourth.

The easiest way to avoid this is with a receiving line held first thing
at the reception site or at the church. A standard receiving line is
formed by the bride and groom, their parents, and the women of the
wedding party. First in line are the official hosts of the party, usually
the parents of the bride. Next to them are the parents of the groom,
usually the semiofficial hosts. Standing next to them are the newlyweds, and next to them the female attendants. The best man may be
included as well.

There are, of course, variations to the basic receiving line. If the
bride and groom are themselves giving the wedding, they may stand
alone. Older couples, or those for whom this is not the first wedding,
may also receive alone. If parents of the bride or groom are divorced
and are uncomfortable standing near one another, usually the mother
stands in the line while the father circulates among the guests. This
is a matter for discussion and decision among the families in the days
before the wedding.

If someone other than the bride's or the groom's families have
helped pay for the wedding, they are the official hosts and have a
right to stand at the head of the receiving line.

On the other hand, if your wedding is small or if you like nothing
more than constantly circulating, the two of you together, you might
not need a receiving line.

Ushers need not stand in the receiving line; stepparents may be
included in the receiving line or not, depending on everyone's feelings. If there are two stepparents involved, and, say, you are partic-

ularly close to one, you must be sure to invite the other, too. If the situation is complicated by more stepparents, you might want to limit the receiving line to just blood parents or the parents responsible for raising a child, otherwise the receiving line will be very long.

As a guest going through a receiving line, your job is to introduce yourself when necessary, greet everyone, perhaps say a very few choice words of joy, and move on.

Close relatives do not need to go through the receiving line but should circulate among the guests.

THE RECEIVING LINE

The order, from left to right, should be as follows:
Mother of the bride
Father of the groom
Mother of the groom
Father of the bride
Bride
Groom
Maid or matron of honor
Best man (optional)
Bridesmaid
Bridesmaid

ORDER OF EVENTS

Knowing what to do and when to do it at the reception is a source of anxiety for many people. However, it is at this event that I feel you can relax the protocol as necessary in an effort to make the event go smoothly. After all, the main purpose of the party is for everyone to have a good time. This means that you try your best not to hurt anyone's feelings. To this end the bride and groom and families and even guests have a few duties.

Seating. If you are having a seated meal, people will need to be seated. The kindest thing you can do is prepare a seating plan with corresponding place cards, so that people have a chance to meet and mingle, yet don't have to be anxious about finding a place. Deciding on a seating plan can be especially important when parents are divorced or when relatives don't get along. Posting a seating chart for guests to consult when they first arrive makes it simple for people to know where to sit. If your meal is casual or the wedding small, you probably need not worry too much about where people will sit.

At most formal or semiformal meals, the bride and groom and the wedding party sit at a table, and the parents and grandparents of the bride and groom at another table. If you have a large family, you might want to place one or two family members at the other tables to act as hosts. If parents are divorced, you might want to seat them at separate tables, with their current spouses and family members or close friends. Sometimes local custom dictates that parents of the bride sit at one table, and parents of the groom at another. It doesn't really matter, so long as everyone is happy with their arrangement.

Toasts. At some point or another at just about every wedding someone proposes a toast to the happiness of the bride and groom (most often, it's the best man who offers the first toast). A number of toasts may be offered. At a seated meal the toasts are usually offered as soon as everyone is seated. At a stand-up buffet or tea, toasts may begin as soon as the guests have passed through the receiving line and have been served drinks. Sometimes a second round of toasts is offered at the cutting of the cake.

If the budget and custom allow, champagne is poured for the first toast. Wine or another beverage is perfectly fine, too. The best man toasts the bridal couple. Everyone except those being toasted raises the glass and drinks to them. A good new custom seems to be developing in which the maid or matron of honor toasts the couple next. The groom offers the next toast, to the bride, followed by the bride's to the groom. The father and mother of the bride and groom often toast next. After that, it's open to friends and family. If the toasting goes on too long, the best man should signal for it to cease and resume later at a pause in the meal or at the cutting of the cake.

Toasts, by the way, may be amusing but should never be crude or bring up embarrassing events that might not be deemed funny by all who hear. Similarly, guests should never make pointed remarks and jabs about either the bride or groom and past behavior.

Dancing. If the wedding has a seated meal, dancing often takes place between courses or toward the end of the meal. If the reception does not offer a seated meal, the bridal couple take to the dance floor for their first dance after everyone has gone through the receiving line.

This is the signal that the dancing has begun. The bride and groom usually take a few turns around the floor or complete a song. The bride's father claims the second dance while the groom dances with the bride's mother. This dance may be followed by one between the bride and her new father-in-law. At some point the bride should dance with all the ushers, close friends, and family. At a very large wedding it is not possible to dance with every man in attendance. Aside from the first dance, there need not be anything rigid about the order of dancing. It's more important to be tactful and dance first with those whose feelings might be bruised should you not.

Cutting the Cake. The ceremony of cutting the cake takes place before dessert is served at a seated dinner or toward the end of the reception for a buffet or tea. The bride and groom usually cut the first piece, after which someone else usually takes over. Then they share the piece they've cut. They are not required to feed each other. Often toasts are made at this juncture, too.

After the first piece, usually taken from the bottom tier, the top layer of the cake may be removed, saved, and frozen for the couple to eat on their first wedding anniversary.

How to Cut a Round-Tiered Wedding Cake

1. Start on the bottom tier. Cut straight down through the cake in a circle at the meeting of the second tier and the bottom.

2. Cut vertical slices about one inch apart all around the bottom tier. Transfer to dessert plates to serve.

(How to Cut a Round-Tiered Wedding Cake, cont'd.)

3. Cut the second tier in the same manner. If the top tier has already been removed, make the circle cut two to three inches in from the edge.

4. Repeat with any remaining tiers, and then start over again at the bottom.

At an especially elaborate wedding, small boxes of wedding cake or groom's cake are sent home with the guests as mementos. Sometimes table favors with the names of the bride and groom and the date are sent home.

Technically, no guest is supposed to leave before the cake is cut, but luckily this rather silly convention is falling away. If, for instance, the meal goes on into the wee hours and your babysitter expects to be home imminently, there is no reason why you can't give the bride and groom your best wishes, thank the hosts of the party, and leave when needed.

Departing. It used to be considered very bad form to leave the wedding before the bride and groom. They were expected to leave promptly after the principal festivities and the party would go on without them. These days, when often the couple have worked hard to put the event together, they want to stay to enjoy the party to the fullest. And yet, many people do want to see the bride and groom off, and so the thoughtful couple will either leave the reception fairly early or will make a ritual that will allow people to greet them one last time as they leave.

Some people use the tossing of the bouquet as an exit point. This ritual, which you need not feel obliged to do if you don't want to, involves the bride gathering unmarried women around her, turning her back to them and tossing her bouquet into the crowd. The person who catches it ostensibly will be the next married. Women who wish to save their bouquets shouldn't do it, or should have a second bouquet made up to throw.

Many couples put great time and effort into planning their exit. With a little creativity it can be a high point of the festivities. Once

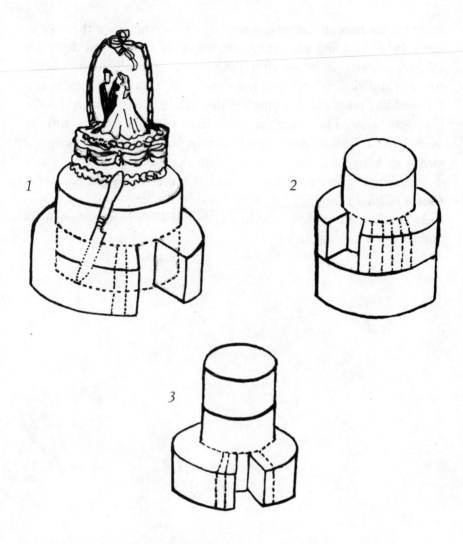

Fig. 6.4 Cutting a round-tiered wedding cake

it is deemed the appropriate time to get ready to leave, the bride excuses herself and goes to change into her travel clothes, as does the groom. They then exit to the cheers and fond wishes of their guests. They may be pelted with flower petals, birdseed, or confetti, or showered with bubbles.

One final note on the reception. The duration of most wedding parties is best at no more than five hours. After that, people are tired and families become cliquish. One way to accommodate the urge to keep the party going and really entertain your nearest and dearest is to have a party at home after the reception at which the out-of-towners and close friends can relax and visit. This is only practical if the wedding takes place during the day and the reception ends early. One good way to keep the reception from running too late into the evening yet still allow close friends, family, and out-of-towners a good visit is to have breakfast or brunch with them the next day.

Weddings, when thoughtfully and considerately planned, are a source of fond memories for more than just the bride and groom and their families. After all, a wedding is one of life's happiest events—and its joy is contagious.

7

MILESTONES AND TRANSITIONS

We mark the stages of life from birth to death with various forms of acknowledgment. Some are celebrations, some are matters of course, others are difficult adjustments. As with all things, however, the more we can keep the feelings and needs of those we encounter in mind, the better we manage the happy as well as the sad milestones of life.

BIRTH

Is there anything so joyous as the birth of a child? Certainly not to any parent or grandparent. For many of us, having children puts life into perspective by giving us a glimpse of the endless possibilities ahead and our small role in them. When we celebrate the birth of a baby, we are all in a small way affirming the worth of our own lives.

BABY SHOWER

One of the ways people celebrate an awaited birth is with a baby shower, a party intended to help equip new parents with some of the gear soon to be needed. Such gatherings, traditionally the preserve of women, are also a celebration of the baby soon to be born. In the past, showers were given only for the firstborn, the thinking being that once a family is equipped, a shower for subsequent babies would be superfluous. Also, it was regarded an imposition to ask friends to give a subsequent baby a present, even though close friends and family usually wish to anyway.

Today, however, people have begun to have showers for second and third children as a celebration of the impending birth. The gifts given at these parties tend to be a little different from those for the first; they often focus more on the comfort and pampering of mother and baby than on practical goods.

Another thing that has changed is that fathers are more often involved in showers than they used to be. Given the increased role that fathers now play, this seems only right and natural.

When planning a baby shower, there are a few important things to keep in mind. A baby shower should be given well into the second or third trimester of the pregnancy, when it is clear that the pregnancy is proceeding nicely and the mother-to-be feels well.

Many people like to make a baby shower a surprise. This can be a lot of fun, but only if the needs of the mother-to-be are kept in mind. The first thing to consider is, Does she like surprises? If she doesn't, you probably would do better to let her in on the plans. If she does, it's often a good idea to use a ruse involving some special event so that the woman is prepared and looks and feels her best.

Baby showers are usually given by friends of the parents-to-be and often take place during the day or, if most everyone works, during the evening. They usually include refreshments of some kind or a light meal. People gather, talk, eat, sometimes play games, and open presents. Usually there is much talk of babies, including updates and war stories.

In some parts of the country and among some ethnic groups, the custom is to give a baby shower after the birth. Among some groups the party may be held ahead of time, but the presents cannot be delivered to the house until after the birth.

Should a woman have a difficult pregnancy or one during which the health of the baby is in question, it may be kindest to delay a shower until after the birth, when mother and baby are out of danger.

Guests invited to a baby shower are expected to bring a gift. It need not be elaborate. Often guests chip in to buy an expensive piece of equipment. Unless the sex of the infant is known, shower presents should be neutral in color and style. If you are invited to a shower and cannot attend, you are not obligated to send a present.

ANNOUNCING A BIRTH

When a baby is born the telephone lines and grapevine usually work overtime spreading the good news. But beyond the immediate family and friends, the rest of one's world is usually informed by way of a birth announcement.

Birth announcements come in a wide variety of styles, from those that are preprinted with only the particulars to be filled in to specially printed ones. Printed ones are usually the most formal but can also be very creative.

When buying preprinted announcements, try to avoid those that are too coy or cutesy, unless it really suits your taste.

Traditional birth announcements are among the most charming of all. These announcements consist of a printed announcement and a small card with the baby's name. The cards are printed or engraved on white or off-white stock and the two cards are attached with a small satin ribbon. The ribbon may be color coded for sex, or not, as may the edge of the card. The wording of such a card often looks like this:

Mr. and Mrs. Hugh Howard
take great pleasure in announcing
the birth of
Sarah Miller
born November 10, 1990

Parents often include the weight and length of the baby at birth, as well.

Receiving a baby announcement does not obligate you to send a gift, although many people welcome the opportunity to send one.

It's a time-old practice to name sons after their fathers or other male relatives. If the boy is named after his father, the father becomes a "senior" (Sr.) and the son becomes "junior" (Jr.). When the father is a junior, the son becomes "the third" (3rd or III). If the father dies, the son may choose to keep the "junior," to differentiate himself from his father, or drop it. A boy who is named after a grandfather or other relative becomes "the second" (II), "the third" (III), and so on. When a girl is named after her mother or other relative, no generational title is used.

BABY CEREMONIES

Soon after the birth of a baby, many cultures and religions celebrate with a religious ceremony, officially welcoming the child into
the world and the ways of the particular group. Christian babies are
often christened or baptized anywhere from a few weeks to a few
months after birth, depending on the customs of the group. Anyone
invited to a ceremony honoring a baby, especially one held in a house
of worship, should wear appropriately dressy clothes.

At a christening or baptism, the baby, dressed in white, is taken
to a church where she or he becomes the focus of a ceremony that
may or may not be part of the regular service. The clergy person
welcomes the infant into the church, usually by reciting prayers and
pouring or sprinkling water over the baby's head. Parents and sometimes godparents (people who sponsor the child if the group requires
it) are charged by the clergy with the responsibilities of properly
rearing the child. Afterward the parents typically hold a reception at
home or in a church hall.

In the Jewish religion, baby boys undergo a circumcision ceremony
on the eighth day after birth. The ceremony usually is held in the
morning with a reception after for close friends and family held at
home. Guests bring baby presents and godparents usually give a lasting gift, such as something in silver, or a contribution to a college or
trust fund.

Jewish girls are often honored with a naming ceremony held any-
time from the first Sabbath after birth until several weeks afterward.
The simple ceremony is usually followed by a reception, at home or
in the synagogue, to which gifts may be brought.

Hindus hold a naming ceremony for babies usually between six
and eight months old. The ceremony, called a "rice-eating ceremony,"
marks the first time a baby eats solid food. Such ceremonies are usually held at home, often with a reception that begins before and con-
tinues after the ceremony. Guests, dressed as for any religious service,
bring gifts to the child.

Many Islamic families honor newborns with a ceremony called an
akikah. The ceremony, which varies widely from culture to culture,
may take place at home or in a general-purpose room of a mosque.
If the ceremony takes place in a mosque, men dress as for any reli-

gious ceremony, or at least in slacks and a shirt. Women cover their heads and do not wear slacks, short sleeves, or skirts above the knee. Guests should not wear any jewelry of a religious nature, or that shows signs of the zodiac, faces or heads of people or animals. Guests bring the infant a gift. A reception often follows the ceremony.

RITES OF PASSAGE

FIRST COMMUNION

In the Roman Catholic church children take communion for the first time when they are six or seven, after a year of religious preparation. First communion is an opportunity for family and community celebration. Family, close family friends, and special friends of the celebrant are invited. The ceremony takes place in the church and is usually followed by a reception at the church hall which may, in turn, be followed by others at the homes of the individual children receiving communion.

Boys wear dark suits and girls wear white dresses and veils or white headpieces, depending on local custom.

Parents often have private parties at home, following the service, to which family and friends are invited. Guests often present gifts to the celebrant, usually with a religious connotation, such as a cross or prayerbook, or something else serious such as a piece of jewelry or savings bond. Toys are not appropriate.

CONFIRMATION

During the teen years, usually between the ages of eleven and fifteen, and after months of preparation, Protestant and Catholic children are welcomed into the church as members with full privileges in a ceremony called a confirmation. The group ceremony is often followed by a reception in the church parlor and may be followed again by a party held for family and close friends at home. Parents, godparents, and other close friends may give gifts with religious connotation or those of lasting value.

Reform Jewish children are also confirmed in their faith at age thirteen.

BAR AND BAT MITZVAH

Orthodox, Conservative, and some Reform Jewish boys celebrate the coming of age at thirteen (usually the first Saturday after the boy's birthday) with a ceremony called a bar mitzvah, which means "son of the commandment" in Hebrew. Conservative and Reform girls celebrate with a bat mitzvah for "daughter of the commandment."

The event, the result of months of religious instruction, involves the child reading from the Torah as part of the regular Saturday service. The service is followed by a reception, open to all, which may include a luncheon at the synagogue. Later, in the evening after the Sabbath or the following afternoon, an elaborate party is usually given.

Only those who receive invitations attend the party given later. Invitations are often formal. Depending on the formality of the event and the time of day, people dress as for any dressy party.

Everyone invited to a bar mitzvah is expected to take a gift, usually something of lasting value, including money.

QUINCEAÑERA

When a girl turns fifteen in communities with a large Hispanic population, there is often a grand celebration called *quinceañera*. There may be a religious ceremony at which the girl reaffirms church vows, but such a service is usually followed by a big party.

Similar to a debutante ball, the party may be formal, with male guests wearing either black or white tie and women long gowns. A girl's first waltz with her father is often a highlight of the evening, after which general dancing begins. Gifts of lasting value or money are given, depending on the customs of the community.

SWEET SIXTEEN PARTIES

In some communities sweet sixteen parties are held for girls turning sixteen, an age often associated with the beginning of young adulthood. These parties, usually given by a girl's parents, can be elaborate (such as a dance given at a hall or in a club) or modest (such as a slumber party for a girl's close friends) or anything in between.

DEBUTANTE DANCES

At debutante dances girls of eighteen are formally acknowledged to be in society. These dances can be presented for groups of girls—the most common approach—or privately. The most formal events are balls, the least formal afternoon tea dances. Many such parties are sponsored by charities, which thus benefit from any proceeds. Parents of the debutantes are asked to contribute a certain amount of money to the charity as part of the privilege of having their daughters presented to society.

THE PROM

For many teenagers, the first and sometimes last formal dance they attend is a high school prom. A prom, short for promenade, is a chance for kids to pretend for a night to be sophisticated adults. Just like adult parties, they can be quite lavish.

People usually arrange dates for the big night several weeks in advance. For many people it seems very important to have a date, and it is usually up to the boys to do the asking. This can, of course, be awkward for shy boys and shy girls alike. The customs of the particular school may dictate how a boy is supposed to ask a girl for a date, and if girls feel comfortable asking boys for dates. One way to get around a possible awkward pairing and hurt feelings is for a group of friends, boys and girls mixed, to go together.

Girls and boys both may invite a date from another community or school. If they do this, they should expect to pay the expense of tickets to the dance, dinner, and possibly transportation to the event itself. An out-of-town guest pays for the cost of transportation and room if necessary, but the kind host tries to arrange accommodation with family or a friend, or helps pay for a hotel room.

Usually the boy pays for most of the costs of the evening, including any tickets needed, flowers, dinner, and transportation, if rented. Exceptions exist, of course, but these should be discussed in advance.

Traditionally, both boys and girls dress in formal clothes. Girls wear evening dresses. Boys wear black tie. Girls usually buy their outfits, complete with accessories, while boys usually rent theirs.

Boys usually give their dates flowers, often a corsage. Flowers can be either delivered during the afternoon of the dance, or the boy can bring them with him. He should check with his date to see what she prefers in the way of flowers: loose flowers, a small bouquet, or a corsage. A girl may give her date a boutonniere, a single flower to wear on the lapel, if she and he wish.

Often couples or groups of friends go to dinner, often at a nice restaurant, before the dance begins. Usually the boy pays for his and his date's dinner, unless the couple have agreed in advance to share the cost. Everyone should pay attention to his or her behavior at table, being sure to use good table manners and being considerate of the other diners in the restaurant. If a boy is paying for a girl's dinner she should avoid ordering the most expensive item on the menu as well as the very least, unless it is what she really wants. (See also the section on ordering food, page 117.)

The anticipation of a prom evening, or any formal event, and the effort to create a perfect night can fray the nerves of even a level-headed person. It is an opportunity to experience an evening out of the ordinary and one should feel special, even slightly elevated from the day to day, but one should try to keep it all in perspective. It will be an evening of fun, but it won't make or break a social reputation— unless you act really foolish.

After all the preparations, it will suddenly be showtime. Walk a little slower, stand a little taller, and enjoy wearing your fine clothes. Observe the scene around you and act accordingly. Overlook petty behavior in others, and avoid it yourself. Use your best manners—a prom is a wonderful excuse to behave like an adult. On the other hand, don't take the evening so seriously you forget to have fun. Remember, you're at a *promenade,* a magical time when, for an evening, you try a walk about a world from which the child is excluded.

ANNIVERSARY PARTIES

I think a wedding anniversary is always something to celebrate, whether it's a major one or not. Most couples celebrate minor anniversaries and early anniversaries privately or with a small party. Major anniversaries such as a twenty-fifth, fortieth, or fiftieth tend to be given by the couple's children, although the couple may do it for themselves if they wish.

Invitations to major anniversary parties may be issued by telephone or in writing, depending on the size and formality of the party. Pre-printed invitation cards, in which you fill in the particulars, may be used, as can formal invitations or handwritten notes. An invitation obligates guests to bring a gift, unless the invitation states something like "Mother and Dad will be most pleased with your presence as a present." (For more information, see the section on anniversary gifts, page 216.)

Many people like to surprise relations or friends with a special party. Surprise parties are great for people who like them, not so for those who don't. Some people who give surprise parties do so because *they* like them.

If you plan to give a surprise party, determine the wishes of the guests of honor. This is especially true of older people, some of whom get overwhelmed easily by crowds. Maybe a small party with taped wishes from far-flung friends might be a better idea for these people. As with all surprise parties, make sure that the recipients are prepared for some sort of special event before springing a load of people on them. No one likes to be surrounded by well-dressed strangers when dressed in gardening clothes.

RETIREMENT PARTIES

When a person retires after a long career it's often nice to honor him or her with a party. These often take place with people from the person's place of employment and are thus a mixture of social and business relationships. Such parties can also be strictly business related or all friends and family.

Anyone can give a retirement party, from fellow office workers to loving family. The party can be at the office, a restaurant, at home, anywhere you think appropriate to the crowd. The party itself can be a small gathering or a large one and can be a simple reception or a seated dinner.

However you choose to structure the party, make sure the focus is a celebration of a job well done. Sometimes such parties are bittersweet for the honoree, and organizers and should be filled with good cheer but also aware of a certain poignancy.

Usually toasts are given to honor the recipient. These often relate an anecdote or joke.

If retiring from a company after long service, the retiree is usually given a present by the management. The traditional gift was a gold watch, but today it may be something related to the person's outside hobbies, interests, or even extra cash.

FAMILY REUNIONS

When my grandmother became too old to travel to her various relations I decided it was time we went to her. I organized our first annual family weekend picnic at her house. It's become our most eagerly awaited family event, as members travel from all parts of America to join in.

Everyone brings food—some made at home, some purchased, some cooked on-site. And then we visit and eat and share and visit some more.

When Grandma was alive she was our guest of honor, and we didn't let her do much work. She was seated on a throne that we had made by decorating a favorite chair of hers. She was allowed to direct or help as she wished, but it was our gift to her and ourselves.

I think family reunions are a wonderful way to mark a family's progress, and they can be tailored to suit the needs and distances of almost anyone. They usually take place over a weekend and usually during the day so that families with children can attend.

There is no right way and no wrong way to make a reunion, so long as it suits everyone's wishes and gets people together so that they can share each other's company.

THE END OF LIFE

Everyone deals with death in his or her own way. In our culture, there is no universal method for coping with the end of life. Not everyone will keen and wail; nor will most people show a stiff upper lip and carry on as though nothing has happened. Certain ethnic groups have mourning practices that help ease the process for the survivors, but there is no national standard.

The one thing that our culture has done almost universally is make death as abstract as possible. We don't view it as something inevitable and natural, but as something to be overcome. Perhaps this notion has grown from a secret hope that if we ignore Death we won't have to meet up with him. This is a shame, since a lifelong acceptance of death's inevitability can only make it easier when someone we know dies, or when we prepare ourselves for our own demise.

One practical way to prepare for our own ends which can help our families is to take care of our affairs long in advance of death. There are human considerations: Try to heal old wounds with family and friends. This can be a monumental task, but if you can do it well before death, the life left will be enhanced in countless ways. But there are practical considerations, too.

Consult a financial adviser on how best to disburse your assets. Make a will. Plan your funeral and make your burial wishes known in writing. You might even want to choose and buy a burial plot. Arrange for funeral expenses to be paid. All of this may sound morbid, but if done well in advance it need not be, and the help it will give to the grieving family when the time does come will be immense. So often, we find ourselves having to read the mind of a loved one after he or she is gone in order to determine the best course of action.

Even if the dead or dying party hasn't reached metaphysical understanding and peace nor resolved all the practical issues, there are some practicalities the survivors need to focus on when someone near to them dies. Three steps must be taken immediately in order to set in motion the planning of the funeral. First, family members must be notified; second, the deceased person's lawyer must be contacted; and third, an undertaker must be called to make arrangements for the body.

PLANNING A FUNERAL

The first thing the family must do in the event of a loved one's death is to plan the funeral. It's not as daunting a prospect as it might seem at first. All clergy are trained to provide guidance and help in planning a funeral as well as in supporting survivors. Funeral directors are also most adept at guiding people through the steps necessary. Decisions are usually made by the remaining spouse, should there be one, or children of the deceased. In the case of a child, the parents, naturally, are responsible.

Sometimes the deceased has left clear instructions of what is to be done by way of funeral arrangements. The family is duty-bound to honor the person's wishes as much as practically possible. I feel there is one exception, however. I believe that funerals and memorial services are to help the living come to terms with the death of a loved one. If the deceased asked that no funeral be held, and the family feels a service would be helpful, I think they should consider having one. They should try to plan a ceremony that the loved one would not object to, if possible.

Sometimes a memorial service, traditionally held after cremation or burial of the body, or in cases where there is no body, is a good way to remember someone without having a full religious ceremony. Such a service, which can also be called a Service of Thanksgiving, can have a strong element of religion or not, depending upon the family's wishes.

OBITUARIES

An obituary is a newspaper article about a person who has died, usually a prominent person in the community. It is not something that the family pays for or can demand, but often local newspapers welcome basic information about the deceased. If the person who has died played a public role in life, regional or even national papers might also be contacted. Talk to the director of the funeral home or telephone the editorial offices of the newspaper, if you wish, to inquire about procedures. Often a basic bio listing accomplishments, education, survivors, and other particulars can be faxed or delivered.

PUBLIC MOURNING CUSTOMS

Different religions and cultural groups have their own mourning customs, but as with most things in our society, they have become less formal. The practices of each ethnic and religious group differ, but a few things in general have changed.

It is no longer considered important for the family to wear black to the funeral and for the months after a death. People attending a funeral generally wear somber clothes and act in a dignified manner. It is generally not a time for displays of boisterousness or high spirits.

Most funerals are announced in the newspaper. The announcement is often placed by the funeral home, although obituaries are usually the responsibility of the family. Anyone who sees the announcement of the funeral is welcome to attend, unless the announcement states that the service is to be private.

Friends and family usually call on family members, either at home or during calling hours at the funeral home before the funeral. Callers should offer a few words of condolence to family members and should sign the guest book, even if no family members are present when they arrive. Guests need not spend a long time talking unless requested to by members of the family. Guests should never ask pointed questions about the death.

If the body is on display, as is the custom with some groups and in some parts of the country, you may or may not view it as you wish.

FUNERAL CUSTOMS

Most funerals follow a general pattern. Family and friends gather at a house of worship or a funeral home. A service is held to honor the deceased, during which a member of the clergy offers prayers. Eulogies may be offered and hymns sung, depending on the religion and denomination. The service may be elaborate, as in a Catholic mass, or very simple with no more than a few prayers said.

In some religions, such as Christianity and Buddhism, it is customary to send flowers to the funeral. Alternately, a donation may be made to charity instead, if the family requests. In the Jewish, Islamic, and Hindu religions, flowers are not sent to the funeral. Hindus often bring flowers to the house and place them at the feet of the deceased. Islamics usually send flowers to the family after the funeral.

Jewish custom requires that a body be buried as soon as possible after death, often the next day. This means that people who are less than intimate friends or who live some distance away may not hear of the funeral until it is over. They may still pay a condolence call on the family, as they usually retire for a period of public mourning to a relative's home for several days (three for Reform, seven for most Conservative and Orthodox Jews). During this time, called "sitting shiva," friends may call, being sure to grant the mourners privacy, often not even shaking hands or even asking how they are faring.

Hindu tradition also requires that a body be buried immediately.

Friends call and visit family members to offer condolences. The body usually remains at home until it is taken to the place where it will be cremated. The service is held there, usually with an open coffin.

Muslims are usually buried within two or three days of death. Friends often call and offer condolences to the bereaved before the funeral, which is usually conducted at a funeral home by an imam. The casket is never open and the body is never cremated. Visitors are welcome to call on the bereaved any time during the following forty days, the official period of mourning. Visitors usually sit in silence while someone reads aloud.

Buddhist tradition differs from other customs in one significant way. People do not call on the family before the funeral to offer condolences; they do so after. The funeral service resembles a Christian funeral in many ways, taking place in a funeral home or temple, with a eulogy and prayers offered by a priest. The casket is usually open, with guests expected to view the body and bow slightly in appreciation of the reminder of the impermanence of life. The body can be interred or cremated. Buddhists also hold a ceremony forty days after the funeral at which time the soul is thought to be released.

PRIVATE MOURNING

Since mourning is an internal process that differs from one person to another, finding one's own way of accepting a death is necessary. Gone are the days when a close family member of a recently deceased person could not accept a social invitation for at least a year. These days, a person can do as much or as little as he or she feels—within a few limits.

In order to be caring and considerate, keep in mind the solemnity of your recent loss. A woman who appears at a party in a revealing dress two weeks after her husband's death, thus announcing her immediate availability, sends the world a rather unfeeling message. A man who openly squires women around town within a few weeks of his wife's death similarly communicates a selfish position. It is generally considered disrespectful to look openly for a new mate immediately after the funeral. Allowing a few months for both spouse and friends to mourn usually eases the possibility of censure.

The thoughtful friend takes cues from the person in mourning regarding when and how much social activity would be appreciated, offering appropriate consolation along the way. If a bereaved person is not ready for a party a few months after a death, but would appreciate a walk, lunch out, or just a talk, the considerate friend tries to be useful in these ways.

In general, the thoughtful friend checks in with the bereaved on a regular basis, offering to do whatever the friend would find a comfort. You might even send a note saying something like "Let me be your 911." You don't have to make a pest of yourself, but neither should you assume that once the funeral or official period of mourning is over, everything is fine again. People get a lot of attention in the period immediately surrounding the death, but it tends to quickly wane. For many people, the hard adjustments are just beginning at that point.

As the person who has suffered the loss of a loved one, there is of course the most necessary process of grieving. People grieve in their own ways and on their own schedules. After a certain period, however, most people begin to emerge from the maelstrom of loss and the healing process begins. Some people find it useful to join support groups of other grieving people. Some become interested in going out and meeting new people, taking classes, volunteering, getting a new job, or any other of a thousand other things.

For anyone who has ever lost a loved one, life is never *just* as it was before. The death will always be felt, but a full life and happiness can still be had. Many people find that they actually experience a growing feeling of independence and self-confidence once they are able to let go of the grief and use that energy to create a new life. It may not be easy to establish new patterns and find new interests, but the power created by the grieving process can be harnessed to find new interests and revitalize old ones.

THE CONDOLENCE NOTE

A note of sympathy written to a friend or relation on the death of a loved one is not merely a social convention but a useful tool in the grieving process. A handwritten condolence note means ten times more than any commercial sympathy card. The note need not be long, but when writing a note, you should try to recall some memory or feeling associated with the person, one of yours or the bereaved person's. (For more information, see Letters of Condolence, page 31.) The bereaved is responsible for sending a handwritten note of thanks for all flowers and condolence notes. (See also the section on thank-you notes, page 30).

TRANSITIONS

In everyone's life there are transitions, some happy, some sad, but all sharing the element of change. That element of change, bringing with it the fear of the unknown, is something we humans often wish didn't exist. But life *is* change and the more we can do to prepare for it gracefully, the easier it can be.

LEAVING HOME

There comes a time in everyone's life when you have to leave home. That step from childhood to adulthood is exciting, yet it can be difficult and sad, especially for those left at home. For those on the exciting end of leaving, my advice is to keep in touch. If your parents ask you to call once a week, please do so. If they ask that you write, make the effort.

For those staying I would ask that you respect the privacy of the person, usually child, now out on his or her own. Be as supportive as you can. Your child is stretching and learning how to be a grown-up, and you may still be needed as backup. Chances are good that if you've done your job well, the training you instilled will be used and useful, helping to ease the way for the emerging adult. Besides, there is not a whole lot you can change at this late date.

If your child has moved a distance away, you might want to send care packages containing some favorite items. Young people away at college often get homesick, and such tokens of love can ease the difficulties in adjusting. They can be good therapy for the sender, too.

Writing letters is another good method for easing homesickness. A good newsy letter or E-mail message can be read at a convenient moment, such as when a wave of nostalgia washes over the recipient.

It can also be reread. Letters and messages don't have to replace phone calls but can be sent in addition.

DIVORCE

Sadly, despite high hopes and good intentions, many marriages end. For most people facing divorce, the experience is fraught with feelings of failure and isolation. A person in the throes of divorce needs the support and understanding of friends and family.

A couple who decides to get a divorce tells their families first, then close friends. Family and close friends will probably know or hear all the grisly details, but try not to overburden them with your travails, and leave the world at large out of it.

No formal announcement of divorce is ever issued. Word gets out. For friends whom you don't see often but keep up with annually, you can mention the fact simply in the next letter or holiday card. Don't detail events, just announce the decision, perhaps with a qualifying sentence. Such an announcement might look something like this: "Luke and I separated in the spring, and our divorce will be final soon. It's been a rough time for both of us, but I'm looking forward to things settling down soon."

Sometimes one of the partners is glad to be free of the marriage. Relief from an untenable situation is natural, of course, but you should try to keep in mind that the other party may still be wounded, and thus to discuss it with acquaintances may be unfair. A divorce party or printed announcements is never in good taste.

By all means call on close friends for support, but once the official channels have been entered, you will need to accept the finality of the divorce, even if it was not what you wanted. Your duty, then, is not to try to work out the marriage in the lawyer's offices, but to work out whatever arrangements need to be made to bring the marriage to a clean and final end.

Once the divorce is final, pick up the pieces of your life and start to remold them. If you still feel wounded, try to keep a positive "I'm on the move forward" attitude instead of dwelling on the injustice of the situation. That will speed your recovery. Perhaps you might join a new group, take a class, make new friends—something to break the old patterns. You need not feel pushed to date until you are ready, if ever, but you do need to move on, for your sake as well as that of your family and friends.

Being a Friend. As a friend helping another through a divorce, be as supportive as you can. Listen, offer to help out, take your friend out to a movie, play, art show, concert, and do it again and again. Listen and respond as necessary. Keep the conversation moving forward if you can, rather than repeatedly dwelling on the unhappiness.

During a divorce most people's emotions are fragile and often volatile. To criticize the spouse can be read at one time or another as a criticism of your friend. For instance, if you say something along the lines of "I always thought the bum was no good," you set your friend up for thinking, "What's wrong with me that I ever loved him (or her)?" or "Where does he/she get off telling me I'm such a dope?" The other reason not to speak ill of the spouse is that you never know: When the anger abates the two of them might be friends again or even be reconciled. It happens, and the sharp words some people uttered can come back to bite them.

Telling the Children. Few things are more painful than telling children that you and their other parent can no longer live with each other. While this is primarily a parenting issue rather than one of etiquette in the strictest sense, certain principles of commonsense consideration do apply.

To *pretend* that you and your spouse still love each other is unfair to your children. They intuitively know when things are not right and to tell them everything is fine only makes them confused and unable to trust their own feelings.

Children do not need to know all the details of your reasons for separation, but they do need basic age-appropriate information. Try not to dwell on your negative feelings toward the other parent.

You may also be called on to help your children deal with the advent of your or an ex-spouse's new partner. You may encounter frustration and anger from your children and perhaps even in yourself. This is natural, but try your best not to show your irritation to your children. They need to feel as positive about the situation as possible, and as in every other instance, how you treat them will directly affect how they feel, respond, and in turn treat others.

Dealing with Your In-Laws. If you have children you will probably still have relations with your in-laws after the divorce. Try to maintain a cordial relationship and try to discuss the ex-spouse as little as possible. If your ex-in-laws insist on discussing the situation, you will need to tell them kindly but firmly that you are trying to remake your life and going over old wounds only makes it harder.

Unless there are outstanding reasons, your children need their grandparents as much as their grandparents need them. Try to keep communication and visitation frequent and friendly. Feel free to lay some ground rules about what you feel they should and should not discuss with your children. This goes for your own parents and relatives as well.

ILLNESS

At one time or another we are all faced with serious illness, either our own or someone else's. During such times we feel the need of support from family and friends most keenly. We also sometimes need to know how to be good patients.

Hospital Visits. When visiting a friend in the hospital, little gifts are often appreciated. Such token gifts should be small, since space is almost always limited. A small pot of flowers or a flowering plant can cheer up a room, but check first to see if these are allowed the patient (allergies, certain medications, and the use of oxygen can be restricting). Other good ideas include blank note cards with postage stamps, magazines, nice body lotion, and books on tape.

People often appreciate a special service. A call ahead of time asking if there is a special wish for something from the outside world, any errands to be run or chores to be done that would ease the patient's mind can be helpful.

When visiting, it's a good policy in general to limit the visit to fifteen minutes, unless pressed to stay. While there, make sure you don't disrupt the hospital routine—when the staff needs to perform a task, just step into the hall for a moment or two, or go have a cup of coffee in the cafeteria and come back. Take your cues from the patient. If he or she looks tired or suddenly ill, cut the visit short. If you have a cold or the flu, stay away. Make a phone call instead.

Keep the conversation upbeat without ignoring the patient's

situation. Not only do you bring news from the outside, but be prepared to listen. Sometimes people need to talk through their experiences. Sometimes they don't want to talk at all.

Patients who are too ill to receive visitors still often appreciate cards or calls. Family members taking care of them also appreciate a call asking if there is anything that *they* need.

Don't underestimate the power of touch. Being ill causes great anxiety. Holding a hand, giving a hug, or gentle stroking of a sick person can ease anxiety and promote overall comfort for both of you. Of course, don't just assume that you can touch someone, especially if you have had a reserved relationship.

Don't infantalize an ill person. When we see someone ill and with diminished powers, we sometimes have the tendency to treat them as children. Remember, just because someone is incapacitated doesn't mean they are essentially any different from before. Don't assume that because a person is lying in bed that he or she has become deaf, blind, or simpleminded. Even if a person has lost mental acuity, he or she is still due respect.

Being a Good Patient. There is an art to being a good patient and it requires a balancing act of being firm, fair, and sweet. A good patient treats everyone who works in the hospital with respect—but then the well-mannered person does this anyway. Staff members will invariably treat you better if you make an effort to learn their names and to thank them for services they've done you. Hospitals are very busy places, and they are often understaffed, so if you can keep non-urgent requests to a minimum or make them at a relatively quiet time, the staff will usually be happy to oblige you.

You are also there to be nursed, so when you really need something you must stand firm, in the nicest possible way, of course. If you haven't been badgering the staff with demands you are more likely to have your needs met.

Once you have recovered, you might want to thank staff members who have been especially helpful during your stay. A note to the staff and their superiors, a certain treat that you know staff members particularly like, or a donation toward a needed piece of equipment are all things that people appreciate.

When friends come to visit there are a few guidelines that can make the time most pleasant. Try not to dwell on your illness. People are often curious, but they rarely want grisly details and endless explanations. Keep such discussions brief. Instead, try to steer the conversation to other topics. Ask about what's going on in the world outside, with the friends you have in common, or about your visitor's interests.

Most visitors will be aware of not staying too long, but when you feel tired or ill or your visitor just doesn't seem to know when to leave, kindly tell your friend that you need to rest or see a staff member.

Home Visits. When someone is ill at home but well enough to receive company, a visitor often can make the whole day brighter.

When planning a visit to someone at home, you have some more latitude in what you can do and bring. When a friend is home you might offer to bring lunch over or to bring a dinner for the family that just needs to be reheated. Offer to take the kids for the afternoon. Maybe a little housework would be appreciated, or errands run. When planning a trip to the grocery store, you might call and offer to do a friend's shopping. Maybe your friend has paperwork that needs catching up on that you can help with.

Remember to keep visits brief, and look for signs of discomfort as your signal to leave.

Friends with long-term illnesses may need the extra help of friends on a regular basis. Offer to help drive to a treatment, doctor's appointment, or physical therapy session. You might be able to organize a group of friends to help out on a regular basis with some of the tasks of daily life.

Entering an Assisted Living Facility or a Nursing Home. There comes a time for many people when running a household is just too hard. Illness, age, and loneliness may all contribute to a decision to leave home for a room or apartment in a long-term care facility.

For most, this is a difficult time. For some, it signals another step toward the inevitable end. For others, it is a chance to concentrate their energies on living, but without much of the work of running a household. For the person or persons moving, or for the relatives who are left to sort everything out, it is a time of intense emotional upheaval and pure work, for moving is hard work. Rarely is it a time of great joy.

As a friend, almost anything you can do to help out will be appreciated. It may be as simple as returning library books, or as intense as cleaning out the closets. Offer what time and talents you have and don't feel bad about not doing it all.

If you're the person moving, don't hesitate to ask for help from family, friends, and neighbors. Sometimes a family manager can be a great help in many ways. These are professionals who help elderly people with a variety of needs, including managing monthly finances, grocery shopping, transporting people to doctor's appointments, moving, and many other tasks of daily life. One advantage that a professional manager brings to the situation is detachment. Often such a life change taps into a wealth of messy family dynamics, and someone who serves as an adjunct can accomplish much more with much less fuss than family members. Professional managers usually work for an hourly rate.

Friends and family also need to provide emotional support. Say you are the adult child of someone breaking up housekeeping after fifty years and you find it difficult to see overall changes made and items of sentimental value disbursed; now, imagine what your parent is going through.

Friends can help by calling or visiting the person to discuss concerns or just to talk about the events of the day. Take the person out for a needed break. You can go to a movie, out for lunch, for a walk or drive. Even if you can't get out much, a regular phone call can do a world of good.

Once people are established in new homes, they need the services of friends and family on a regular basis. It can be very isolating leaving friends and changing one's patterns. Be supportive and visit frequently if you can. If a friend is well enough, go out to do anything that you both like to do. You can also just visit.

When taking a present to a friend in a nursing home or retirement apartment, remember that space is limited, yet rooms need to be humanized. A framed picture of family or friends, a beautiful and cozy afghan, a favorite treat are often all appreciated. For a friend who loves to read, a special book, a trip to the library, or a Walkman with a book on tape can really add quality to life.

Life in a long-term care facility *can* be fulfilling. If a person is active, many facilities offer a range of events on a regular basis. Take advantage if you can. Keep in touch with friends who live nearby.

Friends, too, need to keep in touch. I know of one small-town newspaper that publishes the names of the nursing home's residents and their visitors each week. No one in that town gets forgotten! The challenge, at any stage of life, is to stay involved with people.

8

GIVING AND RECEIVING GIFTS

One of the great joys of life from infancy onward is the giving and receiving of gifts. It is an art that we all practice in various ways, some conscious and some not. For parents, those precious moments after a child is born may be rich with an understanding that a great gift has just been received. Sometimes the death of a loved one makes us aware of a gift we have lost. In between such awesome moments, our lives may seem punctuated by the giving and receiving of more conscious gifts. These presents, large and small, add fun, intrigue and spice to life.

GENERAL GIFT-GIVING GUIDELINES

Giving thoughtful gifts can be aided by a few general guidelines. The sensitive person tries to tailor each gift to its recipient. There are a few exceptions, such as when an employer has a policy about what gifts are sent and when. In most cases, however, you would do well to try to imagine how the recipient will use the gift or where it will live.

In general, unless you know the tastes and needs of the recipient very well, it's best to do some research and use a little common sense to find out what is really needed or wanted. For instance, both parties would be embarrassed if you gave candy to a person with diabetes or someone who is conscientiously dieting. You are more likely to please if you give something that relates to a person's passions, hobbies, or career.

Try to keep in mind that people are often more sensitive than they appear and can easily construe certain gifts as criticism. For instance, if you know a friend loves to cook, feel free to give a cookbook. But if you know the person finds cooking a great effort, steer clear of culinary gifts.

Gag gifts can strike unrecognized sensitivities. Any joke gifts relating to a person's physique or personal habits should be avoided. Unless you are really sure of your audience, keep silly gifts to a minimum and opt instead for a gift you're sure will be appreciated.

In general, presents that require care should be avoided unless you know the wishes of the recipient well. If, for instance, you wish to give your godchild a pet, check with the parents in advance.

Ostentatious gifts are usually in poor taste, as it embarrasses everyone present, sometimes even the person giving it. When faced with an ostentatious present the question arises, Is the present a reflection of the giver's guilt or ego, or is it truly meant for the recipient?

Including a card with most gifts is important. If there is more than one gift being opened, the card can help avoid confusion over who gave what. Often recipients like to keep cards as a keepsake, and a well-worded note can turn a simple gift into something of lasting value.

If you take a house gift to a dinner party, you generally don't need a card as you usually hand it over personally as you meet the hosts.

GENERAL GIFT-RECEIVING GUIDELINES

The recipient of a present has an obligation just as much as the giver. Your first task is to thank the giver for any gift you receive. If the giver is present, so much the easier, for it is quickly done. For a gift opened out of the giver's presence, a thank-you is still required, at least by phone and preferably by handwritten note.

Even if you really don't like a particular gift, you still must think of something to say or write. After quickly studying the object try to come up with something pleasant to say, even if it's only "What a nice round shape this is," or some such innocuous but pleasant phrase.

Sometimes I find it easier to write to thank someone after I've had the time to compose my thoughts. I might discuss the event and how much fun it was, describing it briefly ("I was so delighted with seeing all of you at Martha's house—we all laughed so hard and ate so well!"). If you really like a present, it's usually easy to say so ("The candles are so lovely and colorful . . ."), and then to mention how you intend to use it ("The whole set will show off my holiday table so nicely at our annual Open House . . ."). If you don't care for a gift, a simple phrase such as one thanking the giver for the time and effort spent choosing the gift, or the usefulness of the gift, its elegant form, its pleasing color, or other such attribute shows appreciation ("You were so thoughtful to give me those brilliant red mittens; they do look warm indeed . . ."). (For more information, see the section on thank-you notes, page 30.)

Your second obligation as the receiver of a gift is to appear pleased. Usually this is easy, but on occasion it can be difficult. You don't have to lie, but you may have to use some creative language, body as well as verbal (embrace those ugly towels for a moment and remark, "They feel so fuzzy!"). Never let your smile flag. Proudly display the gift for as long as your guest is present (after the giver has gone, retire the towels to a closet).

Often presents are given at a party, such as a birthday, at which half the fun of giving a gift is to watch the recipient open it. The graceful way to open the gifts at such a party is to gather the gifts together and open them all at once. The recipient then reads each card and shows the gift. If someone gives money, you thank them warmly, but do not mention the amount.

At a very large party at which you are apt to receive a lot of envelopes, such as at a wedding or bar mitzvah, the presents need not be opened on the spot since to do so might interrupt the flow of the party. They can be held until later and opened with other gifts.

There are times when gifts should be opened right away and with little fanfare. One such case is when you are brought a house gift at a dinner party. Such gifts are usually presented to the host or hostess when guests arrive. You open them right then and thank the giver warmly, but do not make a display of it, since it is not specifically a gift-giving occasion and other guests may not have brought anything.

SOCIAL GIFTS

A variety of occasions call for the giving of gifts. The expected birth or the actual arrival of a baby, birthdays, weddings, and other events all present both the obligation and the opportunity to find and give appropriate gifts. Here are some guidelines for selecting and giving gifts at such occasions.

BABY GIFTS

Lucky is the baby who gets inundated with gifts from loving and admiring friends and family. Unless you are experienced in giving gifts to babies and their families, you might find yourself bewildered by the choices. The array of goods available is positively mind-boggling. Here is a simple guide.

Baby Showers. Clothes are often welcome. If the sex of the baby is known you may buy clothing specific to a boy or girl. Otherwise, it's better to select something in a unisex style of a color other than pink or light blue. Blankets, quilts, soft toys, crib mobiles, and first books are also popular choices. Sometimes friends pool together to buy a piece of baby equipment. If you do this, try to determine the taste and needs of the parents or make sure that the present can be exchanged.

I know one person who carries on the tradition of her mother and grandmother and makes receiving blankets. She takes a beautiful square of flannel and crochets around the edges to seal them. They're simple, elegant, useful, and worth passing down.

Some people feel it is bad luck to give baby presents before the birth. If you feel this way and are invited to a shower, give the mother a present instead. Popular choices include a basket of soothing toiletries, a special mug and a selection of the mother-to-be's favorite teas, a certificate for services such as an afternoon of babysitting, or an indulgence such as a gift certificate for a manicure or a facial.

Baby gifts presented to a child in honor of a christening or other ceremony are usually intended to outlast babyhood. A silver spoon, cup, rattle, or picture frame, often engraved with the child's initials or name and date of birth, are traditional and lovely presents that will be cherished throughout life—more so as the child grows older. A savings bond makes another excellent long-lasting gift.

Parents acknowledge all baby gifts with a handwritten note unless they come from close family and friends whom you can thank in person. (For more information, see the section on thank-you notes, page 30.)

A PRESENT TO HONOR THE NEW MOTHER

Sometimes thoughtful and generous husbands like to honor their wives with a special piece of jewelry to mark the birth of a child. One way is to give a ring or other piece of jewelry set with the baby's birthstone. When such rings are simple, these can often be worn together with the wedding band.

Once a family is complete, a ring or pin can be made up with a setting that contains the birthstone of each child. This can be given to celebrate a special birthday or Mother's Day. (See also the section on birthstones and flowers, page 210.)

BIRTHDAYS

Birthdays seem especially important when we are children—I know one almost-six-year-old child who begins planning her next birthday the day after her current one. But there is no reason they can't be cause for celebration throughout life.

Children's Birthday Presents. For very small children, parents usually make the decisions of what to give their children's friends. When children reach the age of five or six, they are usually old enough to help in the decision. You might want to have several things on hand or in mind and let them pick one, or solicit their opinions.

Some children at age five or so enjoy helping to wrap their friends' presents. Why not let them help, even if their folds aren't sharp and they use ten pieces of tape where three would do. It makes them participants in the process of giving.

Older children often can be hard to buy for, as their interests narrow. If you can find out what piques a teenager's interest, you're home free. Sports, music equipment, tickets to events, and gift certificates to music, department, and bookstores are all good bets.

A SENTIMENTAL JOURNEY THROUGH CHILDHOOD

Gifts from grandparents and other relatives are often of real emotional value to children. So, if you're a grandparent, why not make the most of this by creating a memory book or box for each grandchild?

Decorate a box or binder and gradually fill it with sentimental mementos. You can include the front page of the paper from the day the child was born and for subsequent birthdays. Drawings, photographs, report cards, letters, locks of hair from first haircuts, all kinds of things can be included. Parents can make these too, of course, or help you in assembling materials. Then pick an event—the first day of school, a bar or bat mitzvah, a sweet sixteen party, a Christmas celebrated at your house, or some other appropriate time—to give them the lovingly assembled gift.

Adult Birthdays. Many people celebrate big birthdays, such as 40, 50, and 65, with a party. Usually friends bring presents, and finding the right birthday present for an adult can be tricky. If you know the taste of your friend, it's easy of course. If you don't, stick to safe things, such as a bottle of nice wine, flowers, candles, a pretty vase, food items, and such. Big birthdays are often celebrated with gag gifts but these must be carefully chosen, too, so as not to offend. When in doubt, play it safe and skip the gag.

BIRTHSTONES AND FLOWERS

Month	Stone	Flower
January	Garnet	Snowdrop
February	Amethyst	Primrose
March	Aquamarine, blood-stone, jasper	Violet
April	Diamond	Daisy
May	Emerald	Hawthorn
June	Pearl, moon-stone	Rose
July	Ruby	Water lily
August	Sardonyx, peridot, carnelian	Poppy
September	Sapphire	Morning glory
October	Opal	Water lily
November	Topaz	Chrysanthemum
December	Turquoise, lapis lazuli	Holly

CONFIRMATION, BAR OR BAT MITZVAH

When a child undergoes a religious rite of passage during adolescence, it is customary to give a gift when invited to the ceremony. As with the ceremonies of babyhood, gifts should be of lasting value. Traditional gifts for children include a bible or prayer book engraved with the child's name or initials, a cross, medal, or other religious symbol to be worn on a chain. Other thoughtful choices include a fine book and a good pen-and-pencil set or a savings bond. Another traditional gift for children being bar and bat mitzvahed is money.

When choosing other gifts for adolescents you may wish to consult a child's wish list, the child's parents and friends, or give a gift certificate, as children's tastes often are narrowly focused.

WEDDING GIFTS

Anyone who receives an invitation to a wedding and attends the wedding is expected to provide a gift. People who receive an invitation and do not attend the wedding are not obligated to send a present, although they usually do. Those who receive a wedding announcement have no gift-giving obligation.

Wedding presents need to be chosen with special care, since they serve a variety of functions. They help equip the bride and groom; they send a message to the couple and their parents that you share in the importance of the occasion; and they should please the recipients.

Wedding gifts tend to be more lavish than some others, but they should always be in keeping with what the giver can afford. An expensive gift from someone who can ill afford it is unnecessary and can be embarrassing to the recipients. A stingy gift from someone who is well-off makes the givers look miserly.

When buying a wedding gift it helps to know the taste of the bride and groom, as well as their needs and wishes. This is where consulting the bridal registry of major stores in your area is a real help. Even if you don't buy from the registry, you will have a good idea of the sorts of things the couple likes.

One good way to get more for your money is to pool contributions from a group of friends or fellow office workers to buy a large present for the bride and groom. A word of advice, however: Check with the couple to make sure you buy something they want or need. I know of one couple who were given a large antique pine table by a group of friends because the newlyweds liked antiques. Unfortunately, the person who organized the purchase chose something to his own taste, and the bride and groom were left with something large, expensive, and nonreturnable.

If at all possible, try to buy a wedding gift that is returnable. People often receive duplicates of presents, or would rather exchange a gift they don't cherish for one precisely to their tastes.

Presents for second weddings are often less traditional than for first weddings, since the couple usually is well equipped. Presents are not strictly necessary for second weddings, but many people like to acknowledge the event with something special. Tickets to a cultural event, a certificate for dinner, a very nice bottle of wine, a subscription to a magazine or publication are a few ideas of nontraditional presents that people often like. Traditional presents are often welcome, but check with the bride and groom before you choose a household item that they might already own.

Wedding gifts are usually wrapped in white, silver, or gold paper with coordinating ribbons, although they may also be wrapped in bright colors and patterns. Presents should be sent or taken to the bride's home or the couple's shared home before the wedding. If you can't manage to send it ahead of time, a gift may be sent any time up to a year after the wedding.

Increasingly, people take presents to the wedding reception. This practice has become so common that the bride and groom should establish a place to put the gifts at the reception and make arrangements to have someone to collect the gifts at the end of the party and keep them until the couple return from their honeymoon.

Among some ethnic groups, giving money as a present is customary. Often an envelope with a card and check or cash is presented to the bride or groom at the reception. Even among groups where such monetary gifts are not usual, there are times that money is appreciated. If you don't know the couple terribly well or do know that what they would like most is money with which to buy the things they need, you can send a card with a check enclosed.

All wedding gifts must be acknowledged with a handwritten thank-you note. Yes, it's a pain to write a lot of notes. But remember, people go to a lot of trouble and expense to provide gifts they hope the bride and groom will like, and failing to thank them is terribly unkind. There is also the practical aspect that a thank-you note is the confirmation that the present has been received.

Thank-you notes really need to be handwritten. Never use a preprinted card reading "Thank you for your gift." Make sure you thank each person for the specific gift sent. Notes need not be very long, but they should be personal. If both bride and groom pitch in, it will go much faster. (For more information, see the section on thank-you notes, page 167.)

REGISTERING WITH A BRIDAL REGISTRY

Most department stores have a bridal registry, as do an increasing number of specialty stores—from craft stores to kitchenware shops and catalogs—to help guide wedding guests in their selection of a gift.

Registering is a simple matter. Several months before the wedding, visit the store and meet with the person in charge of the registry, which is often located in the china department. You will be presented with a checklist of items the store carries. You select specific items that are then entered into the company's computer. When guests ask to see your wish list, they are presented with a copy from which they can choose something if they like. If they do, the purchase is noted in the computer to avoid duplicates.

As a bride and groom choosing items, select things in a range of price levels and categories to give guests a real choice. If, for instance, you choose an expensive china pattern, make sure you offset it with things that people without the means to buy a full place setting can buy, such as towels, table linens, cookware, or small appliances.

HOUSEWARMING GIFTS

When friends move into a new house, we often mark the event with a small gift appropriate for the house. Some people send flowers, and this is fine if you don't know the tastes and needs of the new residents very well. A more lasting gift, however, is often an even better way to mark the occasion. Appropriate gifts include seeds, a plant or bulbs for the yard, or a gift certificate from a local nursery or catalog. For the house itself, an address book with local services listed, a stamp holder filled with stamps, or personalized return address labels are often welcome.

If new neighbors have just moved to a new area, a small gift of local interest might be appreciated. You might choose a local newspaper subscription, selection of local road maps, transportation schedules, information on local activities and points of interest, as well as a list of recommended goods and services.

Another thoughtful way to welcome new neighbors is to provide a home-cooked meal they can easily heat and eat during the chaos of moving.

GOING-AWAY GIFTS

When friends move away, people often like to give them a little something that will serve as a keepsake or will make the journey easier. You might choose something specifically related to where you live, such as a book of local history or a locally made object, or something reflecting what you did with your friends. If you had neighborhood cookouts, you could make up a barbecue kit or a selection of a few recipes you all enjoyed. If the family will be going on a long car ride, a survival kit consisting of snacks and entertainments for the children can be fun.

You might gather friends and neighbors and have them create a special memento by decorating a tablecloth or set of place mats with fabric paints or markers.

You can endear yourself to friends who go away on trips by giving them thoughtful little presents, too. For instance, if friends are going abroad, you can present them with a gift of some local currency. This is particularly handy when someone first arrives without much local money on hand. A few dollars in foreign money is also a great way to prepare children for a trip abroad.

A selection of fine toiletries in travel size is another thoughtful and useful gift for the traveler.

HOUSE GIFTS

House gifts are those that say, "Thank you for having me." Often they are presented when you arrive for a party or a weekend. A house gift may be sent after a visit, too, which is especially useful if you didn't know the tastes of your hosts in advance.

It used to be that people routinely sent flowers before a party as a gift to the hostess. The hostess displayed them prominently so that guests could admire them as they arrived. These days that practice is waning as people entertain more informally. Instead, people often take a bouquet of flowers or other gift. If you take flowers, present them in an arrangement tied with a pretty bow or in a vase if you can, so the hostess or host need not leave guests to arrange them.

If you are the guest of honor at a party it is considered most polite to send an arrangement of flowers to your hosts the day of the party. You might want to check to see if the hosts have any special favorites and to coordinate with any decorations they may have planned. If you can find out the florist being used, you may discreetly coordinate through them.

When invited to a dinner party or when you are a house guest, you have lots of options of things to take. A bottle of wine presented to hosts before a dinner party is often appreciated, especially if it is carefully chosen. If you are a house guest, more than one would be appropriate.

When giving gifts of food or drink, be sure to make it clear that you don't expect it to be served at that event. You can say something like, "This is for your wine cellar," in the case of wine or, "Something for your larder" in the case of food.

Other appreciated items include a basket of edible treats or items of personal luxury, such as bath salts and powders. Beautiful candles suited to the decor of the house are welcome. A potted houseplant or a few for the garden often please fellow gardeners. If you make jams, pickles, or relishes, a jar or two of those, especially chosen to suit the taste of your hosts, can be welcome. If you can, wrap the present in festive paper or a pretty bag. This makes even a small token seem special.

VALENTINE'S DAY GIFTS

For those of us who celebrate Valentine's Day, a gift of some kind is necessary. The gift need not be expensive jewelry, but it should be out of the ordinary. For women, chocolates are the traditional choice, but not always well considered if a woman is diet conscious. One alternative approach would be to fill a candy box with something your mate really loves, such as nice jewelry, tapes, a favorite kind of novel, golf balls—whatever he or she would enjoy.

Whatever you choose for woman or man, it should be romantic and purely unnecessary. Flowers from a man who doesn't normally give them are romantic; from a man who brings them home regularly they are not. A romantic meal, either prepared at home or out, is often tenderly appreciated.

A handcrafted and sincere poem of any kind is almost sure to melt a person's heart, no matter how amateurish the writing.

Of course, the best sort of Valentine gift is the kind you give all year to a loved one. Some suggestions of things you might try:

• Make a regular date with your spouse, once each week or month.

• Send silly or romantic cards to your significant other at the office throughout the year (you might leave them unsigned).

• Make a list of ten ways in which you take your partner for granted, then examine how you can show how much you do care. Institute a new method of showing your feelings each week for ten weeks. Then start again.

• Plan a mystery date with your partner. It can be an evening or a weekend. Give only the barest of information in order not to spoil the surprise.

• Surprise your spouse with a present that you both would enjoy, for no particular occasion.

ANNIVERSARY GIFTS

Anniversary gifts are similar to Valentine's gifts in that whatever you choose, the gift should be something that is not necessary to the running of the house. It may be related to the house, however. One couple I know decided to give each other a set of antique china for their fifth anniversary. Yes, it was practical, but it wasn't necessary and it pleased them both.

For a big anniversary, family members might want to pitch in for something the couple wouldn't buy for themselves. It could be a weekend at a wonderful hotel or resort. It could be an evening of dancing or a meal at the fancy new restaurant in town.

Children can make an anniversary book, with a page for each year of marriage. On each page, children can write a specific example of how their parents have shared their lives with them and illustrate it with photographs, mementos like ticket stubs or postcards, or simple drawings. The memories may be funny, sentimental, or both.

Friends can make a similar sort of scrapbook that details the major events they have all shared over the time of the marriage.

Presents geared to traditional gift themes can be lots of fun, too. When one couple I know celebrated their tenth anniversary they had a party and all their friends gave them windup tin toys.

TRADITIONAL ANNIVERSARY GIFT THEMES

Anniversary	Theme
First	Paper
Second	Cotton
Third	Leather
Fourth	Fruit, flowers, linen, silk
Fifth	Wood
Sixth	Sugar, candy, iron
Seventh	Copper or wool
Eighth	Bronze or pottery
Ninth	Pottery or willow
Tenth	Tin, aluminum
Eleventh	Steel
Twelfth	Silk or linen
Thirteenth	Lace
Fourteenth	Ivory
Fifteenth	Crystal or glass
Twentieth	China
Twenty-fifth	Silver
Thirtieth	Pearl
Thirty-fifth	Coral or jade
Fortieth	Ruby
Forty-fifth	Sapphire
Fiftieth	Gold
Sixtieth	Diamond
Sixty-fifth	Diamond
Seventieth	Diamond

OFFICE GIFTS

While most gift giving is related to the social aspects of our lives, business giving often plays an important role, too. Office giving can serve several functions. Gifts to clients and colleagues strengthen ties by telling them you value their business or their assistance and that you like them. Sometimes a gift given to a colleague acknowledges work well done, especially when given after an extra effort has been made, or a deal finalized.

Customs vary from one business to another and one country to another. In some businesses giving presents to signal the consummation of a deal, to celebrate the holidays, or to boost morale is quite common. In others it is forbidden. Federal employees of the United States and employees in many states are forbidden from accepting gifts of value and may not accept gifts in return for favors. This is true for the employees of certain other countries as well. On the other hand, in some parts of the world business is conducted routinely with the help of gifts. Before you give any gifts, check out the policies of your company and of those with which you work.

GIFT-GIVING OCCASIONS FOR CLIENTS AND COLLEAGUES

Here are a few common ones:
- Holiday time
- Completion of a project
- A promotion
- A personal event, such as a wedding, birth of a child, or retirement
- A business event, such as a new job, merger, restructuring, or sale of a company
- When you have committed a gaffe or forgotten something important
- When someone has gone to great trouble on your behalf

Choosing the Right Gift. Whenever possible, business gifts should be creative, interesting, and chosen specifically for each recipient. In general, they shouldn't be too personal, which makes choosing a gift rather tricky.

Corporate gifts (anything that bears a company logo) are usually safe gifts—they can't be construed as bribes—but at times you may wish to supplement these sometimes bland gifts with something that you have chosen.

Gifts of flowers and food are also traditional company gifts. These can be out of the ordinary when they are somehow unusual or the best of their kind. For instance, someone I know owns a small advertising company that uses a bowler hat as its logo. One Christmas he had cookie cutters and homemade cookies made in the shape of his logo and sent to clients. Unusual flowers or arrangements created by an imaginative florist also send a more personal message.

If you know of particular interests or hobbies of a client or coworker you can add to the collection. You wouldn't want to give a present that is too personal, but a book on a favorite subject or a piece of sports equipment, such as tennis or golf balls, could be most appreciated. Tickets to cultural or sporting events are an invaluable and time-honored business gift.

Corporations often provide gifts at holiday time for their employees to give to clients. For really special clients these may be supplemented by something you choose, so long as company policy allows it. During the rest of the year the executive is usually on his or her own with regard to choosing and sending gifts to clients.

Office Collections. One standard method of gathering enough money to buy a substantial gift for a coworker is to hold a collection at which everyone contributes a modest amount. These can be helpful if you don't know what to give a fellow worker or a nuisance if you are asked to shell out for someone you barely know. If you feel strongly about a particular collection, be comforted that you are not obligated to donate, just don't then sign the card that accompanies the gift.

Gifts from Managers to Employees. Generally, a manager gives presents for a birthday or holiday only to those with whom he or she works most closely, such as a secretary or assistant. As with any gift it should be chosen thoughtfully with the person's tastes, interests, and needs in mind. Any such gifts should not be too personal. A fine pen, a book, desk equipment, or something related to a person's interests outside the office are all appropriate.

From Subordinates to Bosses. Employees do not generally give presents to their bosses. Exceptions exist, of course, such as when a secretary or assistant is especially fond of a boss and wishes to return the kindness of a gift. Such gifts should not be expensive or too personal. Executives should never accept expensive gifts from subordinates.

Between Colleagues. Coworkers do often acknowledge holidays and other special events by exchanging gifts. Often guidelines are set to limit the amount that can be spent. Sometimes a grab bag is organized or names are drawn to determine who provides whom with a gift. Gifts are often related to the business and are often humorous. The standard differs, of course, for coworkers who have become more personal friends then business acquaintances.

9

OFFICE ETIQUETTE

Many people spend half or more of their waking hours during the work week in an office. They make their living there, but there's more to it than earning a paycheck. Life in an office is work, but doing it well involves adapting a range of life skills to a set of professional circumstances. How well we adjust our speech, behavior, and, yes, manners to the different demands of office life has an important impact on our ability to function successfully at work.

Work is about money, satisfaction, imagination, integrity, toughness, and a thousand other things. But success in the workplace also involves communication and relationship skills. Again, a working knowledge of office etiquette can only help you in finding the right job and in doing it well.

FINDING A JOB

Whether you are starting out on your first serious job hunt or you're looking to make your next move upward, the process is ritualized and relies on a variety of steps. First, of course, you need to scout out the possibilities.

The best source of job news is usually word of mouth, which tends to come one's way when you already have a job. If you have any professional colleagues (preferably outside of your current company) let them know of your interest in moving. You may call or write. Don't broadcast your desire around the office, but keep it quiet and don't make your wish to change appear too urgent. In the absence of inside knowledge, you might approach professional placement services or employment agencies. Look for ads in the newspapers, trade journals, and other publications. Get the word out among family and friends, too. You never know when Uncle Joe's best friend's company might need someone.

Once you've identified a potential job source, one key to getting a job is employing the proper politesse in querying, interviewing, and securing the job. Some of that is done on paper, some in person.

THE RESUMÉ AND COVER LETTER

For most people, the first step to getting a good job is to prepare a resumé detailing their work experience and education. The style and length of the resumé is determined by the field and the amount of time you have been working. There are plenty of good books and articles (available at the library) that can guide you through the intricacies of creating a selling resumé, but the basic elements to be included are: your name and address, including E-mail and fax number if applicable; your previous work experience; your educational background; and any honors or awards you've received, especially work-related ones.

Every resumé must be freshly typed or printed on good-quality paper. Never send a photocopy. Never fax your resumé and accompanying cover letter unless you specifically know that the company welcomes such transmissions. All the trouble you spent making your resumé look professional will be for nothing if it ends up blurry and crinkled on curled-up fax paper.

The letter you send with the resumé should again be printed on a good-quality paper; avoid using your current company's stationery. You must address the letter to a specific person in a company. To send something to "The Office of Human Resources" won't do. Instead, take the time to get the name of a person who might be useful. This could be an executive in the division for which you wish to work, a well-connected friend of a friend, or the head of the Human Resources department.

Briefly outline in your letter why you are interested in working for that particular company and why you think you would be qualified. Don't go into paragraphs of detail, but summarize your interest and highlight your qualifications. Ask for an appointment. The whole letter should fit on one page, unless there is a truly outstanding reason to go to a second.

Once the letter has been sent, wait for a call. If a call for an interview doesn't come after two weeks, you may phone, ask politely if your letter and resumé were received, and ask for an appointment.

REQUESTING A REFERENCE

In some circumstances a good reference can be critical to landing the job you want. Approach professional acquaintances whom you believe would be helpful and ask if they would be willing to speak on your behalf, if needed. If possible, have several names, so that you don't have to use the same names repeatedly. People are generally happy to speak to an employer or two, but not to a multitude. Send along a copy of your resumé to each person who agrees to give you a reference.

PREPARING FOR THE INTERVIEW

The purpose of sending a letter and resumé is to get you an interview. During the interview you present your best image in the hope that the perfect job will be waiting for you. It's also an opportunity to learn more about the company. While most of the questions may be asked of you, you may ask some too. The general rule of interviewing is that you appear well mannered and professional. To this end I have some helpful suggestions.

Prepare for the interview. Do a little homework on the company, familiarizing yourself with their product lines, philosophy of employment, or other pertinent information related directly to the company. Information can usually be found out at the library, by scanning business magazines or the Internet, and by talking to anyone you know who works there or for a company that does business with your potential employer.

On the day of the interview, dress carefully. Make sure you get up early enough to be thoroughly awake, clean, and tidily dressed (take the time to dry your hair). Make sure that the outfit you wear is appropriate. No see-through blouses or micro-minis for women, no untucked T-shirts or shorts for men. Your clothing and shoes should be spotlessly clean and in good repair. Carry any materials you need in a neat portfolio or briefcase in which everything is easily accessible.

Be on time. I can hardly stress this enough because people who are late send a clear message that they are not to be relied upon.

When the interviewer greets you, stand up (if you've been sitting), look the person in the eye, offer a cordial greeting, extend your hand, and shake hands firmly.

When you enter the interviewer's office stand until invited to sit. Sit where you are asked to sit. If the seat you are directed to proves to be uncomfortable—say, the sun is shining directly into your eyes— you may ask politely if you may move, explaining why.

Do not place anything on the interviewer's desk unless you are asked to show samples of your work.

Ignore any interruptions that might occur during your interview. If someone telephones or comes into the office, take no notice; look away to indicate that you are not listening.

Listen to the interviewer, who will usually guide the conversation, and take your cues from him or her, including when to end the interview. At some point it may be appropriate for you to ask questions about the job or the company.

Your demeanor should be professional. Present your credentials and the reasons you should be hired with confidence. Try not to underplay your accomplishments or overplay them *too* much. Avoid bringing your personal life into the interview, unless specifically asked. Do not drop the names of important people you know.

Be sensitive to signs that your interview is at an end and make a graceful exit. Thank the interviewer and shake hands. If you feel the interview has gone especially well you may ask whether you may call soon or when a decision is likely to be made.

As always, be pleasant to everyone you meet at the office. Don't turn on the charm as soon as you meet the interviewer and then cast a stony glance at the receptionist as you leave. Being courteous to everyone should be a habit. Good habits become as well known in a company as bad ones.

Send a note of thanks to the person who interviewed you. Such a note is not merely courteous (reason enough in itself) but also will put your name in front of the interviewer again. The note should be brief and businesslike.

CONDUCTING THE INTERVIEW

If you are the interviewer you have a few responsibilities, too. Try not to keep people waiting very long for an interview. Yes, you may have the power to keep someone waiting, but it is a hollow kind of respect you will engender.

During the interview try to put the interviewee at ease. The classic ploy of seating someone in a low chair so that you tower over them is rather childish. Try not to let other business intrude on the interview. Request that all phone calls but the most urgent be held until you are through.

Never ask inappropriate questions. Such questions include any that relate to a person's particular tastes and personal life, unless they are mentioned on the resumé. In many places, it is illegal for you to ask anyone's religion, age, national origin, marital status, or future family plans.

Hiring and Not Hiring. So now you've interviewed the candidates and found the perfect person. You call the person and make a firm offer. Once the offer is accepted, you exchange pleasantries. As the hirer, you mention how you are looking forward to working with the person, and how you believe both she or he and the company will benefit. You might mention that other members of the company are delighted by the qualifications presented. The new employee should mention how happy he or she is to join the team.

At managerial and executive levels a small lunch may be arranged to introduce a new member to other members of the office. This may take place on the day the offer is accepted or on the employee's first day of work. The new employee should expect to pay for his or her share of the lunch and should offer when the check comes. The new employee shouldn't be surprised if the offer is rejected, and will then accept the lunch with a gracious thank-you.

Suppose you've interviewed six people and found the right person to hire. The other five, however, may be waiting for your call. If you know during the interview that you won't be hiring someone, don't lead him or her on with unreal expectations.

If you really haven't made up your mind during the interview, you owe it to the people you have interviewed, especially at an executive level, to tell them yourself. Never dodge the responsibility by refusing to return phone calls, suddenly being unable to speak on the phone, or shoving the task off to another employee. This is cowardly and rude.

Make the call and say something simple like: "Thank you for your time and patience, but I'm sorry to tell you we won't be offering you the job." You needn't go into great detail but if you can give an honest but carefully worded answer for the reason, do so. Instead of saying, "Your personality would clash with that of other workers," you could say, "I feel that you might find yourself in conflict with other members of our team who are already in place." If a person is overqualified or underqualified for the job, you may easily say just that.

THE NEW JOB

So you've gotten the job you wanted; now it's time to start. The first few days or months of any new job are naturally a little disorienting. Even when you are welcomed warmly you may be surrounded by a sea of new faces, new tasks, new methods. You may find yourself in a decidedly taciturn office, where no one seems to notice there's someone new. Hard as it is, relax and try to take each day as it comes.

The first day or few days at a new job, you will probably want to try to fit in as well as you can, while surveying the scene. Wear clothes that are fairly conservative until you get the range of the place, remembering that new employees have to be more careful of appearance than old hands because they are as yet unknown and thus are a focus for speculation.

During the first few days you may be overwhelmed by the number of new people you meet. Keep smiling and when you forget someone's name, candidly say something like, "I'm so sorry, I've forgotten your name. It will take me a little while to get everyone straight in my mind." If you encounter a superior whose name you don't know, you might want to wait and ask a fellow worker.

Accept invitations to lunch—they are a good way to get to know other workers—but avoid settling into a clique. As with many aspects of life, getting in with a particular crowd and limiting yourself to them can keep your horizons unnecessarily limited. A good approach is to get to know as many people in the office as you can before making particular friends with anyone. Office gossip is often rife, but avoid the temptation to pay much heed to rumors until you have your own experiences.

GOODWILL IN THE OFFICE

Few things take you as far with as little effort as practicing the art of civility in the office. This certainly doesn't mean stiff formal manners, but always keep very much in your mind that basic word *respect*. If you respect your fellow workers, regardless of their level on the organization chart, learning the nuances of office behavior in your particular shop will come easily.

Many workplaces are rife with politics. You may think that management doesn't pay attention to the needs of subordinates, but executives are constantly taking the pulse of everyone in their divisions regardless of whether it appears so or not. Therefore it is in every employee's interest to work efficiently and diligently at all times, airing their concerns thoughtfully when necessary.

Inversely, executives who treat their subordinates in a less than civil manner set themselves up for poor staff morale, reduced efficiency, and lower cooperation. Treating people well makes for a win-win situation for everyone.

GREETINGS AND CONVERSATION

In most offices people exchange greetings and the odd pleasantry when they first see one another during the day. Simple greetings may be exchanged by everyone, subordinate and superior alike. People say "good night" to colleagues and other staff they encounter at the end of the day. Beyond that, the level of conversation appropriate to the workplace is determined by the individual office. Rarely, however, is it considered appropriate to chat with a fellow worker in the office for more than a few minutes at a time on matters unrelated to work.

If you find that someone seems to want to talk more than you feel is right and is thus hindering your work, you will have to devise a tactful way to let him or her know that it's time to get back to work. You might try barely nodding, while continuing to work, or even better saying something like: "I can't talk right now. I have to get this out in a few minutes," or "I'm sorry, I'm really busy right now, how about if we save our conversation until lunchtime?"

INTRODUCTIONS

Subordinates are always introduced to superiors regardless of sex or age. Everyone shakes hands when they are introduced and subordinates rise if they are seated.

Listen carefully when introductions are made to see if titles are used. If someone says, "Mr. Jones, I would like you to meet our newest staff member, Celia Smith," you know right away that Mr. Jones will not be known as Ted to you, at least not yet.

When introducing peers to one another the order does not matter. If you are introducing someone new, it is helpful to identify where or with whom the employee will be working. The correct response to an introduction is "How do you do."

Every company has its own policy about the formality of names. Some companies instruct their employees to address each other by first name. If you don't know the policy it's better to err on the side of conservatism and use titles, especially for superiors, until you know. Americans tend to be more informal when addressing colleagues, so if you find yourself dealing with people abroad, be aware that they more than likely will be comfortable using titles.

SHAKING HANDS

People shake hands more in business than in social situations. The person who is acting as host in a meeting or conversation is the person who extends a hand first. Among colleagues little notice is taken of who extends a hand first. In the past, women never took the initiative, but that is definitely outmoded. Handshakes should be firm but not bone-breaking. Nothing telegraphs ineffectuality more quickly than a limp and sweaty handshake from a man or woman.

LISTEN AND LEARN

It may sound simplistic, but you can learn a great deal about how the dynamics of an office and company work by paying attention to what those around you say and do. Sometimes this means not offering up all of your opinions until you have the views of others. Sometimes it means putting aside your own agenda entirely and listening.

You might have to look beyond the words to what other people—coworkers, superiors, subordinates—are saying. I don't mean reading your thoughts into what is being said; I mean focusing on the underlying issues that may be at hand rather than the superficial.

PROFESSIONAL RELATIONSHIPS

Some people are unable to resist the temptation to treat those who are in a position below theirs on the company organization chart as inferiors. That's wrongheaded. Perhaps it makes insecure people *feel* powerful to treat others as inferior, but all it really does is show up their small-mindedness. Where does it get you to treat, say, a mailroom clerk as if his or her job isn't important? Will the clerk respect you? Will the clerk do a better job for you? The work a person performs does not identify him or her as a human being. This goes for the president of the company as well as the janitorial staff. A person is a person deserving of respect no matter what job he or she does.

Also, what goes around, comes around. If you treat someone well, they are more likely to work hard and respect you. If you treat someone badly, they are more likely to resent you, doing nothing to help you. We all rely on one another. If the people in support positions don't feel that they are part of the overall team, what are the chances that they will do a good job?

If a person repeatedly acts badly—treating coworkers as inferior, intentionally disregarding the intentions and feelings of others, infringing on the domain of fellow workers—he or she risks losing the respect of all those with whom he or she comes in contact.

Of course we all know people who bully and shove their way to the top, treating everyone around them like dirt. There will always be such people, and some of them will make it to the top, but what a price they pay along the way! Once at the top what do they have but the enmity of all around them. We have to assume that they like it that way. We may have to deal with them, but we don't have to be like them. And you don't have to be an ogre to get ahead.

So how do you treat everyone with respect? It starts with simple things. When someone does something for you, say "thank you." When you need something done you say "please." You look people in the eye when you speak with them. You don't require people to perform tasks that are not in their job descriptions. When asking someone to do something, you need to give enough instruction and enough time for the person to do the job properly. Don't pit one employee against another.

Make sure you don't ask your staff to work harder than you do. People are more willing to work hard, and even devote extra time and energy, if they know that you put in the same kind of time or effort.

Take into account that other people have lives outside the office and that asking them to work extra hours may be burdensome. Employees should understand that while their outside life is important, it is not part of office life. Sometimes emergencies do come up and people have to deal with them, but not routinely.

Be receptive to employees' needs and concerns. Perhaps you are a person who invites open oral communication. Perhaps you prefer issues of concern laid out in a memo. Whatever your preferred method of communication, let your staff know. When presented with problems or concerns, act to correct the situation if you can. Communicate with the people concerned to alert them to what you have done.

BE WORTHY OF RESPECT

While everyone has the right to respect, we must work to earn and keep it. First and foremost, we must do our jobs.

Don't abuse the privileges of a job. Don't bring your home life to work. During working time, your first obligation is to the job and the people you work with. Do your job with as much diligence as you can, anticipating needs that might arise. Take serious problems to your superiors and try to work out solutions. Offer suggestions when warranted, and accept criticism with grace.

GIVING AND ACCEPTING CRITICISM

At times, just about everyone in a management position finds himself or herself having to criticize the work of employees. This may take the form of a regular evaluation or review, or it may involve addressing a specific problem. Effectively handling reviews or solving problems requires sensitivity and sometimes creativity.

People work well when they believe they are good at what they do. When offering criticism you need to keep from undermining an employee's confidence, otherwise you both lose. To do this, you need to offer suggestions tactfully. Instead of saying, "Your work is always late, shape up," you might say something like, "I've noticed recently that you seem to run out of time when deadlines loom. Is there something we can do which will allow you to meet those targets?"

Asking employees how they would correct a problem gives them an element of control. Listen to the ideas put forth. If the solution offered makes sense, you might try it; if not, offer your methods for correcting the problem.

Save criticism for important issues and keep the focus of a critical session to one or two elements.

Criticism can be important to advancement. Not to provide useful criticism or help for an employee with a specific correctable problem is unfair to that person. Conclude any critical session by offering valid praise and complimenting the employee's strong points.

Accepting criticism is much harder than giving it. Everyone wants reinforcement for a job well done. Most people are faced with evaluative reviews and occasional work problems, so it's almost impossible to escape hearing criticism now and again. To a certain degree, how you handle it depends on how it is given and what your relationship is to the person reviewing you. But in general, try to remember that most criticism is given in an effort to improve the job being done. Try your best to take it in that spirit and accept the criticism gracefully.

In an evaluative review your boss might ask for your ideas on how to improve elements of your job and performance. This is your turn to be diplomatic, as your response can be read as criticism of your boss. Make useful suggestions and express them in a positive way.

At the end of the session, thank your supervisor for the honesty and suggestions for improving the situation. Bad managers do exist, however, and if you feel yourself constantly subjected to unfair criticism, it might be time to take the issue to a higher authority or to look for a new job. If such a situation develops, try your best to keep your cool, venting in the privacy of home, if you need to. Remaining pleasant and in command of your work is the best way to secure a good recommendation when looking for a new job or for getting senior management to pay attention to your claims.

OFFICE CONDUCT

In general, people should act with professional decorum toward everyone at work. This means treating everyone in a friendly manner, respecting their work and their space. Workers don't gossip about or bad-mouth others, set up cliques, or exclude fellow employees from conversations.

An effective worker or manager doesn't lose emotional control. There's no quicker way to lose respect than to throw a temper tantrum in the office.

Everyone should use proper spoken language, avoiding too much slang and any profanity. Profanity has no place in a business setting.

No one should expect the office to be a dating service or a forum for working out personal problems. To use sexual attraction as a tool for advancement or as a requirement for a job is demeaning to all involved. It is also illegal.

To avoid even the suspicion of impropriety, try to avoid situations that could be misread. Such situations include working late in an empty office with a boss or subordinate, traveling in pairs, having frequent meals with a boss or subordinate, or frequently working behind closed doors with one person.

PERSONAL RELATIONSHIPS

These days, many eligible men and women meet at work. That means that it's almost impossible to keep romance out of every office. In fact, many strong relationships and marriages have grown from office roots. However, handling an office romance can be a tricky balancing act.

My first piece of advice: Enter into an intimate relationship with a coworker only after much consideration and with great care. Make sure that you both understand the extent of the relationship and the boundaries. Is this a relationship growing out of mutual trust and affection? Or is this an exercise of power? Are there people either in the office or outside who are likely to be hurt by your relationship?

Discretion is at the base of every successful office relationship. If the personal intrudes on the professional, you're in for trouble. This is true even for plain old friendships.

Rule number one: Leave the spats, moon June looks, and physical contact at home. You do not need to share your relationship with the rest of the office. If you can't keep them separate, one of you had better start looking for another job, or you risk making you and all those around you suffer.

Another reason for the careful separation of work and personal life is the issue of what happens if the romance goes sour. Hurt feelings and recriminations can do great damage in an office, not only to the people directly involved but to those who work with them.

Need it be said that romantic relationships between people who are otherwise married or seriously attached are rarely a good idea.

WRITTEN BUSINESS COMMUNICATIONS

Every written word you dispatch—via letter, fax, or E-mail—reflects on you and your company. Communication is at the core of business and human relations. For that reason, we need to pay close attention to the various elements of communication in order to make the most of our working time.

BUSINESS LETTERS

For a long time business letters were a specialized form of letter writing that was rather stilted and filled with jargon. Today, the most effective letters use standard language and echo the speech rhythms of the people who write them. That's not to say that business letters are written in modern slang. No, there is still an art to the carefully crafted letter, but it's no longer arcane or awkward.

A business letter has six parts: heading, inside address, greeting, body of the letter, closing, and signature. Each element is simple, yet when put together they form a specific form of communication.

The heading contains the sender's address, usually printed on the stationery, and the date.

The inside address includes the addressee's name, followed on the next line by the title, followed by the company name, street address, city and state (or country), and postal code.

The greeting opens the letter itself. Most letters begin with "Dear" followed by the person being addressed. Acceptable business greetings include: Dear Ms. Jackson (or Mrs. or Miss if you know she uses Miss); Dear John; Dear Sir or Madam; Gentlemen (or Ladies or Ladies and Gentlemen). Any title that a person uses in front of his or her name should be used.

It is always best to write to a specific person, making sure the name is spelled correctly. This may sound minor, but don't you find it irritating when your name is misspelled? When you don't know someone's name, you may put the title instead, such as "Dear Operations Manager" or some such. Your company may have guidelines on how they want their business letters to be phrased.

The body of the letter conducts the business. Most business letters are brief, from a single paragraph to a page. Every sentence should be complete and logical. Today's business style of writing is more personally expressive than in days gone by, when a business letter was full of stuffy idioms. Business letters are still all business, however, but the writing should be simple, clear, and direct.

BUSINESS LETTERS

Phrases to avoid	Better choices
I beg to enclose	I enclose
Please find enclosed	I enclose
Will send same	I will send you
Yours of the fifth (or whatever date)	Your letter of August 5
Hoping to hear from you	I hope to hear from you
Thanking you	Thank you

SAMPLE BUSINESS LETTER

RED ROCK MARKETING, INC.
619 Stonewall Road   East Lansing, Michigan 66294

October 19, 1999

Ms. Mary Ann Ryan
Vice President
GB Associates
210 State Road
Great Barrington, MA 02830

Dear Ms. Ryan:

I am pleased to send along to you the prospectus that we discussed on the phone on October 1. As you can see, Red Rock Marketing directly serves the needs of businesses like yours. I've highlighted the areas that we might want to discuss further.

If convenient for you, I will call within the next week or so to set up an appointment.

I look forward to continuing our discussion.

Cordially,

Lynn McLaren

Lynn McLaren
President

Toward the end of the letter you may wish to include a personal sentence. It might relate to your most recent conversation or something general, like an upcoming holiday. The letter itself should not be chatty—that's unprofessional—but a cordial ending is fine.

It used to be that closings were very formal; today, they are much less so. "Very truly yours" or "Very sincerely" are about as formal as you see these days. More common closings include "Best regards," "Sincerely," and "Cordially."

The signature of a business letter consists of the full name and title of the sender, typed below the handwritten signature.

SENDING AND RECEIVING FAXES

The advent of the facsimile (fax) machine has, along with E-mail, played a role in the ongoing revolution in the way people in business communicate. No longer do we have to rely on the mail to send letters, drafts of contracts, and other documents. Today they are routinely delivered, almost instantaneously, over phone lines.

Just about any document can be sent by fax. Depending on company policy, you may need to prepare a cover sheet that clearly identifies the person for whom the fax is intended in order that it can be routed correctly by the receiver's mail room (this is often where a company's fax machines are located).

Some companies provide their employees with standardized fax cover sheets. Such a sheet looks a little like a traditional interoffice memo. At the top of the sheet it says "To:" and "From:" and possibly "Re:". You fill in the blanks. Usually the number of pages is also cited. When sending a letter by fax it's helpful to type at the bottom left: "By fax" or "By facsimile."

When composing a fax, keep in mind that people other than the addressee will probably see your document. That means you won't want to include anything privileged or too personal. You should also be aware that what arrives on the other end doesn't look as professional as a cleanly typed document on good bond paper. There is loss of clarity in the faxing process; the thermographic paper that some fax machines still use is thin and curls easily. The image doesn't always last either, so when you send something that warrants saving, send it by mail. Some people send a fax and then back it up by sending a copy by mail.

A fax is by its nature an informal and public tool, and tempting though it may be to send all correspondence by fax, there are a number of instances for which it is not appropriate. As mentioned, any time you send something of lasting importance or something that may require signatures, such as a contract, you need to send it conventionally. Resist the urge to send your resumé by fax, unless specifically asked to, and even in that special circumstance you should follow up with a paper document. Thank-you letters for job interviews, as well as most personal communications, including congratulatory notes, should be sent by post.

MEMOS AND REPORTS

Memorandums and reports are the other two standard forms of office communication. Memos are less formal than reports and usually serve to keep people in an office informed. Reports usually give full details of an issue. As with all business writing, memos and reports are written to convey facts and should be clearly organized, concise, and, when needed, persuasive.

Good writing skills are a great asset for writing both memos and reports. One advantage of such communications is that they inform colleagues and managers without requiring a lot of time. Take into account your audience when preparing a memo or report. Check your wording to make sure it isn't convoluted, condescending, or self-indulgent. Clear, grammatical sentences of well-chosen and correctly spelled words are easier to read and more persuasive than those that are sloppy, cliché-ridden, or defensive. Always check over your work at least twice before sending something out.

E-MAIL

There's no doubt about it, computers allow us to accomplish any number of things that only a few years ago were done at a fraction of the speed. Instant electronic communication is a classic case in point: E-mail (electronic mail) allows you to type a message into your computer and with a click of your mouse send it to someone else's computer.

E-mail is really just another method of writing a letter, memo, or note. In keeping with the rapidity with which E-mail is delivered, I recommend you keep sentences, lines, and paragraphs short. Use single spacing within a paragraph, double spacing between. That said, your messages should still consist of thoughtfully considered sentences that are clearly and concisely written.

One of the reasons for keeping sentences lines and paragraphs short is the issue of word wrap. There are few things more irritating than receiving a missive that looks like a haiku poem. This happens when someone has typed in lines that are set by his or her computer at ninety characters long. Other computers that receive the messages may be set for sixty-five characters per line. The receiving computer does not automatically delete the returns sent at ninety-character-long lines, so you end up with some pretty hard-to-read copy.

One of the drawbacks of E-mail as opposed to regular letters is that unless you are a very good writer, it is difficult to convey emotions or subtleties since many of the elements we use when writing, such as exclamation marks, italics, and underlines, are not available in many E-mail programs.

Someone has come up with a solution to this little problem: emoticons. Also known as smileys, these are little sideways faces made from the regular type characters on a typewriter. Such symbols look like this:

:-)	happiness
:-(	sadness
;-)	wink
:-o	surprise
>:-(	anger

Some people love emoticons—and there are dozens of these symbols—while others find them irritating. However you view them, they are a little like being nudged in the ribs: "Get it? Get it?" In business correspondence it's best to omit the use of smileys and let your words do the talking.

Once you send your missive out, don't necessarily expect an immediate response. Perhaps you're the kind of person who likes to check your E-mail several times a day. Other people may only check theirs every few days. Try to give the recipients of your messages at least a couple of days to respond. With practice you'll get to know the habits of people you correspond with regularly.

As with regular mail, the receiver of an E-mail should respond to a message as soon as possible. If you have an angry response, resist the temptation to fire back your answer in the heat of the moment. This is even more of a temptation electronically, because it's all so immediate. But try to resist, simmer down, and think through your response before sending it off.

It's tempting to use E-mail more than is necessary. When you are communicating with friends and electronic acquaintances at home, this is your own business, but when it's at the office, be careful not to overuse the service. A colleague down the hall may not need three messages a day, and friends outside the office probably don't need them on company time.

Finally, remember that while it may seem that an E-mail message is as private as a letter, it isn't. Particularly in a business setting, there's a perception that E-mails are public communications; people routinely send messages on to other people, sometimes carelessly so. So be discreet.

"NETIQUETTE" AND THE INTERNET

If your office is truly in the computer age you may have access via the Internet, a huge network of computers linked all over the world, to the World Wide Web, the software that allows people to communicate, transact business, and access information in a mind-numbing array of areas. Often the terms Internet and World Wide Web are used interchangeably. Most people use the Internet for fun, participating in discussions, reading other peoples' opinions, even buying things.

Perhaps the World Wide Web's most useful function in business is as a research tool. Like any tool, there are some rules about how best to use it and not use it so that the people affected are best served.

It's sometimes hard to remember that even though it is an electronic medium, the Internet and the World Wide Web are run by people. People have feelings and emotions even when they are communicating through a computer.

There is even a term for the do's and don'ts of using the Internet: "netiquette." Not surprisingly, the underlying rule of netiquette is the

Golden Rule: Treat others as you wish to be treated. Even though you will never meet most of the people you encounter in the electronic world, you still need to be courteous.

When you ask for something from someone always type "please" and "thank you." Thank anyone who has sent you information. Needless to say, you should never make fun of people, insult them, yell at them, or whisper behind their backs, even electronically.

When first starting out using the Internet, you might want to wait before contributing to any discussion groups (that's known as "lurking") to see how and in what way something is said. When you finally do contribute or request information, make sure that you use upper- and lowercase letters. That's because ALL CAPS is read as SHOUTING IN CYBERSPACE!

You might want to keep in mind that people often pay for their time on-line, and that you shouldn't waste it.

Sometimes people express some pretty strong opinions on the Internet. Avoid responding to them, especially those that are rude or insulting (known as "flames").

TEN RULES OF NETIQUETTE

According to Virginia Shea, author of *Netiquette,* these are the essential rules to follow when using the Internet:

1. Remember the human—the medium is impersonal but the receiver is not.
2. Adhere to the same standards of behavior on-line that you follow in real life.
3. Know where you are in cyberspace.
4. Respect other people's time and bandwidth.
5. Make yourself look good on-line.
6. Share expert knowledge.
7. Help keep flame wars (exchanges of insults) under control.
8. Respect other people's privacy.
9. Don't abuse your power.
10. Be forgiving of other people's mistakes.

VERBAL BUSINESS COMMUNICATION

How you speak signals a great deal to the people you work with. The employee who speaks clearly, thoughtfully, and with proper diction is far more likely to catch the attention of promotion-minded bosses. Clients who encounter well-spoken employees tend to trust the person, and by extension, the company. Employees who speak in a sloppy manner without gathering their thoughts together before opening their mouths, then mumbling using poor grammar, profanities, and excessive jargon or slang may have more to overcome to earn respect and advancement.

When you speak, think before you utter. What do you wish to say, how best might you phrase it? Speak clearly and slowly enough to be understood, not so slowly that you sound condescending. Look your conversant in the eye. Even if you are apprehensive, try to avoid nervous laughter. Use your normal tone of voice and avoid sounding ponderous or preachy.

Your body language conveys information in a conversation, too. If you slouch and hang your head while speaking with someone in person, the message conveyed is one of diffidence at best. If you cannot look someone in the eye, you can't expect that person to trust you. Your facial expression should match the intent of the conversation.

USING THE TELEPHONE

For many people the telephone is the mainstay of their work communications. It's often the device that introduces them to people outside the office and maintains the relationships that develop.

For this reason, what you say and how you say it are important. It doesn't matter whether you are a secretary in your first job or a high level executive, a pleasant and efficient phone manner garners respect. And respect gets you action.

How you sound on the phone is important. As with any conversation, speak clearly and at a moderate pitch and speed. The tone of voice should be upbeat (but not irritatingly so), conveying a sense of security and efficiency. An abrupt or gruff manner is very off-putting, especially since on the phone there is no body language to read that might counteract it.

Answering the Telephone. When answering the phone, greet the caller pleasantly. If you screen calls for a boss, follow the company policy or say something along the lines of "Special Projects, Betsy Miller speaking," or "Heather Jones's office, Betsy Miller speaking." Your name alone or the department name are also acceptable. When using only your name, use your first and last name, avoiding any title. A simple "Hello" conveys no orienting information to your caller.

Try to be helpful to anyone who calls. If you don't know the person the caller wishes to speak to, make an effort to locate the person. Never put them off by saying "Wrong department" and then hanging up. At the very least, offer to route the call back to a main switchboard.

Making Calls. If someone places your calls for you, don't waste the time of the person you call by keeping him or her waiting on the line. This may seem like something a person would do to show how powerful he or she is, but it is only rude. Who are you to say that someone else's time is not as valuable as yours?

When making a call, always identify yourself as soon as someone answers. You can say: "Hello, this is Mary Burke. May I speak to Martha Whiteman, please?" If the person you wish to speak to answers the phone, after the greeting you identify yourself: "Hello, Martha? This is Mary Burke." If you don't know the person, you may wish to be a little formal and say, "Hello, Ms. Whiteman? This is Mary Burke, of Amity Electronics."

Just as at home, if you reach a wrong number when you call, don't just hang up. Verify the number you called, so that you won't dial it again, then apologize and hang up.

Basic phone manners are the same whether you are at work or home. You don't interrupt people, speak to third parties, or do so many things that you are distracted and can't pay attention. If you need to take another call, ask the first caller's permission, put her or him on hold briefly, ask if you can call the second person back or make very quick work of the call, and get back to the first. Apologize briefly to the first caller when you resume.

Now and again we all find ourselves in a long-winded conversation. One gracious way to get out of it is to say, "I don't want to take up any more of your time, so I'll say good-bye now." Those who really can't take a hint may need a stronger clue, such as "I'm sorry, I must go now."

End all business calls in a businesslike manner. Say "good-bye." Save the slang and cute stuff for home.

Leaving Messages. Whether you leave a message with a person, such as a secretary or assistant, or voice mail—essentially an answering machine—the procedure is the same. State your name and leave a brief message. If you're talking to a machine, you may wish to leave the time and date, although many office voice-mail systems automatically note when you called.

When recording a message to greet incoming calls, be pleasant and businesslike. If you know when you will be back, mention it on your message; this will keep the caller from anxiously awaiting your call. At home you may not want to mention how long you will be gone for security reasons, but at an office this isn't an issue.

When you take a message for someone else, start by saying politely something like, "I'm sorry, she's not in the office at the moment. May I take a message?" Then write down the information and read it back to the person calling. Make sure you repeat the phone number. Say "thank you" before hanging up.

Speaker Phones. If you have a phone with the capacity to be used as a speaker, resist the temptation to use it unless you have the permission of the person you are speaking with. The quality of the sound is almost always poor and not many people are charmed by the notion that their voices can be heard by anyone in a room when they are not physically present. It can also convey the message "You're not important enough for me to give you my full attention."

Cellular Phones and Beepers. Resist the temptation to use these marvels of technology for anything other than essential business during business hours. When giving out your cellular or beeper number, be selective and give instructions. You might say, "Call me when you know the results of the Walker deal," or some such. Instruct your staff that you are not to be reached except in the case of an emergency, unless otherwise instructed. Then outline what constitutes an emergency.

It's a good idea to follow a couple of basic rules. First, do not use an office cell phone or beeper outside of business hours. Second, don't use them unnecessarily. For instance, there is no need to call someone to say, "I'll see you in five minutes."

Whenever you do use a cellular phone in public, speak quietly. Strangers will not be impressed by anything in your conversation.

Turn off cellular phones and beepers in public, if possible. Few things are more irritating than being intruded upon while on a train, in a play, show, or movie, or at a dinner party or restaurant. If it is so important to conduct business, do it where it won't interfere with other people.

A final note: Manners—in the office, at home, anywhere—are about attitude. Good etiquette is a state of mind, born of consideration, cooperation, and generosity. Courtesy is about regard for others, and when you put all of these behaviors together, what you have is civility.

To put it another way, a world without manners would be uncivilized. So let's do it the better way, and use commonsense etiquette.

10

Commonsense Advice: Fifteen Ways to Make the World a More Civilized Place

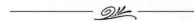

1. Approach life with an attitude of respect, thus treating *everyone* you encounter with thoughtful regard.

2. Remember that the more civilized you are the more respect you engender from others.

3. Try to remain patient with the world around you and resist the temptation to react when presented with bad behavior.

4. Be aware that your actions—good and bad—affect those around you.

5. How you present yourself to the world is how most people will know you.

6. Think before you speak.

7. The written word, no matter how brief, resonates longer than the spoken.

8. You don't have to be an ogre to succeed in business.

9. Spend time regularly with family and friends, giving continued support when needed.

10. Teaching children how to behave with consideration is a gift both to the children and the world around them.

11. Considerate table manners benefit those who use them and those who view them.

12. Careful planning and a relaxed attitude will help you sail through most social situations.

13. The secret to successful entertaining is to make others feel comfortable.

14. Try to keep the focus of major events, particularly weddings, on the important elements and don't fuss the details.

15. Have fun.

INDEX